COLLECTED POEMS
(1800-1822)

BY

ROBERT BLOOMFIELD

FACSIMILE REPRODUCTIONS

WITH AN INTRODUCTION

BY

JONATHAN N. LAWSON

Five Volumes in One

GAINESVILLE, FLORIDA

SCHOLARS' FACSIMILES & REPRINTS

1971

SCHOLARS' FACSIMILES & REPRINTS

1605 N.W. 14TH AVENUE

GAINESVILLE, FLORIDA 32601 U.S.A.

HARRY R. WARFEL, GENERAL EDITOR

Grateful acknowledgment is made to the following for permission to reprint books in their possession:

THE BRITISH MUSEUM: *The Farmer's Boy, Rural Tales,* and *May Day with the Muses.*

JONATHAN N. LAWSON: *Wild Flowers* and *The Banks of the Wye.*

L.C. Catalog Card Number: 79-161927

ISBN 0-8201-1088-4

CONTENTS

Introduction

The Farmer's Boy (1800)

Rural Tales, Ballads, and Songs (1802)

Wild Flowers (1806)

The Banks of the Wye (1811)

May Day with the Muses (1822)

INTRODUCTION

Of England's "uneducated poets," as Southey called them, none was more popular or more widely lauded in his own time and is now generally ignored than Robert Bloomfield (1766-1823). The history of his early years appears in Capel Lofft's preface to *The Farmer's Boy; A Rural Poem;* knowledge of later years must be drawn from his published letters and from the manuscript letters in the British Museum. When in 1781 he left his uncle's farm in Suffolk to enter the shoemaker's trade in London, he brought with him an intense fondness for the country, its traditions, and its solitude. Having "educated" himself, discovered poetry, and penned his first rough verses, Bloomfield began *The Farmer's Boy* in May, 1796. The lengthy seasonal tale of Giles, the rural lad who resembles Bloomfield in spirit and humility, is his best remembered work.

The ambitious plan was to finish the poem in a year, and much of it was composed while Bloomfield cobbled. The whole of "Winter" and part of "Autumn" were, in fact, composed in his head long before he had time to write them down. Thus, he rejected blank verse for the couplet form which facilitated remembering long passages of poetry (Brit. Mus. Add. MS. 28,266 fol. 85). It was, however, April 22, 1798, before *The Farmer's Boy* was finished.

Bloomfield's first intention was that the poem be nothing more than a present for his mother. A memento of the rural life he had known, it contained much that would be familiar to her. When it occurred to him that many sillier things were sometimes printed, he took his manuscript (full of regional errors in spelling and grammar) to such bookmen as William Lane and to W. Bent, publisher of the *Universal Magazine*. His efforts to have a copy of the poem printed for his mother were rescued from failure by Capel Lofft, who found him a publisher and revised the orthography. The publication of his poem did not produce in Bloomfield the ingenuousness that might have appeared in a less humble man, and a troublesome but unaffected shyness caused him both to hate and to love his sudden notoriety.

The great and unexpected popularity of *The Farmer's Boy* brought Bloomfield to the notice of sundry public figures including the Duke of Grafton, lord of the manor in which the poet had lived, who granted him a small annuity. The time Bloomfield had for the shoemaking still vital to the support of his family was usurped by new friends, well-wishers, and the curious. His financial situation was such that he never amassed any fortune; when he did have some gain from his publications, his generosity led him to provide for various of his relatives and to spend what remained on small conveniences for his immediate family. Bloomfield's own constitutional infirmity, the generally poor health of his family, and the expenses of treating a lame son helped keep him from all but modest comforts.

Although the critical reception of *The Farmer's Boy* was mixed, it pleased Wordsworth and Coleridge at first and won Bloomfield the friendship and praise of George Dyer, Samuel Rogers, Dr. Edward Jenner, and later John

INTRODUCTION

Clare. Robert Southey, with the express purpose of furthering Bloomfield's career, reviewed the poem warmly. A host of minor literary figures responded by bringing him presentation copies of their works as his popularity grew; thus despite his complaints about time lost, the shoemaker's intellectual and literary interests became more extensive. His letters and the memoranda printed in *The Remains* (1824) reveal him studying a range of subjects from the activities of the garden spider to the history and construction of aeolian harps. The harps held such fascination for him that he wrote a study of them (1808) and eventually managed a small income selling harps of his own manufacture.

Bloomfield's most productive period (1796-1811) was during his thirties and early forties, when almost all of his works were either published, written, or planned. By May, 1798, he had finished *The Farmer's Boy* and had begun the poems which would comprise *Rural Tales, Ballads, and Songs*. In a letter prefixed to Add. MS. 28,265, Bloomfield records the approximate time of their composition. "Richard and Kate" (October, 1798), "The Miller's Maid" (Spring, 1799), "The French Mariner" (Spring, 1799), "Dolly" (Summer, 1799), "Nancy" (Summer, 1799), and "Market Night" (March, 1800) were all composed prior to the publication of *Farmer's Boy*. "The Widow to her Hour Glass" (May, 1800), "The Fakenham Ghost" (July, 1800), "A Visit to Whittlebury Forest" (Autumn, 1800), "A Word to Two Young Ladies" (October, 1800), "Rosy Hannah" (October, 1800), and possibly "Lucy" came at regular intervals through the fall of 1800, while "Walter and Jane" (Spring, 1801), "Hunting Song" (Spring, 1801), "Winter Song" (Summer, 1801), and "A Highland Drover" (about October, 1801) were written during the spring through fall. "On Hearing of the Translation of Part of *The Farmer's Boy* into Latin" Bloomfield sent in a letter to his brother George on February 24, 1801 (*Correspondence*, 1870, p. 7). The completed volume appeared in January, 1802, after a prolonged quarrel with Capel Lofft over the nature of Lofft's laudatory notes that were to be attached to each poem. At Bloomfield's request, the notes remain in the smaller octavo volumes despite the publisher's desire to remove them from the entire edition.

Wild Flowers; or Pastoral and Local Poetry contains what was Bloomfield's next separate publication of note. The poem, "Good Tidings; or, News from the Farm," was first published in 1804 and was "improved" by the poet before its inclusion in *Wild Flowers*. Bloomfield, who lost his father and a nephew to smallpox, was an early and possibly influential supporter of Dr. Jenner's then controversial smallpox vaccine. Accordingly by 1800 he began to have his children vaccinated, and by January, 1802, finding Jenner's cause a "glorious" one, he began his vaccine poem. Jenner himself, while following the progress of Bloomfield's work on the poem, called, corresponded, and invited the poet to tea. In 1803 at a celebration in honor of Jenner's birthday, Bloomfield sang a song he had composed for the occasion (*Remains*, 1824. Vol. I, p. 49), and the following year, again on Jenner's birthday, he recited most of "Good Tidings" at the anniversary meeting of the Royal Jennerian Society. Bloomfield fortunately thought better of his working titles "Vaccine Rose" and "On Vaccination."

The other poems in *Wild Flowers* are not so easily dated as those in *Rural Tales*. The subject of "Barnham Water" had Bloomfield's attention on October 1, 1801,

INTRODUCTION

and by October 13 the poem was ready to be shown to Capel Lofft (Add. MS. 28,268 foll. 108-110). Aside from "My Old Oak Table," recorded in the published work as December, 1803, and "Love of the Country," recorded as June, 1804, Bloomfield dated only "Shooter's Hill"—June, 1803—in the manuscript draft of the book (Add. MS. 28,266 foll. 71-74). On March 7, 1806, Bloomfield sent a copy of the volume to the Right Hon. C. J. Fox, hoping to find in that quarter the same approbation he found for *Rural Tales* (*Correspondence*, p. 37). Fox however, appears to have been ill at the time, but the volume did receive ready praise from the Earl of Buchan who sent a laudatory address to the publishers with his permission to print it in the second edition (*Correspondence*, pp. 38-41).

Bloomfield's public silence from 1806 until the appearance of *The Banks of the Wye* in 1811 was not a mark of inactivity. His Wye tour in 1807 with friends and correspondents, Mr. and Mrs. Lloyd Baker, R. B. Cooper who eventually illustrated the volume, and others, set him to writing a prose journal and a poetical record of the trip as well as attempting a series of sketches of memorable scenes. Working on the sketches and some lines of the poem through the winter, he could report to Mrs. Baker in January of 1808 the completion of 700 lines (Add. MS. 28,268 fol. 147). The prose journal he found too full of his own talk to be of general interest. By April he had composed 1,100 lines of the poem, but felt remorse at not writing more quickly (*Ibid.* foll. 254-255). His progress was further slowed by other publishing business and by chronic rheumatism, headaches, and bad dreams. After revising and expanding the poem, he finally became convinced in January, 1811, of its fitness to be published (*Ibid.*, fol. 295). Bloomfield's mind was at ease in August, 1811, when he announced to Mrs. Baker that the printing task was finished (*Ibid.*, fol. 306).

The first edition sold well enough at first, but just at the point Bloomfield thought a second would be called for, a bookseller returned 500 copies which were redistributed (*Ibid.*, fol. 316). The death of Mr. Hood, the principal partner in the publishing company, and the relinquishment of the firm by the remaining partners to a young man who quickly went bankrupt further delayed the second edition and ruined the poet's financial expectations. The death of the Duke of Grafton and the temporary cessation of Bloomfield's annuity increased his despair. The second edition with its considerable revisions did not appear until 1813 when the publishing firm was in new hands.

The years remaining until the publication of *May Day with the Muses* in 1822 were painful ones for Bloomfield. Faced with a nagging poverty that had forced him out of London to cheaper lodgings in Shefford, with death among his children, and with his own illness and partial blindness, he fell back for a while to reissuing editions of his earlier work and publishing a children's book which he had written much earlier. Bloomfield, for the sake of his family, felt that he had to live long enough to receive the bookseller's half of his copyrights when they reverted to him, if not "to dig in the earth for my lost muse" (*Ibid.*, fol. 334). Dreaming of new poems in his old style, he wrote that "some Country tales, and spiced with love and courtship, might yet please, for Rural life by the art of Cooking may be made a relishing and highly flavour'd dish, whatever it may be in reality" (*Ibid.*, fol. 351). Such was his financial desperation while composing the pieces in *May Day with the Muses* that in September, 1816, Sir Samuel

Egerton Brydges and a few more of Bloomfield's supporters opened a subscription in his behalf. The appeal was to purchase for him an annuity and so relieve him from his embarrassment. Although the subscription drew considerable notice, the poet's embarrassment continued.

For all of his troubles, Bloomfield did continue his writing and was composing "Alfred and Jennet" in May, 1813 (*Ibid.*, fol. 332v). By the spring of 1819 he had the working title of "Oakly Hall" and was "going on boldly" with it (*Ibid.*, fol. 394). Bloomfield decided to offer the work to Messrs. Baldwin and Longman early in September. Later in the month, however, he felt that any future presentation might win a more profitable reward if he wrote the entire work out including the preface. This he resolved to do by Christmas (*Ibid.*, fol. 406). It could have been *May Day*, then, which he offered to John Murray in May, 1820, for the poet had heard that the publisher paid Crabbe three thousand pounds for his *Tales* (*Ibid.*, fol. 399v).

In 1821 the work was considerably delayed at the engraver's for the designs, and it was not until February of 1822 that the printers began to work on it. When the edition appeared in the spring, it was Baldwin's firm, not Murray's, which published it. A second edition of *May Day with the Muses* in 1822 and the preparation of *Hazelwood Hall; A Village Drama* in 1823 followed. Bloomfield died August 19, 1823.

Despite illness and hypochondria, Bloomfield wrote his last letters with warm humor about the past and the future. His love of the country, of the rural traditions, and his distaste for the effects of urban life on its people and on the countryside remained his standards. That he practiced in verse a great part of what Wordsworth would advise in his Preface, and that he did it with enough whimsied humor and objectivity to save himself from a great indulgence in sentimentalism is typical of this poet who wisely respected his own limitations yet never quite accepted them.

The *Farmer's Boy* reproduced here is an octavo format adaptation of the quarto first issue and is printed from a typesetting reimposed after the quarto issue. This octavo differs from the quarto edition in having a title page that ascribes the illustrations to Anderson, in bearing the names of additional booksellers, and in having the title page vignette placed as a frontispiece. Most of the 26,000 copies of the work sold during its first three years—there were fourteen separate editions during Bloomfield's lifetime—appear to have been of the smaller octavo format which subsequent editions offered in addition to the quartos and demy-octavos. The *Rural Tales*, *Wild Flowers*, and *Banks of the Wye* herein reproduced are of that popular smaller octavo size in which so many of Bloomfield's readers met him.

The *Rural Tales* includes the disputed notes by Capel Lofft which were not printed in the large copies of the first issue—those first to be seen by the public. The laudatory notes, Bloomfield thought, would seem less out of place here in the smaller copies. This is the third of three separate issues dated 1802 and is followed by what is marked as the Second Edition. A large paper quarto with some extra-large paper copies printed from the same typesetting was first issued. It was followed by a smaller edition in quarto format (probably octavo in quarto) set from the same type. The small and more popular octavo here is not so attractive as the larger copies but is of interest for the notes.

The small octavo *Wild Flowers* that I have chosen

INTRODUCTION

has page *ix* misnumbered *xi* as in the first issue, while the engraving for "Abner and the Widow Jones" is bound as a frontispiece. *Banks of the Wye* has an engraving mistakenly called "VIEW of the WYE through a GATEWAY at CRICKHOWEL" in this small octavo. With the Second Edition, Corrected, of 1813, the river is properly identified as the Usk.

Farmer's Boy, Rural Tales, and *May Day with the Muses* are reproduced from copies in the British Museum. *Wild Flowers* and *Banks of the Wye* are from my personal library.

For a research grant which enabled me to read at the British Museum in May, 1969, and later to ready these materials, I am deeply indebted to the Research Foundation at Texas Christian University. To the British Museum for permission to reproduce three of the works of Bloomfield and to the Mary Couts Burnett Library at T. C. U. for assistance in assembling materials I owe further thanks. Robert F. Ashby, F. L. A., County Librarian, Surrey County Library, England, whose facsimile edition of Bloomfield's Correspondence and whose counsel on details of bibliography have been most helpful, has my lasting gratitude as has Professor Jim W. Corder of Texas Christian University who first introduced me to Robert Bloomfield.

JONATHAN N. LAWSON

Texas Christian University
May, 1970

THE
FARMER'S BOY

THE
FARMER'S BOY;

A RURAL POEM,

IN FOUR BOOKS.

BY
ROBERT BLOOMFIELD.

" A Shepherd's Boy....he seeks no better name."

With Ornaments engraved in Wood by Anderson.

LONDON:

PRINTED BY T. BENSLEY, BOLT-COURT, FLEET-STREET;
FOR VERNOR AND HOOD, POULTRY;
T. C. RICKMAN, UPPER MARY-LE-BONE-STREET; INGRAM, BURY;
AND BOOTH, NORWICH.

MDCCC.

PREFACE.

HAVING the satisfaction of introducing to the Public this very pleasing and characteristic POEM, the FARMER's BOY, I think it will be agreeable to preface it with a short Account of the manner in which it came into my hands: and, which will be much more interesting to every Reader, a little History of the Author, which has been communicated to me by his Brother, and which I shall very nearly transcribe as it lies before me.

In *November* last year I received a MS. which I was requested to read, and to give my opinion of it. It had before been shewn to some persons in *London:* whose indifference toward it may probably be explained when it is considered that it came to their hands under no circumstances of adventitious recommendation. With some a person must be rich, or titled, or fashionable as a literary name, or at least fashionable in some respect, good or bad, before any thing which he can offer will be thought worthy of notice.

I had been a little accustomed to the effect of prejudices: and I was determined to judge, in the only just and reasonable way, of the Work, by the Work itself.

PREFACE.

At first I confess, seeing it divided into the four Seasons, I had to encounter a prepossession not very advantageous to any writer, that the Author was treading in a path already so admirably trod by THOMSON; and might be adding one more to an attempt already so often, but so injudiciously and unhappily made, of transmuting that noble Poem from Blank Verse into Rhime;....from its own pure native Gold into an alloyed Metal of incomparably less splendor, permanence, and worth.

I had soon, however, the pleasure of finding myself relieved from that apprehension: and of discovering that, although the delineation of RURAL SCENERY naturally branches itself into these divisions, there was little else except the General Qualities of a musical ear; flowing numbers, Feeling, Piety, poetic Imagery and Animation, a taste for the picturesque, a true sense of the natural and pathetic, force of thought, and liveliness of imagination, which were in common between Thomson and this Author. And these are qualities which whoever has the eye, the heart, the awakened and surrounding intellect, and the diviner sense of the Poet, which alone can deserve the name, must possess.

But, with these general Characters of true Poetry, " *The Farmer's Boy* " has, as I have said, a character of its own. It is discriminated as much as the circumstances and habits, and situation, and ideas consequently associated, which are so widely diverse in the two Authors, could make it different. Simplicity, sweetness, a natural tenderness, that *molle atque facetum* which HORACE celebrates in the Eclogues of VIRGIL, will be found to belong to it.

PREFACE.

I intend some farther and more particular CRITICAL RE-MARKS on this charming Performance. But I now pass to the Account of the Author himself, as given me by his Brother:....a Man to whom also I was entirely a stranger:....but whose Candor, good Sense, and brotherly Affection, appear in this Narrative; and of the justness of whose Understanding, and the Goodness of his Heart, I have had many Proofs, in consequence of a correspondence with him on different occasions which have since arisen, when this had made me acquainted with him, and interested me in his behalf.

In writing to me, Mr. GEORGE BLOOMFIELD, who is a Shoemaker also, as his Brother, and lives at BURY, thus expresses himself.

"As I spent five years with the Author, from the time he was thirteen years and a half old till he was turned of eighteen, the most interesting time of life (I mean the time that instruction is acquired, if acquired at all), I think I am able to give a better account of him than any one can, or than he can of himself: for his Modesty would not let him speak of his Temper, Disposition, or Morals."

"ROBERT was the younger Child of GEORGE BLOOMFIELD, a *Taylor*, at HONINGTON.* His Father died when he was an infant under a year old. His Mother ** was a Schoolmistress, and instructed her own Children with the others. He thus learned to read as soon as he learned to speak."

---

* This Village is between *Euston* and *Troston*, and about nine miles N. E. of *Bury*. L.
** ELIZABETH, Daughter of ROBERT MANBY. Vide Note at the end of this Preface.

PREFACE.

" Though the Mother was left a Widow with six small Children, yet with the help of Friends she managed to give each of them a little schooling."

" ROBERT was accordingly sent to Mr. RODWELL,* of Ixworth, to be improved in *Writing:* but he did not go to that School more than two or three months, nor was ever sent to any other; his Mother again marrying when ROBERT was about seven years old."

" By her second Husband, JOHN GLOVER, she had another Family."

" When *Robert* was not above *eleven* years old, the late Mr. W. AUSTIN, of SAPISTON, † took him. And though it is customary for Farmers to pay such Boys only 1s. 6d. per week, yet he generously took him into the house. This relieved his Mother of any other expence than only of finding him a few things to wear: and this was more than she well knew how to do."

" She wrote therefore," Mr. G. BLOOMFIELD continues, " to me and my Brother NAT (then in London), to assist her; mentioning that he, ROBERT, was so small of his age that Mr. AUSTIN said he was not likely to be able to get his living by hard labour."

---

* This respectable Man is senior Clerk to the Magistrates of the Hundred of BLACKBOURN, in which Honington is situated, and has conducted himself with great propriety in this and other public employments. L.

† This little Village adjoins to HONINGTON. L.

PREFACE.

Mr. G. BLOOMFIELD on this informed his Mother that, if she would let him take the Boy with him, he would take him, and teach him to make shoes: and NAT promised to clothe him. The Mother, upon this offer, took coach and came to LONDON, to Mr. G. BLOOMFIELD, with the Boy: for she said, she never should have been happy if she had not put him herself into his hands.

"She charged me," he adds, "*as I valued a Mother's Blessing, to watch over him, to set good Examples for him, and never to forget that he had lost his Father.*" I religiously confine myself to Mr. G. BLOOMFIELD's own words; and think I should wrong all the parties concerned if in mentioning this pathetic and successful Admonition, I were to use any other.

Mr. G. BLOOMFIELD then lived at Mr. *Simm's,* No. 7, *Fisher's-court, Bell-alley, Coleman-street.* "It is customary," he continues, "in such houses as are let to poor people in *London,* to have light Garrets fit for Mechanics to work in. In the Garret, where we had two turn-up Beds, and five of us worked, I received little ROBERT."

"As we were all single Men, Lodgers at a Shilling per week each, our beds were coarse, and all things far from being clean and snug, like what *Robert* had left at SAPISTON. *Robert* was our man, to fetch all things to hand. At Noon he fetched our Dinners from the Cook's Shop: and any one of our fellow workmen that wanted to have any thing fetched in, would send him, and assist in his work and teach him, for a recompense for his trouble."

PREFACE.

"Every day when the Boy from the Public-house came for the pewter pots, and to hear what Porter was wanted, he always brought the yesterday's *Newspaper*.* The *reading* of the Paper we had been used to take by turns; but after *Robert* came, he mostly read for us,....because his time was of least value."

"He frequently met with words that he was unacquainted with: of this he often complained. I one day happened at a Book-stall to see a small Dictionary, which had been very ill used. I bought it for him for 4d. By the help of this he in little time could read and comprehend the long and beautiful speeches of BURKE, FOX, or NORTH.

"One *Sunday*, after an whole day's stroll in the country, we by accident went into a dissenting *Meeting-house* in the *Old Jewry*, where a Gentleman was lecturing. This Man filled little *Robert* with astonishment. The House was amazingly crowded with the most genteel people; and though we were forced to stand still in the Aisle, and were much pressed, yet *Robert* always quickened his steps to get into the Town on a Sunday evening soon enough to attend this Lecture.

"The Preacher lived somewhere at the West End of the Town....his name was FAWCET. His language," says Mr. G. BLOOMFIELD, " was just such as the *Rambler* is written in; his Action like a person acting a Tragedy; his Discourse rational, and free from the Cant of Methodism.

* There was then, neither as a resource for the exigencies of finance, nor as a Principle of supposed Policy, that unhappy Check which prevails now on the circulation of *Newspapers*, and other means of *popular* Information. L.

PREFACE. vii

"Of him *Robert* learned to accent what he called *hard words*; and otherwise improved himself; and gained the most enlarged notions of PROVIDENCE.

"He went sometimes with me to a *Debating Society* * at *Coachmaker's-hall,* but not often; and a few times to *Covent-garden Theatre.* These are all the opportunities he ever had to learn from Public Speakers. As to *Books,* he had to wade through two or three Folios: an *History of England, British Traveller,* and a *Geography.* But he always read them as a task, or to oblige us who bought them. And as they came in sixpenny numbers weekly, he had about as many hours to read as other boys spend in play."

"I at that time," proceeds his Brother, "read the *London Magazine;* and in that work about two sheets were set apart for a *Review....Robert* seemed always eager to read this Review. Here he could see what the Literary Men were doing, and learn how to judge of the merits of the Works that came out. And I observed that he always looked at the *Poet's Corner.* And one day he repeated a *Song* which he composed to an old tune. I was much surprised that a boy of sixteen should make so smooth verses: so I persuaded him to try whether the Editor of our Paper would give them a place in *Poet's Corner.* And he succeeded, and they were printed. And as I forget his other early productions, I shall copy this."

---

* It is another of the Constitutional Refinements of these times to have fettered, and as to every valuable purpose, silenced, these Debating Societies. They were at least, to say the lowest of them, far better amusements than drunkenness, gambling, or fighting. They were no useless Schools to some of our very celebrated Speakers at the Bar and in Parliament: and, what is of infinitely more importance, they contributed to the diffusion of Political Knowledge and Public Sentiment. L.

PREFACE.

THE MILK-MAID,

ON THE FIRST OF MAY.

I.

Hail, MAY! lovely MAY! how replenish'd my pails!
    The young Dawn overspreads the East streak'd with gold!
My glad heart beats time to the laugh of the Vale,
    And COLIN's voice rings through the woods from the fold.

II.

The Wood to the Mountain submissively bends,
    Whose blue misty summits first glow with the sun!
See thence a gay train by the wild rill descends
    To join the glad sports:....hark! the tumult's begun.

III.

Be cloudless, ye skies!....Be my Colin but there,
    Not the dew-spangled bents on the wide level Dale,
Nor Morning's first blush can more lovely appear
    Than his Looks, since my wishes I could not conceal.

IV.

Swift down the mad dance, while blest health prompts to move,
    We'll count joys to come, and exchange Vows of truth;
And haply when Age cools the transports of Love,
    Decry like good folks the vain pleasures of youth.

V.

No, no; the remembrance shall ever be dear!
    At no time LOVE with INNOCENCE ceases to charm:
It is transport in Youth....and it smiles through the tear,
    When they feel, in their children, it's first soft alarm.

PREFACE.

The Writer of this Preface doubts whether he has been successful in adding the last Stanza to this beautiful and simply expressive Song. But he imagined that some thought of this kind was in the mind of the Author: and he was willing to endeavour to express it. The Breast which has felt Love, justly shrinks from the idea of its total extinction, as from annihilation itself. And there is even an high social and moral use in that order of Providence which exalts Sensations into tender and benign Passions; those Passions into habitual Affections yet more tender; and raises from those Affections *Virtues* the most permanent, the most necessary and beneficent, and the most endearing: thus expanding the sentiment into all the Charities of domestic and social Life.

" I remember," says Mr. G. BLOOMFIELD, continuing his Narrative, " a little piece which he called *the Sailor's Return:* * in which he tried to describe the feelings of an honest Tar, who, after a long absence, saw his dear native Village first rising into view. This too obtain'd a place in the Poet's Corner."

" And as he was so young," his Brother proceeds, " it shews some Genius in him, and some Industry, to have acquired so much knowledge of the use of words in so little time. Indeed at this time myself and my fellow workmen in the Garret began to get instructions from him, though not more than sixteen years old." †

" About this time there came a Man to lodge at our Lodgings that was troubled with fits. ROBERT was so much hurt

---

* It is much to be wished that this may be discovered. L.
† What simple magnanimity and benevolence in this Remark. L.

PREFACE.

to see this poor creature drawn into such frightful forms, and to hear his horrid screams, that I was forced to leave the Lodging. We went to *Blue Hart-court, Bell-alley.* In our new Garret we found a singular character, James Kay, a native of *Dundee.* He was a middle-aged man, of a good understanding, and yet a furious *Calvinist.* He had many Books,....and some which he did not value: such as the SEASONS, PARADISE LOST, and some *Novels.* These Books he lent to ROBERT; who spent all his leisure hours in reading the *Seasons,* which he was now capable of reading. I never heard him give so much praise to any Book as to that."

" I think it was in the year 1784 that the Question came to be decided between the *journeymen Shoemakers;* whether those who had learn'd without serving an *Apprenticeship* could follow the Trade." *

" The Man by whom *Robert* and I were employ'd, Mr. CHAMBERLAYNE, of *Cheapside,* took an active part against the lawful journeymen; and even went so far as to pay off every man that worked for him that had joined their Clubs. This so exasperated the men, that their acting Committee soon looked for *unlawful men* (as they called them) among *Chamberlayne's* workmen."

* That is *as journeymen:* for there was no Question that they could not as *Masters* on their *own* account. That a person may work as a *journeyman* without having served an apprenticeship, had already been determined, T. 9. G. 3. *Beach* v. *Turner.* Burr. Mansf. 2449. A person also who has not served an Apprenticeship may be a *partner,* contributing money, or advice and attention to the accounts and general concerns of the Trade, provided that he does not actually exercise the Trade, and that the acting partner has served. Vide *Reynolds* v. *Chase,* M. 30. G. 2. Burr. Mansf. 2. 1 Burn J. P. Apprent. §. 12. L.

PREFACE.

They found out little *Robert*, and threatened to prosecute *Chamberlayne* for employing him, and to prosecute his Brother, Mr. *G. Bloomfield,* for teaching him. Chamberlayne requested of the Brother to go on and bring it to a Trial; for that he would defend it; and that neither *George* nor *Robert* should be hurt.

In the mean time *George* was much insulted for having refused to join upon this occasion those who called themselves, exclusively, the *Lawful Crafts. George,* who says he was never famed for patience, (it is not indeed so much as might be sometimes wished, very often the lot of strong and acute minds to possess largely of this virtue,) took his pen, and addressed a Letter to one of the most active of their Committee-men (a man of very bad character). In this, after stating that he took *Robert* at his Mother's request, he made free as well with the private character of this man as with the views of the Committee. "This," says *George,* " was very foolish; for it made things worse: but I felt too much to refrain."

What connects this episodical circumstance with the character of our Author follows in his Brother's words.

" *Robert* naturally fond of Peace, and fearful for my personal safety, begged to be suffered to retire from the storm.

" He came home; and Mr. AUSTIN kindly bade him take his house for his home till he could return to me. And here, with his mind glowing with the fine Descriptions of rural scenery which he found in THOMSON's SEASONS, he again retraced the very fields where first he began to think. Here,

PREFACE.

free from the smoke,* the noise, the contention of the City, he imbibed that Love of rural Simplicity and rural Innocence, which fitted him, in a great degree, to be the writer of such a thing as *the Farmer's Boy*."

" Here he lived two Months:....at length, as the dispute in the trade still remained undecided, Mr. DUDBRIDGE offered to take *Robert* Apprentice, to secure him, at all events, from any consequences of the Litigation."

He was bound by Mr. *Ingram*, of *Bell-alley*, to Mr. *John Dudbridge*. His Brother *George* paid five shillings for *Robert*, by way of form, as a premium. Dudbridge was their Landlord, and a *Freeman* of the *City* of *London*. He acted most honourably, and took no advantage of the power which the Indentures gave him. *George Bloomfield* staid with *Robert* till he found he could work as expertly as his self.

Mr. GEORGE BLOOMFIELD adds, " When I left *London* he was turned of eighteen; and much of my happiness since has arisen from a constant correspondence which I have held with him."

" After I left him, he studied *Music*, and was a good player on the *Violin*."

" But as my Brother *Nat* had married a *Woolwich* woman, it happened that *Robert* took a fancy to a comely young woman †

---

* But one word is altered in this Description; which reminds one of the
  Omitte mirari beatæ
  Fumum et opes Strepitumque Romæ.   L.

† MARY. Her surname before marriage is mentioned in the next Page.

of that Town, whose Father is a boat-builder in the Government yard there. His name is CHURCH."

" Soon after he married, *Robert* told me, in a Letter, that ' he had sold his Fiddle and got a Wife.' Like most poor men, he got a wife first, and had to get household stuff afterward. It took him some years to get out of ready furnished Lodgings. At length, by hard working, &c. he acquired a Bed of his own, and hired the room up one pair of stairs at 14, *Bell-alley, Coleman-street*. The Landlord kindly gave him leave to sit and work in the light *Garret*, two pair of stairs higher."

" In *this* Garret, amid six or seven other workmen, his active Mind employed itself in composing *the Farmer's Boy*."

" In my correspondence I have seen several *poetical* effusions of his; all of them of a good moral tendency; but which he very likely would think do him little credit: on that account I have not preserved them."

" ROBERT is a *Ladies Shoemaker*, and works for DAVIES, *Lombard-street*. He is of a slender make; of about 5 *F*. 4 *I*. high; very *dark* complexion....His MOTHER, who is a very religious member of the *Church* of *England*, took all the pains she could in his infancy to make him pious: and as his Reason expanded, his love of God and Man increased with it I never knew his fellow for mildness of temper and Goodness of Disposition. And since I left him, universally is he praised by those who know him best, for the best of Husbands,

PREFACE.

an indulgent Father, and quiet Neighbour. He is about thirty-two years old, and has three Children."

Mr. GEORGE BLOOMFIELD concludes this clear, affectionate, and interesting Narrative, by a very kind Address to the Writer of this Preface. But, pleased as I am with the good opinion of a Man like him, I must not take praise to myself for not having neglected or suppressed such a Work when it came into my hands. And I have no farther merit than that of seeing what it was impossible for an unprejudiced Mind not to see, and of doing what it was impossible not to do.

But I join with him cordially in his prayer, " that GOD, *the Giver of thought,* may, as mental light spreads, raise up many who will turn a listening ear, and will not despise

" *The short and simple Annals of the Poor.*"

Very few words will complete what remains to be added.

Struck with the Work, but not less struck with the Remark, which is become a Proverb, of the Roman Satirist, that " *it is not easy* * for those to emerge to notice whose circumstances obscure the observation of their Merits," I sent it to a Friend, whom I knew to be above these prejudices, and who has deserved, and is deserving, well of the Public, in many other instances, by his attention to Literature and the elegant Arts. He immediately expressed an high satisfaction in it, and communicated it to Messrs. VERNOR and HOOD. They adopted

---

* *Haud facile emergunt quorum virtutibus obstat Res angusta domi.*

PREFACE.

it upon terms honorable to themselves, and satisfactory to the Author, and to me in his behalf. They have published it in a manner which speaks abundantly for itself; both as to the typographical accuracy and beauty, and the good taste and execution of the Ornaments in Wood.

My part has been this, and it has been a very pleasing one: to revise the MS. making occasionally corrections with respect to Orthography, and sometimes in the grammatical construction. The corrections, in point of Grammar, reduce themselves almost wholly to a circumstance of provincial usage, which even well educated persons in *Suffolk* and *Norfolk* do not wholly avoid; and which may be said, as to general custom, to have become in these Counties almost an established Dialect:....that of adopting the plural for the singular termination of verbs, so as to exclude the *s*. But not a line is added or substantially alter'd through the whole Poem. I have requested the MS. to be preserv'd for the satisfaction of those who may wish to be satisfied on this head.

The *Proofs* have gone through my hands. It has been printed slowly: because most carefully; as it deserv'd to be printed.

I have no doubt of its Reception with the Public: I have none of its going down to Posterity with honor; which is not always the Fate of productions which are popular in their day.

Thus much I know:....that the Author, with a spirit amiable at all times, and which would have been revered by Antiquity,

PREFACE.

seems far less interested concerning any Fame or Advantage he may derive from it to himself, than in the pleasure of giving a printed Copy of it, as a tribute of duty and affection, to his MOTHER; in whose pleasure, if it succeeds, his filial heart places the gratification of which it is most desirous. It is much to be a POET, such as he will be found:....it is more to be such a MAN.

CAPEL LOFFT.

TROSTON, n. BURY, SUFFOLK.
21 Dec. 1799.

** ELIZABETH MANBY, the Mother of the Author of this POEM, was sister to the wife of Mr. WILLIAM AUSTIN. I had written to Mr. GEORGE BLOOMFIELD to request the name, before Marriage, of his Mother. This gained me an Answer, which I have great pleasure in adding.

" The late Mr. AUSTIN's wife was a Manby (my Mother's sister). And it may seem strange that, in the FARMER's BOY, *Giles* no where calls him *Uncle*, but *Master*. .... The treatment that my Brother *Robert* experienced from Mr. *Austin* did not differ in any respect from the treatment that all the Servant Boys experienced who lived with him. Mr. *Austin* was Father of fourteen Children by my Aunt (he never had any other wife). He left a decent provision for the five Children that survived him: so that it could not be expected he should have any thing to give to poor Relations. And I don't see a possibility of making a difference between GILES and the Boys that were not related to Mr. *Austin:* for he treated all his Servants exactly as he did his Sons. They all worked hard; all lived well. The DUKE had not a better Man Tenant to him than the late Mr. *Austin*. I saw numbers of the Husbandmen in tears when he was buried. He was beloved by all who knew him. But I imagine *Robert* thought that when he was speaking of Benevolence that was universal, he had no occasion to mention the accidental circumstance of his being related to the Good Man of whom he sung."

SPRING.

ARGUMENT.

Invocation, &c. Seed time. Harrowing. Morning walks. Milking. The Dairy. Suffolk Cheese. Spring coming forth. Sheep fond of changing. Lambs at play. The Butcher, &c.

v. 83...8.

SPRING.

I.

O come, blest Spirit! whatsoe'er thou art,
Thou rushing warmth that hovers round my heart,
Sweet inmate, hail! thou source of sterling joy,
That poverty itself cannot destroy,
Be thou my Muse; and faithful still to me,
Retrace the paths of wild obscurity.
No deeds of arms my humble lines rehearse,
No *Alpine* wonders thunder through my verse,

SPRING.

Invocation....Simple character of Giles. v. 9.

The roaring cataract, the snow-topt hill,
Inspiring awe, till breath itself stands still:
Nature's sublimer scenes ne'er charm'd mine eyes,
Nor Science led me through the boundless skies;
From meaner objects far my raptures flow:
O point these raptures! bid my bosom glow!
And lead my soul to ecstacies of praise
For all the blessings of my infant days!
Bear me through regions where gay Fancy dwells;
But mould to Truth's fair form what Memory tells.

    Live, trifling incidents, and grace my song,
That to the humblest menial belong;
To him whose drudgery unheeded goes,
His joys unreckon'd as his cares or woes:
Though joys and cares in every path are sown,
And youthful minds have feelings of their own;
Quick springing sorrows, transient as the dew;
Delights from trifles, trifles ever new.

SPRING.

v. 27.   *Euston in Suffolk, and its neighbourhood, the Scene.*

'Twas thus with GILES: meek, fatherless, and poor;
Labour his portion, but he felt no more;
No stripes, no tyranny his steps pursu'd;
His life was constant, cheerful, servitude:
Strange to the world, he wore a bashful look,
The Fields his study, Nature was his book;
And, as revolving SEASONS chang'd the scene
From heat to cold, tempestuous to serene,
Though every change still varied his employ,
Yet each new duty brought its share of joy.

   Where noble GRAFTON spreads his rich domains,
Round *Euston's* water'd vale, and sloping plains,
Where woods and groves in solemn grandeur rise,
Where the kite brooding, unmolested flies;
The woodcock and the painted pheasant race,
And sculking foxes, destin'd for the chace;
There Giles, untaught and unrepining, stray'd
Through every copse, and grove, and winding glade;

SPRING.

Benevolent character of Giles's Master....Spring begins. v. 45.

There his first thoughts to Nature's charms inclin'd,
That stamps devotion on th' inquiring mind.
A little farm his generous Master till'd,
Who with peculiar grace his station fill'd;
By deeds of hospitality endear'd,
Serv'd from affection, for his worth rever'd:
A happy offspring blest his plenteous board,
His fields were fruitful, and his barns well stor'd,
And fourscore ewes he fed, a sturdy team,
And lowing kine that grazed beside the stream:
Unceasing industry he kept in view;
And never lack'd a job for Giles to do.

FLED now the sullen murmurs of the North,
The splendid raiment of the SPRING peeps forth;
Her universal green, and the clear sky,
Delight still more and more the gazing eye.
Wide o'er the fields, in rising moisture strong,
Shoots up the simple flower, or creeps along

SPRING.

v. 63.   *Giles goes out to plow.*

The mellow'd soil; imbibing as it goes
Fresh sweets from frequent showers and evening dews;
That summon from its shed the slumb'ring ploughs,
While health impregnates every breeze that blows.
No wheels support the diving pointed share;
No groaning ox is doom'd to labour there;
No helpmates teach the docile steed his road;
(Alike unknown the plow-boy and the goad;)
But, unassisted through each toilsome day,
With smiling brow the plowman cleaves his way,
Draws his fresh parallels, and wid'ning still,
Treads slow the heavy dale, or climbs the hill:
Strong on the wing his busy followers play,
Where writhing earth-worms meet th' unwelcome day;
Till all is chang'd, and hill and level down
Assume a livery of sober brown:
Again disturb'd, when Giles with wearying strides
From ridge to ridge the ponderous harrow guides;

SPRING.

Harrowing....Giles and his Horses rest.   v. 81.

His heels deep sinking every step he goes,
Till dirt usurp the empire of his shoes.
Welcome green headland! firm beneath his feet;
Welcome the friendly bank's refreshing seat!
There, warm with toil, his panting horses browse,
Their shelt'ring canopy of pendent boughs,
Till rest, delicious, chase each transient pain,
And new-born vigour swell in every vein.
Hour after hour, and day to day succeeds,
Till every clod and deep-drawn furrow spreads
To crumbling mould; a level surface clear,
And strew'd with corn to crown the rising year;
And o'er the whole Giles once transverse again,
In earth's moist bosom buries up the grain.
The work is done; no more to man is given;
The grateful farmer trusts the rest to Heaven.
Yet oft with anxious heart he looks around,
And marks the first green blade that breaks the ground;

SPRING.

v. 99.   *Rooks.*

In fancy sees his trembling oats uprun,
His tufted barley yellow with the sun;
Sees clouds propitious shed their timely store,
And all his harvest gather'd round his door.
But still unsafe the big swoln grain below,
A fav'rite morsel with the rook and crow;
From field to field the flock increasing goes;
To level crops most formidable foes:
Their danger well the wary plunderers know,
And place a watch on some conspicuous bough;
Yet oft the sculking gunner by surprise
Will scatter death amongst them as they rise.
These, hung in triumph round the spacious field,
At best will but a short-lived terror yield:
Nor guards of property; (not penal law,
But harmless riflemen of rags and straw);
Familiariz'd to these, they boldly rove,
Nor heed such centinels that never move.

SPRING.

Wood Scenery.   v. 117.

Let then your birds lie prostrate on the earth,
In dying posture, and with wings stretch'd forth;
Shift them at eve or morn from place to place,
And death shall terrify the pilfering race;
In the mid air, while circling round and round,
They'll call their lifeless comrades from the ground;
With quick'ning wing, and notes of loud alarm,
Warn the whole flock to shun the' impending harm.

   This task had *Giles*, in fields remote from home:
Oft has he wish'd the rosy morn to come.
Yet never fam'd was he nor foremost found
To break the seal of sleep; his sleep was sound:
But when at day-break summon'd from his bed,
Light as the lark that carol'd o'er his head,
His sandy way deep-worn by hasty showers,
O'er-arch'd with oaks that form'd fantastic bow'rs,
Waving aloft their tow'ring branches proud,
In borrow'd tinges from the eastern cloud,

SPRING.

v. 135.   *Various Birds....Their song and appearance.*

(Whence inspiration, pure as ever flow'd,
And genuine transport in his bosom glow'd)
His own shrill matin join'd the various notes
Of Nature's music, from a thousand throats:
The blackbird strove with emulation sweet,
And Echo answer'd from her close retreat;
The sporting white-throat on some twig's end borne,
Pour'd hymns to freedom and the rising morn;
Stopt in her song perchance the starting thrush
Shook a white shower from the black-thorn bush,
Where dew-drops thick as early blossoms hung,
And trembled as the minstrel sweetly sung.
Across his path, in either grove to hide,
The timid rabbit scouted by his side;
Or bold cock-pheasant stalk'd along the road,
Whose gold and purple tints alternate glow'd.
But groves no farther fenc'd the devious way;
A wide-extended heath before him lay,

SPRING.

Bringing in of Cows to be milked.   v. 153.

Where on the grass the stagnant shower had run,
And shone a mirror to the rising sun,
(Thus doubly seen) lighting a distant wood,
Giving new life to each expanding bud;
Effacing quick the dewy foot-marks found,
Where prowling Reynard trod his nightly round;
To shun whose thefts 'twas Giles's evening care,
His feather'd victims to suspend in air,
High on the bough that nodded o'er his head,
And thus each morn to strew the field with dead.

   His simple errand done, he homeward hies;
Another instantly its place supplies.
The clatt'ring dairy-maid immers'd in steam,
Singing and scrubbing midst her milk and cream,
Bawls out, "*Go fetch the cows:...*" he hears no more;
For pigs, and ducks, and turkies, throng the door,
And sitting hens, for constant war prepar'd;
A concert strange to that which late he heard.

SPRING.

v. 171.   *Order of the Cows returning.*

Straight to the meadow then he whistling goes;
With well-known halloo calls his lazy cows:
Down the rich pasture heedlessly they graze,
Or hear the summon with an idle gaze;
For well they know the cow-yard yields no more
Its tempting fragrance, nor its wint'ry store.
Reluctance marks their steps, sedate and slow;
The right of conquest all the law they know:
Subordinate they one by one succeed;
And one among them always takes the lead,
Is ever foremost, wheresoe'er they stray;
Allow'd precedence, undisputed sway;
With jealous pride her station is maintain'd,
For many a broil that post of honour gain'd.
At home, the yard affords a grateful scene,
For Spring makes e'en a miry cow-yard clean.
Thence from its chalky bed behold convey'd
The rich manure that drenching winter made,

SPRING.

Milking.   v. 189.

Which pil'd near home, grows green with many a weed,
A promis'd nutriment for Autumn's seed.
Forth comes the Maid, and like the morning smiles;
The Mistress too, and follow'd close by Giles.
A friendly tripod forms their humble seat.
With pails bright scour'd, and delicately sweet.
Where shadowing elms obstruct the morning ray,
Begins their work, begins the simple lay;
The full-charg'd udder yields its willing streams,
While *Mary* sings some lover's amorous dreams;
And crouching *Giles* beneath a neighbouring tree
Tugs o'er his pail, and chants with equal glee;
Whose hat with tatter'd brim, of knap so bare,
From the cow's side purloins a coat of hair,
A mottled ensign of his harmless trade,
An unambitious, peaceable cockade.
As unambitious too that cheerful aid
The mistress yields beside her rosy maid;

SPRING.

v. 207.   *The Dairy.*

With joy she views her plenteous reeking store,
And bears a brimmer to the dairy door;
Her cows dismiss'd, the luscious mead to roam,
Till eve again recall them loaded home.
And now the DAIRY claims her choicest care,
And half her household find employment there:
Slow rolls the churn, its load of clogging cream
At once foregoes its quality and name;
From knotty particles first floating wide
Congealing butter's dash'd from side to side;
Streams of new milk through flowing coolers stray,
And snow-white curd abounds, and wholesome whey.
Due north th' unglazed windows, cold and clear,
For warming sunbeams are unwelcome here.
Brisk goes the work beneath each busy hand,
And *Giles* must trudge, whoever gives command;
A *Gibeonite*, that serves them all by turns:
He drains the pump, from him the faggot burns;

Suffolk Cheese. v. 225.

From him the noisy hogs demand their food;
While at his heels run many a chirping brood,
Or down his path in expectation stand,
With equal claims upon his strewing hand.
Thus wastes the morn, till each with pleasure sees
The bustle o'er, and press'd the new-made cheese.
 Unrivall'd stands thy country CHEESE, O *Giles!*
Whose very name alone engenders smiles;
Whose fame abroad by every tongue is spoke,
The well-known butt of many a flinty joke,
That pass like current coin the nation through;
And, ah! experience proves the satire true.
Provision's grave, thou ever craving mart,
Dependant, huge Metropolis! where Art
Her poring thousands stows in breathless rooms,
Midst pois'nous smokes and steams, and rattling looms;
Where Grandeur revels in unbounded stores;
Restraint, a slighted stranger at their doors!

SPRING.

v. 243.   *Suffolk Cheese.*

Thou, like a whirlpool, drain'st the countries round,
Till London market, London price, resound
Through every town, round every passing load,
And dairy produce throngs the eastern road:
Delicious veal, and butter, every hour,
From Essex lowlands, and the banks of Stour;
And further far, where numerous herds repose,
From Orwell's brink, from Weveny, or Ouse.
Hence Suffolk dairy-wives run mad for cream,
And leave their milk with nothing but its name;
Its name derision and reproach pursue,
And strangers tell of "three times skim'd sky-blue."
To cheese converted, what can be its boast?
What, but the common virtues of a post!
If drought o'ertake it faster than the knife,
Most fair it bids for stubborn length of life,
And, like the oaken shelf whereon 'tis laid,
Mocks the weak efforts of the bending blade;

The procession of Spring. v. 261.

Or in the hog-trough rests in perfect spite,
Too big to swallow, and too hard to bite.
Inglorious victory! Ye Cheshire meads,
Or Severn's flow'ry dales, where plenty treads,
Was your rich milk to suffer wrongs like these,
Farewell your pride! farewell renowned cheese!
The skimmer dread, whose ravages alone
Thus turn the mead's sweet nectar into stone.

NEGLECTED now the early *daisy* lies;
Nor thou, pale *primrose*, bloom'st the only prize:
Advancing SPRING profusely spreads abroad
Flow'rs of all hues, with sweetest fragrance stor'd;
Where'er she treads, LOVE gladdens every plain,
Delight on tiptoe bears her lucid train;
Sweet *Hope* with conscious brow before her flies,
Anticipating wealth from Summer skies;
All Nature feels her renovating sway;
The sheep-fed pasture, and the meadow gay;

SPRING.

v. 279. Sheep....Range of pasture.

And trees, and shrubs, no longer budding seen,
Display the new-grown branch of lighter green;
On airy downs the shepherd idling lies,
And sees *to-morrow* in the marbled skies.
Here then, my soul, thy darling theme pursue,
For every day was Giles a SHEPHERD too.
   Small was his charge; no wilds had they to roam,
But bright enclosures circling round their home.
Nor yellow-blossom'd furze, nor stubborn thorn,
The heath's rough produce, had their fleeces torn;
Yet ever roving, ever seeking thee,
Enchanting spirit, dear Variety!
O happy tenants, prisoners of a day!
Releas'd to ease, to pleasure, and to play;
Indulg'd through every field by turns to range,
And taste them all in one continual change.
For though luxuriant their grassy food,
Sheep long confin'd but loathe the present good;

SPRING.

Lambs at play.   v. 297.

Instinctively they haunt the homeward gate,
And starve, and pine, with plenty at their feet.
Loos'd from the winding lane, a joyful throng,
See, o'er yon pasture how they pour along!
Giles round their boundaries takes his usual stroll;
Sees every pass secur'd, and fences whole;
High fences, proud to charm the gazing eye,
Where many a nestling first assays to fly;
Where blows the woodbine, faintly streak'd with red,
And rests on every bough its tender head;
Round the young ash its twining branches meet,
Or crown the hawthorn with its odours sweet.
Say, ye that know, ye who have felt and seen
Spring's morning smiles, and soul-enliv'ning green,
Say, did you give the thrilling transport way?
Did your eye brighten, when young lambs at play
Leap'd o'er your path with animated pride,
Or gaz'd in merry clusters by your side?

SPRING.

v. 315.   *Lambs at play.*

Ye who can smile, to wisdom no disgrace,
At the arch meaning of a kitten's face;
If spotless innocence, and infant mirth,
Excites to praise, or gives reflection birth;
In shades like these pursue your fav'rite joy,
Midst Nature's revels, sports that never cloy.
A few begin a short but vigorous race,
And indolence abash'd soon flies the place;
Thus challeng'd forth, see thither one by one,
From every side assembling playmates run;
A thousand wily antics mark their stay,
A starting crowd, impatient of delay.
Like the fond dove from fearful prison freed,
Each seems to say, " Come, let us try our speed;"
Away they scour, impetuous, ardent, strong,
The green turf trembling as they bound along;
Adown the slope, then up the hillock climb,
Where every molehill is a bed of thyme;

SPRING.

Contrast of their near approaching fate. v. 333.

There panting stop; yet scarcely can refrain;
A bird, a leaf, will set them off again:
Or, if a gale with strength unusual blow,
Scatt'ring the wild-brier roses into snow,
Their little limbs increasing efforts try,
Like the torn flower the fair assemblage fly.
Ah, fallen rose! sad emblem of their doom;
Frail as thyself, they perish while they bloom!
Though unoffending innocence may plead,
Though frantic ewes may mourn the savage deed,
Their shepherd comes, a messenger of blood,
And drives them bleating from their sports and food.
Care loads his brow, and pity wrings his heart,
For lo, the murd'ring BUTCHER with his cart
Demands the firstlings of his flock to die,
And makes a sport of life and liberty!
His gay companions *Giles* beholds no more;
Clos'd are their eyes, their fleeces drench'd in gore;

SPRING.

v. 351.   *Conclusion of the first Book.*

Nor can Compassion, with her softest notes,

Withhold the knife that plunges through their throats.

Down, indignation! hence, ideas foul!

Away the shocking image from my soul!

Let kindlier visitants attend my way,

Beneath approaching *Summer*'s fervid ray;

Nor thankless glooms obtrude, nor cares annoy,

Whilst the sweet theme is *universal joy.*

SUMMER.

ARGUMENT.

Turnip sowing. Wheat ripening. Sparrows. Insects. The sky-lark. Reaping, &c. Harvest-field, Dairy-maid, &c. Labours of the barn. The gander. Night; a thunder storm. Harvest-home. Reflections, &c.

SUMMER.

II.

The Farmer's life displays in every part
A moral lesson to the sensual heart.
Though in the lap of Plenty, thoughtful still,
He looks beyond the present good or ill;
Nor estimates alone one blessing's worth,
From changeful seasons, or capricious earth;
But views the future with the present hours,
And looks for failures as he looks for show'ers;
For casual as for certain want prepares,
And round his yard the reeking haystack rears;

Provident turn of the Farmer's mind. v. 11.

Or clover, blossom'd lovely to the sight,
His team's rich store through many a wint'ry night.
What though abundance round his dwelling spreads,
Though ever moist his self-improving meads
Supply his dairy with a copious flood,
And seem to promise unexhausted food,
That promise fails, when buried deep in snow,
And vegetative juices cease to flow.
For this, his plough turns up the destin'd lands,
Whence stormy Winter draws its full demands;
For this, the seed minutely small he sows,
Whence, sound and sweet, the hardy turnip grows.
But how unlike to APRIL's closing days!
High climbs the Sun, and darts his pow'rful rays;
Whitens the fresh-drawn mould, and pierces through
The cumb'rous clods that tumble round the plough.
O'er heaven's bright azure hence with joyful eyes
The Farmer sees dark clouds assembling rise;

SUMMER.

v. 29.   *Showers softening the soil.*

Borne o'er his fields a heavy torrent falls,
And strikes the earth in hasty driving squalls.
" *Right welcome down, ye precious drops,*" he cries;
But soon, too soon, the partial blessing flies.
" *Boy, bring thy harrows, try how deep the rain*
Has forc'd its way." He comes, but comes in vain;
Dry dust beneath the bubbling surface lurks,
And mocks his pains the more, the more he works:
Still midst huge clods he plunges on forlorn,
That laugh his harrows and the shower to scorn.
E'en thus the living clod, the stubborn fool,
Resists the stormy lectures of the school,
Till tried with gentler means, the dunce to please,
His head imbibes right reason by degrees;
As when from eve till morning's wakeful hour,
Light, constant rain, evinces secret pow'r,
And ere the day resume its wonted smiles,
Presents a cheerful easy task for *Giles*.

SUMMER.

Green Corn....Sparrows. v. 47.

Down with a touch the mellow'd soil is laid,
And yon tall crop next claims his timely aid;
Thither well pleas'd he hies, assur'd to find
Wild trackless haunts, and objects to his mind.
 Shot up from broad rank blades that droop below,
The nodding WHEAT-EAR forms a graceful bow,
With milky kernels starting full, weigh'd down,
Ere yet the sun hath ting'd its head with brown;
Whilst thousands in a flock, for ever gay,
Loud chirping *sparrows* welcome on the day,
And from the mazes of the leafy thorn
Drop one by one upon the bending corn;
Giles with a pole assails their close retreats,
And round the grass-grown dewy border beats,
On either side completely overspread,
Here branches bend, there corn o'ertops his head.
Green covert, hail! for through the varying year
No hours so sweet, no scene to him so dear.

SUMMER.

v. 65.   *Scenery....full of life, and inspiring contemplation.*

Here *Wisdom's* placid eye delighted sees
His frequent intervals of lonely ease,
And with one ray his infant soul inspires,
Just kindling there her never-dying fires,
Whence solitude derives peculiar charms,
And heaven-directed thought his bosom warms.
Just where the parting bough's light shadows play,
Scarce in the shade, nor in the scorching day,
Stretch'd on the turf he lies, a peopled bed,
Where swarming insects creep around his head.
The small dust-colour'd beetle climbs with pain
O'er the smooth plantain-leaf, a spacious plain!
Thence higher still, by countless steps convey'd,
He gains the summit of a shiv'ring blade,
And flirts his filmy wings, and looks around,
Exulting in his distance from the ground.
The tender speckled moth here dancing seen,
The vaulting grasshopper of glossy green,

SUMMER.

The Sky-lark. v. 83.

And all prolific *Summer*'s sporting train,
Their little lives by various pow'rs sustain.
But what can unassisted vision do?
What, but recoil where most it would pursue;
His patient gaze but finish with a sigh,
When music waking speaks the *sky-lark* nigh.
Just starting from the corn she cheerly sings,
And trusts with conscious pride her downy wings;
Still louder breathes, and in the face of day
Mounts up, and calls on *Giles* to mark her way.
Close to his eyes his hat he instant bends,
And forms a friendly telescope, that lends
Just aid enough to dull the glaring light,
And place the wand'ring bird before his sight;
Yet oft beneath a cloud she sweeps along,
Lost for awhile, yet pours her varied song:
He views the spot, and as the cloud moves by,
Again she stretches up the clear blue sky;

SUMMER.

v. 101.   *Sky-lark....Corn ripening.*

Her form, her motion, undistinguish'd quite.
Save when she wheels direct from shade to light:
The flutt'ring songstress a mere speck became,
Like fancy's floating bubbles in a dream;
He sees her yet, but yielding to repose,
Unwittingly his jaded eyelids close.
Delicious sleep! From sleep who could forbear,
With no more guilt than *Giles,* and no more care?
Peace o'er his slumbers waves her guardian wing,
Nor conscience once disturbs him with a sting;
He wakes refresh'd from every trivial pain,
And takes his pole and brushes round again.
 Its dark-green hue, its sicklier tints all fail,
And rip'ening harvest rustles in the gale.
A glorious sight, if glory dwells below,
Where Heaven's munificence makes all the show,
O'er every field and golden prospect found,
That glads the ploughman's Sunday morning's round,

SUMMER.

Pleasure from the views of Nature.   v. 119.

When on some eminence he takes his stand,
To judge the smiling produce of the land.
Here Vanity slinks back, her head to hide:
What is there here to flatter human pride?
The tow'ring fabric, or the dome's loud roar,
And stedfast columns, may astonish more,
Where the charm'd gazer long delighted stays,
Yet trac'd but to the *architect* the praise;
Whilst here, the veriest clown that treads the sod,
Without one scruple, gives the praise to God;
And twofold joys possess his raptur'd mind,
From gratitude and admiration join'd.

Here, midst the boldest triumphs of her worth,
Nature herself invites the reapers forth;
Dares the keen sickle from its twelvemonth's rest,
And gives that ardour which in every breast
From infancy to age alike appears,
When the first sheaf its plumy top uprears.

SUMMER.

v. 137.   Reapers....Gleaning.

No rake takes here what Heaven to all bestows:
Children of want, for you the bounty flows!
And every cottage from the plenteous store
Receives a burden nightly at its door.
   Hark! where the sweeping scythe now rips along:
Each sturdy Mower emulous and strong;
Whose writhing form meridian heat defies,
Bends o'er his work, and every sinew tries;
Prostrates the waving treasure at his feet,
But spares the rising clover, short and sweet.
Come, HEALTH! come, *Jollity!* light-footed, come;
Here hold your revels, and make this your home.
Each heart awaits and hails you as its own;
Each moisten'd brow, that scorns to wear a frown:
Th' unpeopled dwelling mourns its tenants stray'd;
E'en the domestic laughing dairy-maid
Hies to the FIELD, the general toil to share.
Meanwhile the FARMER quits his elbow-chair,

SUMMER.

| *The joy of the Farmer.* | v. 155. |

His cool brick-floor, his pitcher, and his ease,
And braves the sultry beams, and gladly sees
His gates thrown open, and his team abroad,
The ready group attendant on his word,
To turn the swarth, the quiv'ring load to rear,
Or ply the busy rake, the land to clear.
Summer's light garb itself now cumb'rous grown,
Each his thin doublet in the shade throws down;
Where oft the mastiff sculks with half-shut eye,
And rouses at the stranger passing by;
Whilst unrestrain'd the social converse flows,
And every breast Love's pow'rful impulse knows,
And rival wits with more than rustic grace
Confess the presence of a pretty face;
For, lo! encircled there, the lovely MAID,
In youth's own bloom and native smiles array'd;
Her hat awry, divested of her gown,
Her creaking stays of leather, stout and brown;...

SUMMER.

v. 173. *The Country Maid.*

Invidious barrier! why art thou so high,
When the slight cov'ring of her neck slips by,
There half revealing to the eager sight
Her full, ripe bosom, exquisitely white?
In many a local tale of harmless mirth,
And many a jest of momentary birth,
She bears a part, and as she stops to speak,
Strokes back the ringlets from her glowing cheek.

Now noon gone by, and four declining hours,
The weary limbs relax their boasted pow'rs;
Thirst rages strong, the fainting spirits fail,
And ask the sov'reign cordial, home-brew'd ale:
Beneath some shelt'ring heap of yellow corn
Rests the hoop'd keg, and friendly cooling horn,
That mocks alike the goblet's brittle frame,
Its costlier potions, and its nobler name.
To *Mary* first the brimming draught is given,
By toil made welcome as the dews of heaven,

SUMMER.

Harvest-field refreshment....The Cart-horse. v. 191.

And never lip that press'd its homely edge
Had kinder blessings or a heartier pledge.
Of wholesome viands here a banquet smiles,
A common cheer for all;...e'en humble *Giles*,
Who joys his trivial services to yield
Amidst the fragrance of the open field;
Oft doom'd in suffocating heat to bear
The cobweb'd barn's impure and dusty air;
To ride in murky state the panting steed,
Destin'd aloft th' unloaded grain to tread,
Where, in his path as heaps on heaps are thrown,
He rears, and plunges the loose mountain down:
Laborious task! with what delight when done
Both horse and rider greet th' unclouded sun!
Yet by th' unclouded sun are hourly bred
The bold assailants that surround thine head,
Poor patient *Ball!* and with insulting wing
Roar in thine ears, and dart the piercing sting:

SUMMER.

v. 209. *Docking of Horses condemned.*

In thy behalf the crest-wav'd boughs avail
More than thy short-clipt remnant of a tail,
A moving mockery, a useless name,
A living proof of cruelty and shame.
Shame to the man, whatever fame he bore,
Who took from thee what man can ne'er restore,
Thy weapon of defence, thy chiefest good,
When swarming flies contending suck thy blood.
Nor thine alone the suff'ring, thine the care,
The fretful *Ewe* bemoans an equal share;
Tormented into sores, her head she hides,
Or angry brushes from her new-shorn sides.
Pen'd in the yard, e'en now at closing day
Unruly *Cows* with mark'd impatience stay,
And vainly striving to escape their foes,
The pail kick down; a piteous current flows.
 Is't not enough that plagues like these molest?
Must still another foe annoy their rest?

SUMMER.

The Gander. v. 227.

He comes, the pest and terror of the yard,
His full-fledg'd progeny's imperious guard;
The GANDER;...spiteful, insolent, and bold,
At the colt's footlock takes his daring hold;
There, serpent-like, escapes a dreadful blow;
And straight attacks a poor defenceless cow:
Each booby goose th' unworthy strife enjoys,
And hails his prowess with redoubled noise.
Then back he stalks, of self-importance full,
Seizes the shaggy foretop of the bull,
Till whirl'd aloft he falls; a timely check,
Enough to dislocate his worthless neck:
For lo! of old, he boasts an honour'd wound;
Behold that broken wing that trails the ground!
Thus fools and bravoes kindred pranks pursue;
As savage quite, and oft as fatal too.
Happy the man that foils an envious elf,
Using the darts of spleen to serve himself.

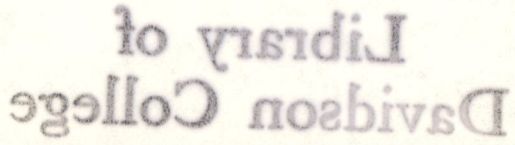

SUMMER.

v. 245.   *Swine....Repose of Twilight.*

As when by turns the strolling *Swine* engage
The utmost efforts of the bully's rage,
Whose nibbling warfare on the grunter's side
Is welcome pleasure to his bristly hide;
Gently he stoops, or lays himself along,
Endures the insults of the gabbling throng,
That march exulting round his fallen head,
As human victors trample on their dead.
   Still TWILIGHT, welcome! Rest, how sweet art thou!
Now eve o'erhangs the western cloud's thick brow;
The far-stretch'd curtain of retiring light,
With fiery treasures fraught, that on the sight
Flash from its bulging sides, where darkness lours,
In Fancy's eye, a chain of mould'ring tow'rs;
Or craggy coasts just rising into view,
Midst jav'lins dire, and darts of streaming blue.
Anon tir'd labourers bless their shelt'ring homes,
When MIDNIGHT, and the frightful TEMPEST comes.

SUMMER.

Midnight....Tempest.   v. 263.

The Farmer wakes, and sees with silent dread
The angry shafts of Heaven gleam round his bed;
The bursting cloud reiterated roars,
Shakes his straw roof, and jars his bolted doors:
The slow-wing'd storm along the troubled skies
Spreads its dark course; the wind begins to rise;
And full-leav'd elms, his dwelling's shade by day,
With mimic thunder give its fury way:
Sounds in his chimney top a doleful peal,
Midst pouring rain, or gusts of rattling hail;
With tenfold danger low the tempest bends,
And quick and strong the sulph'urous flame descends:
The fright'ned mastiff from his kennel flies,
And cringes at the door with piteous cries....

    Where now's the trifler? where the child of pride?
These are the moments when the heart is try'd!
Nor lives the man with conscience e'er so clear,
But feels a solemn, reverential fear;

SUMMER.

v. 281. *Harvest-home.*

Feels too a joy relieve his aching breast,
When the spent storm hath howl'd itself to rest.
Still, welcome beats the long continued show'r,
And sleep protracted, comes with double pow'r;
Calm dreams of bliss bring on the morning sun,
For every barn is fill'd, and HARVEST *done!*

 Now, ere sweet SUMMER bids its long adieu,
And winds blow keen where late the blossom grew,
The bustling day and jovial night must come,
The long accustom'd feast of HARVEST-HOME.
No blood-stain'd victory, in story bright,
Can give the philosophic mind delight;
No triumph please whilst rage and death destroy:
Reflection sickens at the monstrous joy.
And where the joy, if rightly understood,
Like cheerful praise for universal good?
The soul nor check nor doubtful anguish knows,
But free and pure the grateful current flows.

SUMMER.

Freedom and equal joy of the Feast.   v. 299.

Behold the sound oak table's massy frame
Bestride the kitchen floor! the careful dame
And gen'rous host invite their friends around,
While all that clear'd the crop, or till'd the ground,
Are guests by right of custom....old and young;
And many a neighbouring yeoman join the throng,
With artizans that lent their dext'rous aid,
When o'er each field the flaming sun-beams play'd.—
Yet Plenty reigns, and from her boundless hoard,
Though not one jelly trembles on the board,
Supplies the feast with all that sense can crave;
With all that made our great forefathers brave,
Ere the cloy'd palate countless flavours try'd,
And cooks had Nature's judgment set aside.
With thanks to Heaven, and tales of rustic lore,
The mansion echoes when the banquet's o'er;
A wider circle spreads, and smiles abound,
As quick the frothing horn performs its round;

SUMMER

v. 317. *Ancient equality of this Festival.*

Care's mortal foe; that sprightly joys imparts
To cheer the frame and elevate their hearts.
Here, fresh and brown, the hazel's produce lies
In tempting heaps, and peals of laughter rise,
And crackling Music, with the frequent *Song*,
Unheeded bear the midnight hour along.
Here once a year Distinction low'rs its crest,
The master, servant, and the merry guest,
Are equal all; and round the happy ring
The reaper's eyes exulting glances fling,
And, warm'd with gratitude, he quits his place,
With sun-burnt hands and ale-enliven'd face,
Refills the jug his honour'd host to tend,
To serve at once the master and the friend;
Proud thus to meet his smiles, to share his tale,
His nuts, his conversation, and his ale.
 Such were the days,...of days long past I sing,...
When Pride gave place to mirth without a sting;

SUMMER.

Contrast of modern usage.   v. 335.

Ere tyrant customs strength sufficient bore
To violate the feelings of the poor;
To leave them distanc'd in the mad'ning race,
Where'er Refinement shews its hated face:
Nor causeless hated; 'tis the peasant's curse,
That hourly makes his wretched station worse;
Destroys life's intercourse;* the social plan
That rank to rank cements, as man to man:
Wealth flows around him, fashion lordly reigns;
Yet poverty is his, and mental pains.
Methinks I hear the mourner thus impart
The stifled murmurs of his wounded heart:
' Whence comes this change, ungracious, irksome, cold?
' Whence the new grandeur that mine eyes behold?
' The wid'ning distance which I daily see,
' Has Wealth done this?...then wealth's a foe to me;
' Foe to our rights; that leaves a pow'rful few
' The paths of emulation to pursue....

* Vide note at the end of this volume.

SUMMER

v. 353. *Subject continued.*

' For emulation stoops to us no more:
' The hope of humble industry is o'er;
' The blameless hope, the cheering sweet presage
' Of future comforts for declining age.
' Can my sons share from this paternal hand
' The profits with the labours of the land?
' No; though indulgent Heaven its blessing deigns,
' Where's the small farm to suit my scanty means?
' Content, the poet sings, with us resides,
' In lonely cots like mine the damsel hides;
' And will he then in raptur'd visions tell
' That sweet Content with Want can ever dwell?
' A barley loaf, 'tis true, my table crowns,
' That fast diminishing in lusty rounds,
' Stops Nature's cravings; yet her sighs will flow
' From knowing this,...that once it was not so
' Our annual feast, when Earth her plenty yields,
' When crown'd with boughs the last load quits the fields,

SUMMER.

Continued.   v. 371.

' The aspect still of ancient joy puts on;
' The aspect only, with the substance gone:
' The self-same Horn is still at our command,
' But serves none now but the plebeian hand:
' For *home-brew'd Ale*, neglected and debas'd,
' Is quite discarded from the realms of taste.
' Where unaffected Freedom charm'd the soul,
' The *separate* table and the costly bowl,
' Cool as the blast that checks the budding Spring,
' A mockery of gladness round them fling.
' For oft the Farmer, ere his heart approves,
' Yields up the custom which he dearly loves:
' Refinement forces on him like a tide;
' Bold innovations down its current ride,
' That bear no peace beneath their shewy dress,
' Nor add one tittle to his happiness.
' His guests selected; rank's punctilios known;
' What trouble waits upon a casual frown!

SUMMER.

v. 389.   *Continued.*

' Restraint's foul manacles his pleasures maim;
' Selected guests selected phrases claim:
' Nor reigns that joy when hand in hand they join
' That good old Master felt in shaking mine.
' HEAVEN bless his memory! bless his honour'd name!
' (The poor will speak his lasting worthy fame:)
' To souls fair-purpos'd strength and guidance give;
' In pity to us still let goodness live:
' Let labour have its due! my cot shall be
' From chilling want and guilty murmurs free:
' Let labour have its due;...then peace is mine,
' And never, never shall my heart repine.'

AUTUMN.

ARGUMENT.

Acorns. Hogs in the wood. Wheat-sowing. The Church. Village girls. The mad girl. The bird-boy's hut. Disappointments; reflections, &c. Euston-hall. Fox-hunting. Old Trouncer, Long nights. A welcome to Winter.

AUTUMN.

III.

AGAIN, the year's *decline*, midst storms and floods,
The thund'ring chase, the yellow fading woods,
Invite my song; that fain would boldly tell
Of upland coverts, and the echoing dell,
By turns resounding loud, at eve and morn
The swineherd's halloo, or the huntsman's horn.

    No more the fields with scatter'd grain supply
The restless wand'ring tenants of the STY;

AUTUMN.

Wood-scenery....Swine and pigs feeding on fallen acorns. v. 9.

From oak to oak they run with eager haste,
And wrangling share the first delicious taste
Of fallen ACORNS; yet but thinly found
Till the strong gale have shook them to the ground.
It comes; and roaring woods obedient wave:
Their home well pleas'd the joint adventurers leave:
The trudging sow leads forth her numerous young,
Playful, and white, and clean, the briars among,
Till briars and thorns increasing, fence them round,
Where last year's mould'ring leaves bestrew the ground,
And o'er their heads, loud lash'd by furious squalls,
Bright from their cups the rattling treasure falls;
Hot thirsty food; whence doubly sweet and cool
The welcome margin of some rush-grown pool,
The wild duck's lonely haunt, whose jealous eye
Guards every point; who sits prepar'd to fly,
On the calm bosom of her little lake,
Too closely screen'd for ruffian winds to shake;

AUTUMN.

v. 27.   *Wild Ducks among the sedges.*

And as the bold intruders press around,
At once she starts, and rises with a bound:
With bristles rais'd the sudden noise they hear,
And ludicrously wild, and wing'd with fear,
The herd decamp with more than swinish speed,
And snorting dash through sedge, and rush, and reed:
Through tangling thickets headlong on they go,
Then stop, and listen for their fancied foe;
The hindmost still the growing panic spreads,
Repeated fright the first alarm succeeds,
Till Folly's wages, wounds and thorns, they reap:
Yet glorying in their fortunate escape,
Their groundless terrors by degrees soon cease,
And Night's dark reign restores their wonted peace.
For now the gale subsides, and from each bough
The roosting pheasant's short but frequent crow
Invites to rest; and huddling side by side,
The herd in closest ambush seek to hide;

AUTUMN.

Hogs wandering in the wood...Husbandman's prospective care. v. 45.

Seek some warm slope with shagged moss o'erspread,
Dry'd leaves their copious covering and their bed.
In vain may *Giles*, through gath'ring glooms that fall,
And solemn silence, urge his piercing call:
Whole days and nights they tarry midst their store,
Nor quit the woods till oaks can yield no more.
 Beyond bleak *Winter's* rage, beyond the *Spring*
That rolling Earth's unvarying course will bring,
Who tills the ground looks on with mental eye,
And sees next *Summer's* sheaves and cloudless sky;
And even now, whilst Nature's beauty dies,
Deposits SEED, and bids new harvests rise;
Seed well prepar'd, and warm'd with glowing lime,
'Gainst earth-bred grubs, and cold, and lapse of time:
For searching frosts and various ills invade,
Whilst wint'ry months depress the springing blade.
The plough moves heavily, and strong the soil,
And clogging harrows with augmented toil

AUTUMN.

v. 63. *Village Bells.*

Dive deep: and clinging, mixes with the mould
A fat'ning treasure from the nightly fold,
And all the cow-yard's highly valu'd store,
That late bestrew'd the blacken'd surface o'er.
No idling hours are here, when Fancy trims
Her dancing taper over outstretch'd limbs,
And in her thousand thousand colours drest,
Plays round the grassy couch of noontide rest:
Here GILES for hours of indolence atones
With strong exertion, and with weary bones,
And knows no leisure; till the distant chime
Of Sabbath bells he hears at sermon time,
That down the brook sound sweetly in the gale,
Or strike the rising hill, or skim the dale.

  Nor his alone the sweets of ease to taste:
Kind rest extends to all;...save one poor beast,
That true to time and pace, is doom'd to plod,
To bring the Pastor to the HOUSE of GOD:

AUTUMN.

The Church. v. 81.

Mean structure; where no bones of heroes lie!
The rude inelegance of poverty
Reigns here alone: else why that roof of straw?
Those narrow windows with the frequent flaw?
O'er whose low cells the dock and mallow spreads,
And rampant nettles lift their spiry heads,
Whilst from the hollows of the tower on high
The grey-cap'd daws in saucy legions fly.
Round these lone walls assembling neighbours meet,
And tread departed friends beneath their feet;
And new-brier'd graves, that prompt the secret sigh,
Shew each the spot where he himself must lie.
Midst timely greetings village news goes round,
Of crops late shorn, or crops that deck the ground;
Experienc'd ploughmen in the circle join;
While sturdy boys, in feats of strength to shine,
With pride elate their young associates brave
To jump from hollow-sounding grave to grave;

AUTUMN.

v. 99.   *Village Girls....The poor distracted young Woman.*

Then close consulting, each his talent lends
To plan fresh sports when tedious service ends.
Hither at times, with cheerfulness of soul,
Sweet *village Maids* from neighbouring hamlets stroll,
That like the light-heel'd does o'er lawns that rove,
Look shyly curious; rip'ning into love;
For love's their errand: hence the tints that glow
On either cheek, an heighten'd lustre know:
When, conscious of their charms, e'en Age looks sly,
And rapture beams from Youth's observant eye.

 THE PRIDE of such a party, Nature's pride,
Was lovely POLL;* who innocently try'd
With hat of airy shape and ribbons gay,
Love to inspire, and stand in Hymen's way:
But, ere her *twentieth* Summer could expand,
Or youth was render'd happy with her hand,
Her mind's serenity was lost and gone,
Her eye grew languid, and she wept alone;

 * MARY RAYNER, of Ixworth Thorp.

AUTUMN.

The subject continued. v. 117.

Yet causeless seem'd her grief; for quick restrain'd,
Mirth follow'd loud, or indignation reign'd:
Whims wild and simple led her from her home,
The heath, the common, or the fields to roam:
Terror and joy alternate rul'd her hours;
Now blithe she sung, and gather'd useless flow'rs;
Now pluck'd a tender twig from every bough,
To whip the hov'ring demons from her brow.
Ill-fated Maid! thy guiding spark is fled,
And lasting wretchedness waits round thy bed...
Thy bed of straw! for mark, where even now
O'er their lost child afflicted parents bow;
Their woe she knows not, but perversely coy,
Inverted customs yield her sullen joy;
Her midnight meals in secresy she takes,
Low mutt'ring to the moon, that rising breaks
Through night's dark gloom:...oh how much more forlorn
Her night, that knows of no returning dawn!...

AUTUMN.

v. 135.   *Continued.*

Slow from the threshold, once her infant seat,
O'er the cold earth she crawls to her retreat;
Quitting the cot's warm walls in filth to lie,
Where the swine grunting yields up half his sty;
The damp night air her shiv'ring limbs assails;
In dreams she moans, and fancied wrongs bewails.
When morning wakes, none earlier rous'd than she,
When pendent drops fall glitt'ring from the tree;
But nought her rayless melancholy cheers,
Or sooths her breast, or stops her streaming tears.
Her matted locks unornamented flow;
Clasping her knees, and waving to and fro;...
Her head bow'd down, her faded cheek to hide;...
A piteous mourner by the pathway side.
Some tufted molehill through the livelong day
She calls her throne; there weeps her life away:
And oft the gaily passing stranger stays
His well-tim'd step, and takes a silent gaze,

AUTUMN.

Continued. v. 153.

Till sympathetic drops unbidden start,
And pangs quick springing muster round his heart;
And soft he treads with other gazers round,
And fain would catch her sorrow's plaintive sound:
One word alone is all that strikes the ear,
One short, pathetic, simple word,..."*Oh dear!*"
A thousand times repeated to the wind,
That wafts the sigh, but leaves the pang behind!
For ever of the proffer'd parley shy,
She hears the' unwelcome foot advancing nigh;
Nor quite unconscious of her wretched plight,
Gives one sad look, and hurries out of sight....

    Fair promis'd sunbeams of terrestrial bliss,
Health's gallant hopes,...and are ye sunk to this?
For in life's road though thorns abundant grow,
There still are joys poor Poll can never know;
Joys which the gay companions of her prime
Sip, as they drift along the stream of time;

AUTUMN.

v. 171.   *Chicken housed.*

At eve to hear beside their tranquil home
The lifted latch, that speaks the lover come:
That love matur'd, next playful on the knee
To press the velvet lip of infancy;
To stay the tottering step, the features trace;...
Inestimable sweets of social peace!

O Thou, who bidst the vernal juices rise!
Thou, on whose blasts autumnal foliage flies!
Let Peace ne'er leave me, nor my heart grow cold,
Whilst life and sanity are mine to hold.

Shorn of their flow'rs that shed th' untreasur'd seed,
The withering pasture, and the fading mead,
Less tempting grown, diminish more and more,
The dairy's pride; sweet Summer's flowing store.
New cares succeed, and gentle duties press,
Where the fire-side, a school of tenderness,
Revives the languid chirp, and warms the blood
Of cold-nipt weaklings of the latter brood,

AUTUMN.

The Hut.   v. 189.

That from the shell just bursting into day,
Through yard or pond pursue their vent'rous way.
Far weightier cares and wider scenes expand:
What devastation marks the new-sown land!
" From hungry woodland foes go, *Giles*, and guard
The rising wheat; ensure its great reward:
A future sustenance, a Summer's pride,
Demand thy vigilance: then be it try'd:
Exert thy voice, and wield thy shotless gun:
Go, tarry there from morn till setting sun."
    Keen blows the blast, or ceaseless rain descends;
The half-stript hedge a sorry shelter lends.
O for a HOVEL, e'er so small or low,
Whose roof, repelling winds and early snow,
Might bring home's comforts fresh before his eyes!
No sooner thought, than see the structure rise,
In some sequester'd nook, embank'd around,
Sods for its walls, and straw in burdens bound:

AUTUMN.

v. 207. *The pleasures of the Hut.*

Dried fuel hoarded is his richest store,
And circling smoke obscures his little door;
Whence creeping forth, to duty's call he yields,
And strolls the Crusoe of the lonely fields.
On whitethorns tow'ring, and the leafless rose,
A frost-nipt feast in bright vermilion glows:
Where clust'ring sloes in glossy order rise,
He crops the loaded branch; a cumb'rous prize;
And o'er the flame the sputt'ring fruit he rests,
Placing green sods to seat his coming guests;
His guests by promise; playmates young and gay:...
But AH! *fresh pastimes* lure their steps away!
He sweeps his hearth, and homeward looks in vain,
Till feeling *Disappointment's* cruel pain,
His fairy revels are exchang'd for rage,
His banquet marr'd, grown dull his hermitage.
The field becomes his prison, till on high
Benighted birds to shades and coverts fly.

AUTUMN.

The Disappointment. v. 225.

Midst air, health, daylight, can he prisoner be?
If fields are prisons, where is Liberty?
Here still she dwells, and here her votaries stroll;
But disappointed hope untunes the soul:
Restraints unfelt whilst hours of rapture flow,
When troubles press, to chains and barriers grow.
Look then from trivial up to greater woes;
From the poor bird-boy with his roasted sloes,
To where the dungeon'd mourner heaves the sigh;
Where not one cheering sun-beam meets his eye.
Though ineffectual pity thine may be,
No wealth, no pow'r, to set the captive free;
Though *only* to thy ravish'd *sight* is given
The golden path that HOWARD trod to heaven;
Thy slights can make the wretched more forlorn,
And deeper drive affliction's barbed thorn.
Say not, " I'll come and cheer thy gloomy cell
With news of dearest friends; how good, how well:

AUTUMN.

v. 243. *The cruelty of disappointing expectation.*

I'll be a joyful herald to thine heart:"
Then fail, and play the worthless trifler's part,
To sip flat pleasures from thy glass's brim,
And waste the precious hour that's due to him.
In mercy spare the base unmanly blow:
Where can he turn, to whom complain of you?
Back to past joys in vain his thoughts may stray,
Trace and retrace the beaten worn-out way,
The rankling injury will pierce his breast,
And curses on thee break his midnight rest.

 Bereft of song, and ever cheering green,
The soft endearments of the Summer scene,
New harmony pervades the solemn wood,
Dear to the soul, and healthful to the blood:
For bold exertion follows on the sound
Of distant sportsmen, and the chiding hound;
First heard from kennel bursting, mad with joy,
Where smiling EUSTON boasts her good FITZROY,

AUTUMN.

Euston Hall....Fox-hunting. v. 261.

Lord of pure alms, and gifts that wide extend;
The farmer's patron, and the poor man's friend:
Whose mansion glitt'ring with the eastern ray,
Whose elevated temple, points the way,
O'er slopes and lawns, the park's extensive pride,
To where the victims of the chace reside,
Ingulf'd in earth, in conscious safety warm,
Till lo! a plot portends their coming harm.

In earliest hours of dark unhooded morn,
Ere yet one rosy cloud bespeaks the dawn,
Whilst far abroad THE Fox pursues his prey,
He's doom'd to risk the perils of the day,
From his strong hold block'd out; perhaps to bleed,
Or owe his life to fortune or to speed.
For now the pack, impatient rushing on,
Range through the darkest coverts one by one;
Trace every spot; whilst down each noble glade
That guides the eye beneath a changeful shade,

AUTUMN.

v. 279.   *The subject continued.*

The loit'ring sportsman feels th' instinctive flame,
And checks his steed to mark the springing game.
Midst intersecting cuts and winding ways
The huntsman cheers his dogs, and anxious strays
Where every narrow riding, even shorn,
Gives back the echo of his mellow horn:
Till fresh and lightsome, every power untried,
The starting fugitive leaps by his side,
His lifted finger to his ear he plies,
And the view halloo bids a chorus rise
Of dogs quick-mouth'd, and shouts that mingle loud,
As bursting thunder rolls from cloud to cloud.
With ears cropt short, and chest of vig'rous mould,
O'er ditch, o'er fence, unconquerably bold,
The shining courser lengthens every bound,
And his strong foot-locks suck the moisten'd ground,
As from the confines of the wood they pour,
And joyous villages partake the roar.

AUTUMN.

The Fox-hound. v. 297.

O'er heath far stretch'd, or down, or valley low,
The stiff-limb'd peasant, glorying in the show,
Pursues in vain; where youth itself soon tires,
Spite of the transports that the chace inspires;
For who unmounted long can charm the eye,
Or hear the music of the leading cry?

Poor faithful TROUNCER! thou canst lead no more;
All thy fatigues and all thy triumphs o'er!
Triumphs of worth, whose honorary fame
Was still to follow true the hunted game;
Beneath enormous oaks, Britannia's boast,
In thick impenetrable coverts lost,
When the warm pack in fault'ring silence stood,
Thine was the note that rous'd the list'ning wood,
Rekindling every joy with tenfold force,
Through all the mazes of the tainted course.
Still foremost thou the dashing stream to cross,
And tempt along the animated horse;

AUTUMN.

v. 315.   *Not the worst subject of Poetry.*

Foremost o'er fen or level mead to pass,
And sweep the show'ring dew-drops from the grass;
Then bright emerging from the mist below
To climb the woodland hill's exulting brow.
   Pride of thy race! with worth far less than thine,
Full many human leaders daily shine!
Less faith, less constancy, less gen'rous zeal!...
Then no disgrace mine humble verse shall feel,
Where not one lying line to riches bows,
Or poison'd sentiment from rancour flows;
Nor flowers are strewn around Ambition's car:...
An honest dog's a nobler theme by far.
Each sportsman heard the tidings with a sigh,
When Death's cold touch had stopt his tuneful cry;
And though high deeds, and fair exalted praise,
In memory liv'd, and flow'd in rustic lays,
Short was the strain of monumental woe:
" *Foxes, rejoice! here buried lies your foe.** "

   * Inscribed on a stone in Euston Park wall.

AUTUMN.

Midnight....Domestic Fowl....Shortened hours. v. 333.

In safety hous'd, throughout NIGHT's *length'ning* reign,
The Cock sends forth a loud and piercing strain;
More frequent, as the glooms of midnight flee,
And hours roll round, that brought him liberty,
When Summer's early dawn, mild, clear, and bright,
Chased quick away the transitory night:...
Hours now in darkness veil'd; yet loud the scream
Of Geese impatient for the playful stream;
And all the feather'd tribe imprison'd raise
Their morning notes of inharmonious praise;
And many a clamorous Hen and cockrel gay,
When daylight slowly through the fog breaks way,
Fly wantonly abroad: but ah, how soon
The shades of twilight follow hazy noon,
Short'ning the busy day!...day that slides by
Amidst th' unfinish'd toils of HUSBANDRY;
Toils still each morn resum'd with double care,
To meet the icy terrors of the year;

AUTUMN.

v. 351.   *Closing Reflections.*

To meet the threats of *Boreas* undismay'd,
And *Winter's* gathering frowns and hoary head.

 THEN welcome, COLD; welcome, ye *snowy* nights!
Heaven midst your rage shall mingle pure delights,
And confidence of hope the soul sustain,
While devastation sweeps along the plain:
Nor shall the child of poverty despair,
But bless THE POWER that rules the *changing year;*
Assur'd,...though horrors round his cottage reign,...
That *Spring* will come, and Nature smile again.

WINTER.

ARGUMENT.

Tenderness to cattle. Frozen turnips. The cow-yard. Night. The farm-house. Fire-side. Farmer's advice and instruction. Nightly cares of the stable. Dobbin. The post-horse. Sheep-stealing dogs. Walks occasioned thereby. The ghost. Lamb time. Returning Spring. Conclusion.

WINTER.

IV.

WITH kindred pleasures mov'd, and cares opprest,
Sharing alike our weariness and rest;
Who lives the daily partner of our hours,
Through every change of heat, and frost, and show'rs;
Partakes our cheerful meals, partaking first
In mutual labour and in mutual thirst;
The kindly intercourse will ever prove
A bond of amity and social love.

WINTER.

Benevolence springing from mutual sufferings and pleasures. v. 9.

To more than man this generous warmth extends,
And oft the team and shiv'ring herd befriends;
Tender solicitude the bosom fills,
And Pity executes what Reason wills:
Youth learns compassion's tale from every tongue,
And flies to aid the helpless and the young;
When now, unsparing as the scourge of war,
Blasts follow blasts, and groves dismantled roar.
Around their home the storm-pinch'd CATTLE lows,
No nourishment in frozen pastures grows;
Yet frozen pastures every morn resound
With fair abundance thund'ring to the ground.
For though on hoary twigs no buds peep out,
And e'en the hardy bramble cease to sprout,
Beneath dread WINTER's level sheets of snow
The sweet nutritious *Turnip* deigns to grow.
Till now imperious want and wide-spread dearth
Bid Labour claim her treasures from the earth.

WINTER.

v. 27.   *Ice broken and snow cleared for the cattle.*

On GILES, and such as Giles, the labour falls,
To strew the frequent load where hunger calls.
On driving gales sharp hail indignant flies,
And sleet, more irksome still, assails his eyes;
Snow clogs his feet; or if no snow is seen,
The field with all its juicy store to screen,
Deep goes the frost, till every root is found
A rolling mass of ice upon the ground.
No tender ewe can break her nightly fast,
Nor heifer strong begin the cold repast,
Till *Giles* with pond'rous beetle foremost go,
And scatt'ring splinters fly at every blow;
When pressing round him, eager for the prize,
From their mixt breath warm exhalations rise.

If now in beaded rows drops deck the spray,
While *Phœbus* grants a momentary ray,
Let but a cloud's broad shadow intervene,
And stiffen'd into gems the drops are seen;

WINTER.

Night. v. 45.

And down the furrow'd oak's broad southern side
Streams of dissolving rime no longer glide.
   Though Night approaching bids for rest prepare,
Still the flail echoes through the frosty air,
Nor stops till deepest shades of darkness come,
Sending at length the weary laborer home.
From him, with bed and nightly food supplied,
Throughout the yard, hous'd round on every side,
Deep-plunging Cows their rustling feast enjoy,
And snatch sweet mouthfuls from the passing boy,
Who moves unseen beneath his trailing load,
Fills the tall racks, and leaves a scatter'd road;
Where oft the swine from ambush warm and dry
Bolt out, and scamper headlong to their sty,
When *Giles* with well-known voice, already there,
Deigns them a portion of his evening care.
   Him, though the cold may pierce, and storms molest,
Succeeding hours shall cheer with warmth and rest:

| v. 63. | *Christmas Fire.* |

Gladness to spread, and raise the grateful smile,
He hurls the faggot bursting from the pile,
And many a log and rifted trunk conveys,
To heap the fire, and to extend the blaze
That quiv'ring strong through every opening flies,
Whilst smoaky columns unobstructed rise.
For the rude architect, unknown to fame,
(Nor symmetry nor elegance his aim)
Who spread his floors of solid oak on high,
On beams rough-hewn, from age to age that lie,
Bade his *wide Fabric* unimpair'd sustain
Pomona's store, and cheese, and golden grain;
Bade from its central base, capacious laid,
The well-wrought chimney rear its lofty head;
Where since hath many a savoury ham been stor'd,
And tempests howl'd, and Christmas gambols roar'd.
  FLAT on the *hearth* the glowing embers lie,
And flames reflected dance in every eye:

WINTER.

Conversation. v. 81.

There the long billet, forc'd at last to bend,
While frothing sap gushes at either end,
Throws round its welcome heat:...the ploughman smiles,
And oft the joke runs hard on sheepish *Giles*,
Who sits joint tenant of the corner-stool,
The converse sharing, though in duty's school;
For now attentively 'tis his to hear
Interrogations from the Master's chair.

  'LEFT ye your bleating charge, when daylight fled,
' Near where the hay-stack lifts its snowy head?
' Whose fence of bushy furze, so close and warm,
' May stop the slanting bullets of the storm.
' For, hark! it blows; a dark and dismal night:
' Heaven guide the trav'eller's fearful steps aright!
' Now from the woods, mistrustful and sharp-ey'd,
' The *Fox* in silent darkness seems to glide,
' Stealing around us, list'ning as he goes,
' If chance the Cock or stamm'ring capon crows,

WINTER.

v. 99. *Contrast between the inconvenience at Land and a Sea-storm.*

' Or Goose, or nodding Duck, should darkling cry,
' As if appriz'd of lurking danger nigh:
' Destruction waits them, *Giles*, if e'er you fail
' To bolt their doors against the driving gale.
' Strew'd you (still mindful of the unshelter'd head)
' Burdens of straw, the cattle's welcome bed?
' Thine heart should feel, what thou may'st hourly see,
' *That duty's basis is humanity.*
' Of pain's unsavoury cup though thou may'st taste,
' (The wrath of Winter from the bleak north-east,)
' Thine utmost suff'rings in the coldest day
' A period terminates, and joys repay.
' Perhaps e'en now, whilst here those joys we boast,
' Full many a bark rides down the neighb'ring coast,
' Where the high northern waves tremendous roar,
' Drove down by blasts from *Norway's* icy shore.
' The *Sea-boy* there, less fortunate than thou,
' Feels all thy pains in all the gusts that blow;

WINTER.

Effect of the Farmer's kind admonitions.   v. 117.

His freezing hands now drench'd, now dry, by turns;
' Now lost, now seen, the distant light that burns,
' On some tall cliff uprais'd, a flaming guide,
' That throws its friendly radiance o'er the tide.
' His labours cease not with declining day,
' But toils and perils mark his watry way;
' And whilst in peaceful dreams secure *we* lie,
' The ruthless whirlwinds rage along the sky,
' Round his head whistling;...and shalt thou repine,
' Whilst this protecting roof still shelters thine?'
   Mild, as the vernal show'r, his words prevail,
And aid the moral precept of his tale:
His wond'ring hearers learn, and ever keep
These first ideas of the restless deep;
And, as the opening mind a circuit tries,
Present felicities in value rise.
Increasing pleasures every hour they find,
The warmth more precious, and the shelter kind;

WINTER.

v. 135.   *Sleep....renewed labour.*

Warmth that long reigning bids the eyelids close,
As through the blood its balmy influence goes,
When the cheer'd heart forgets fatigues and cares,
And drowsiness alone dominion bears.
  Sweet then the ploughman's slumbers, hale and young,
When the last topic dies upon his tongue;
Sweet then the bliss his transient dreams inspire,
Till chilblains wake him, or the snapping fire:
  He starts, and ever thoughtful of his team,
Along the glitt'ring snow a feeble gleam
Shoots from his lantern, as he yawning goes
To add fresh comforts to their night's repose;
Diffusing fragrance as their food he moves,
And pats the jolly sides of those he loves.
Thus full replenish'd, perfect ease possest,
From night till morn alternate food and rest,
No rightful cheer withheld, no sleep debar'd,
Their each day's labour brings its sure reward.

The Farmer's and Post-horse contrasted.	v. 153.

Yet when from plough or lumb'ring cart set free,
They taste awhile the sweets of liberty:
E'en sober *Dobbin* lifts his clumsy heels
And kicks, disdainful of the dirty wheels;
But soon, his frolic ended, yields again
To trudge the road, and wear the clinking chain.

Short-sighted DOBBIN!...thou canst only see
The trivial hardships that *encompass* thee:
Thy chains were freedom, and thy toils repose,
Could the poor *post-horse* tell thee all his woes;
Shew thee his bleeding shoulders, and unfold
The dreadful anguish he endures for gold:
Hir'd at each call of business, lust, or rage,
That prompt the trav'eller on from stage to stage.
Still on *his* strength depends their boasted speed;
For them his limbs grow weak, his bare ribs bleed;
And though he groaning quickens at command,
Their extra shilling in the rider's hand

WINTER.

v. 171. *The sufferings of the Post-horse continued.*

Becomes his bitter scourge....'tis *he* must feel
The double efforts of the lash and steel;
Till when, up-hill, the destin'd inn he gains,
And trembling under complicated pains,
Prone from his nostrils, darting on the ground,
His breath emitted floats in clouds around:
Drops chase each other down his chest and sides,
And spatter'd mud his native colour hides:
Through his swoln veins the boiling torrent flows,
And every nerve a separate torture knows.
His harness loos'd, he welcomes eager-eyed
The pail's full draught that quivers by his side;
And joys to see the well-known stable door,
As the starv'd mariner the friendly shore.

    Ah, well for him if here his suff'rings ceas'd,
And ample hours of rest his pains appeas'd!
But rous'd again, and sternly bade to rise,
And shake refreshing slumber from his eyes,

Patience recommended from comparison.	v. 189.

Ere his exhausted spirits can return,
Or through his frame reviving ardour burn,
Come forth he must, though limping, maim'd, and sore;
He hears the whip; the chaise is at the door....
The collar tightens, and again he feels
His half-heal'd wounds inflam'd; again the wheels
With tiresome sameness in his ears resound,
O'er blinding dust, or miles of flinty ground.
Thus nightly robb'd, and injur'd day by day,
His piece-meal murd'rers wear his life away.

 What say'st thou, *Dobbin?* what though hounds await
With open jaws the moment of thy fate,
No better fate attends *his* public race;
His life is misery, and his end disgrace.
Then freely bear thy burden to the mill,
Obey but one short law,...thy driver's will.
Affection, to thy memory ever true,
Shall boast of mighty loads that *Dobbin* drew;

WINTER.

v. 207. *The Mastiff.*

And back to childhood shall the mind with pride
Recount thy gentleness in many a ride
To pond, or field, or village fair, when thou
Held'st high thy braided mane and comely brow;
And oft the Tale shall rise to homely fame
Upon thy gen'rous spirit and thy name.
 Though faithful to a proverb, we regard
The midnight chieftain of the farmer's yard,
Beneath whose guardianship all hearts rejoice,
Woke by the echo of his hollow voice;
Yet as the Hound may fault'ring quit the pack,
Snuff the foul scent, and hasten yelping back;
And e'en the docile Pointer know disgrace,
Thwarting the gen'ral instinct of his race;
E'en so the MASTIFF, or the meaner Cur,
At times will from the path of duty err,
(A pattern of fidelity by day;
By night a *murderer*, lurking for his prey;)

A Sheep-biter by night. v. 225.

And round the pastures or the fold will creep,
And, coward-like, attack the peaceful sheep:
Alone the wanton mischief he pursues,
Alone in reeking blood his jaws embrues;
Chasing amain his fright'ned victims round,
Till death in wild confusion strews the ground;
Then wearied out, to kennel sneaks away,
And licks his guilty paws till break of day.

The deed discover'd, and the news once spread,
Vengeance hangs o'er the unknown culprit's head,
And careful *Shepherds* extra hours bestow
In patient *watchings* for the common foe;
A foe most dreaded now, when rest and peace
Should wait the season of the flock's increase.

In part these nightly terrors to dispel,
GILES, ere he sleeps, his little Flock must tell.
From the fire-side with many a shrug he hies,
Glad if the full-orb'd Moon salute his eyes,

WINTER.

v. 243.   *Moon-light....scattered clouds.*

And through the unbroken stillness of the night
Shed on his path her beams of cheering light.
With saunt'ring step he climbs the distant stile,
Whilst all around him wears a placid smile;
There views the white-rob'd clouds in clusters driv'n,
And all the glorious pageantry of heav'n.
Low, on the utmost bound'ry of the sight,
The rising vapours catch the silver light;
Thence Fancy measures, as they parting fly,
Which first will throw its shadow on the eye,
Passing the source of light; and thence away,
Succeeded quick by brighter still than they.
For yet above these wafted clouds are seen
(In a remoter sky, still more serene,)
Others, detach'd in ranges through the air,
Spotless as snow, and countless as they're fair;
Scatter'd immensely wide from east to west,
The beauteous 'semblance of a *Flock* at rest.

The Spectre. v. 261.

These, to the raptur'd mind, aloud proclaim
Their MIGHTY SHEPHERD's everlasting Name.
Whilst thus the loit'rer's utmost stretch of soul
Climbs the still clouds, or passes those that roll,
And loos'd *Imagination* soaring goes
High o'er his home, and all his little woes,
 TIME glides away; neglected Duty calls:
At once from plains of light to earth he falls,
And down a narrow lane, well known by day,
With all his speed pursues his sounding way,
In thought still half absorb'd, and chill'd with cold;
When, lo! an object frightful to behold;
A grisly SPECTRE, cloth'd in silver-grey,
Around whose feet the waving shadows play,
Stands in his path!...He stops, and not a breath
Heaves from his heart, that sinks almost to death.
Loud the owl halloos o'er his head unseen;
All else is silent, dismally serene:

WINTER.

v. 279. *The Explanation.*

Some prompt ejaculation, whisper'd low,
Yet bears him up against the threat'ning foe;
And thus poor Giles, though half inclin'd to fly,
Mutters his doubts, and strains his stedfast eye.
' 'Tis not my crimes thou com'st here to reprove;
' No murders stain my soul, no perjur'd love:
' If thou'rt indeed what here thou seem'st to be,
' Thy dreadful mission cannot reach to me.
' By parents taught still to mistrust mine eyes,
' Still to approach each object of surprise,
' Lest Fancy's formful visions should deceive
' In moon-light paths, or glooms of falling eve,
' This then's the moment when my heart should try
' To scan thy motionless deformity;
' But oh, the fearful task! yet well I know
' An aged ash, with many a spreading bough,
' (Beneath whose leaves I've found a Summer's bow'r,
' Beneath whose trunk I've weather'd many a show'r,)

WINTER.

The terrors of surprise vanish on the use of recollection. v. 297.

' Stands singly down this solitary way,
' But far beyond where now my footsteps stay.
' 'Tis true, thus far I've come with heedless haste;
' No reck'ning kept, no passing objects trac'd....
' And can I then have reach'd that very tree?
' Or is its reverend form assum'd by thee?'
The happy thought alleviates his pain:
He creeps another step; then stops again;
Till slowly, as his noiseless feet draw near,
Its perfect lineaments at once appear;
Its crown of shiv'ring ivy whispering peace,
And its white bark that fronts the moon's pale face.
Now, whilst his blood mounts upward, now he knows
The solid gain that from conviction flows;
And strengthen'd Confidence shall hence fulfill
(With conscious Innocence more valued still)
The dreariest task that winter nights can bring,
By church-yard dark, or grove, or fairy ring;

WINTER.

v. 315.   *Counting of the Sheep in the fold.*

Still buoying up the timid mind of youth,
Till loit'ring Reason hoists the scale of Truth.
With these blest guardians *Giles* his course pursues,
Till numbering his heavy-sided ewes,
Surrounding stillness tranquilize his breast,
And shape the dreams that wait his hours of rest.

   As when retreating tempests we behold,
Whose skirts at length the azure sky unfold,
And full of murmurings and mingled wrath,
Slowly unshroud the smiling face of earth,
Bringing the bosom joy: so WINTER flies!...
And see the Source of Life and Light uprise!
A height'ning arch o'er southern hills he bends;
Warm on the cheek the slanting beam descends,
And gives the reeking mead a brighter hue,
And draws the modest *primrose* bud to view.
Yet frosts succeed, and winds impetuous rush,
And hail-storms rattle through the budding bush;

WINTER.

Turn of the season towards Spring....Ewes and Lambs. v. 333.

And night-fall'n LAMBS require the shepherd's care,
And teeming EWES, that still their burdens bear;
Beneath whose sides tomorrow's dawn may see
The milk-white strangers bow the trembling knee;
At whose first birth the pow'rful instinct's seen
That fills with champions the daisied green:
For ewes that stood aloof with fearful eye,
With stamping foot now men and dogs defy,
And obstinately faithful to their young,
Guard their first steps to join the bleating throng.

But casualties and death from damps and cold
Will still attend the well-conducted fold:
Her tender offspring dead, the dam aloud
Calls, and runs wild amidst the unconscious crowd:
And orphan'd sucklings raise the piteous cry;
No wool to warm them, no defenders nigh.
And must her streaming milk then flow in vain?
Must unregarded innocence complain?

WINTER.

v. 351. *Adopted Lambs.*

No;...ere this strong solicitude subside,
Maternal fondness may be fresh apply'd,
And the adopted stripling still may find
A parent most assiduously kind.
For this he's doom'd awhile disguis'd to range,
(For fraud or force must work the wish'd-for change;)
For this his predecessor's skin he wears,
Till cheated into tenderness and cares,
The unsuspecting dam, contented grown,
Cherish and guard the fondling as her own.
   Thus all by turns to fair perfection rise;
Thus twins are parted to increase their size:
Thus instinct yields as interest points the way,
Till the bright flock, augmenting every day,
On sunny hills and vales of springing flow'rs
With ceaseless clamour greet the vernal hours.
   The humbler *Shepherd* here with joy beholds
The approv'd economy of crowded folds,

WINTER.

The triumph of GILES *as the Year ends.*   v. 369.

And, in his small contracted round of cares,
Adjusts the practice of each hint he hears:
For Boys with emulation learn to glow,
And boast their pastures, and their healthful show
Of well-grown Lambs, the glory of the Spring;
And field to field in competition bring.

    E'en GILES, for all his cares and watchings past,
And all his contests with the wintry blast,
Claims a full share of that sweet praise bestow'd
By gazing neighbours, when along the road,
Or village green, his curly-coated throng
Suspends the chorus of the spinner's song;
When Admiration's unaffected grace
Lisps from the tongue, and beams in every face:
Delightful moments!...Sunshine, Health, and Joy,
Play round, and cheer the elevated Boy!
' *Another* SPRING!' his heart exulting cries;
' *Another* YEAR! with promis'd blessings rise!...

WINTER.

v. 387.   CONCLUDING INVOCATION.

'ETERNAL POWER! from whom those blessings flow,
' Teach me still more to wonder, more to know:
' *Seed-time* and *Harvest* let me see again;
' Wander the *leaf-strewn* wood, the *frozen* plain:
' Let the first Flower, corn-waving Field, Plain, Tree,
' Here round my home, still lift my soul to THEE;
' And let me ever, midst thy bounties, raise
' An humble note of thankfulness and praise!'—

APRIL 22, 1798.

NOTE.

Destroys life's intercourse; the social plan. P. 46, l. 341.

" ALLOWING for the imperfect state of sublunary happiness, which is comparative at best, there are not, perhaps, many nations existing whose situation is so desirable; where the means of subsistence are so easy, and the wants of the people so few....The evident distinction of ranks, which subsists at *Otaheite*, does not so materially affect the felicity of the nation as we might have supposed. The simplicity of their whole life contributes to soften the appearance of distinctions, and to reduce them to a level. Where the climate and the custom of the country do not absolutely require a perfect garment; where it is easy at every step to gather as many plants as form not only a decent, but likewise a customary covering; and where all the necessaries of life are within the reach of every individual, at the expence of a trifling labour;...ambition and envy must in a great measure be unknown. It is true, the highest classes of people possess some dainty articles, such as pork, fish, fowl, and cloth, almost exclusively; but the desire of indulging the appetite in a few trifling luxuries can at most render individuals, and not whole nations, unhappy. Absolute want occasions the miseries of the lower class in some civilized states, and is the result of the unbounded voluptuousness of their superiors. At *Otaheite* there is not, in general, that disparity between the highest and the meanest man, that subsists in England between a reputable tradesman and a labourer. The affection of the Otaheitans for their chiefs, which they never failed to express upon all occasions, gave us great reason to suppose that they consider themselves as one family, and respect their eldest born in the persons of their chiefs. The lowest man in the nation speaks as freely with his king as with his equal, and has the pleasure of seeing him as often as he likes. The king, at times, amuses himself with the occupations of his subjects; and not yet depraved by false notions of empty state, he often paddles his own canoe, without considering such an employment derogatory to his dignity. How long such an happy equality may last is uncertain, and how much the introduction of foreign luxuries may hasten its dissolution cannot be too frequently repeated to Europeans. If the knowledge of a few individuals can only be acquired at such a price as the happiness of nations, it were better for the discoverers and the discovered that the *South Sea* had still remained unknown to *Europe* and its restless inhabitants."

REFLECTIONS ON OTAHEITE, Cook's second Voyage.

THE END.

ELEGANT PUBLICATIONS,

PRINTED FOR AND SOLD BY

VERNOR AND HOOD.

1. THE ANATOMY OF MELANCHOLY, 2 vol. 8vo. a new Edition, on fine wove Paper, with two elegant Frontispieces, engraved by Neagle and Warren, 1l. 1s. boards.

The same Work, Royal Paper, with first Impressions of the Plates, 1l. 15s. boards.

2. ASIATIC RESEARCHES; or, Transactions of the Society instituted in Bengal for inquiring into the History and Antiquities, the Arts, Sciences, and Literature, of Asia. By Sir William Jones, and others. In 5 vol. 8vo. price 2l. 12s. 6d. boards, with all the Plates, &c. printed verbatim from the Bengal Edition.

The same Work, elegantly printed in 5 vol. 4to. price 5l. 5s. boards.

3. HUDIBRAS, in three Parts, corrected and amended, with large Annotations, &c. by Zachary Grey, LL. D. adorned with sixteen Copper Plates, engraved by Ridley from Hogarth's Designs; and twenty-four Head and Tail-pieces, beautifully cut in Wood by Nesbit (Pupil of Bewick), from humorous Designs by Thurston. In 2 vol. 8vo. boards, 1l. 1s.

A few Copies on Whatman's Royal Vellum Paper, with first Impressions of the Plates, boards, 1l. 15s.

4. HUDIBRAS, a beautiful Edition for the Pocket, with ten elegant Wood Cuts by Nesbit, 5s. boards.

Ditto, Royal 12mo. with Plates, 5s. boards.

5. LETTERS OF JUNIUS, a new Edition, printed by Bensley, in the finest style of Typography, ornamented with elegant Head and Tail-pieces, beautifully cut in Wood, and twenty-three Heads and engraved Vignettes, by Ridley. In 2 vol. 8vo. boards, 1l. 1s.

A few Copies on Whatman's Royal Vellum Paper, boards, 1l. 15s.

6. JUNIUS'S LETTERS, 2 vol. 18mo. for the Pocket, with ten elegant Heads. Printed on five wove Paper, 7s. boards.

The same Work, 2 vol. Royal 18mo. elegantly printed, 10s. boards.

7. THE LETTERS OF THEODOSIUS AND CONSTANTIA, before and after her taking the Veil, with an elegant Frontispiece engraved by Neagle, 7s. boards.

The same Work, on Whatman's Royal Vellum Paper, 10s. 6d. boards.

8. Mrs. DOBSON's LIFE OF PETRARCH, 2 vol. 8vo. with eight beautiful Plates, boards, 16s.

The same in Royal 8vo, first Impressions, boards, 1l. 1s.

9. THE ORLANDO FURIOSO OF ARIOSTO, in forty-six Books; translated by John Hoole; 5 vol. 8vo. with elegant Engravings by Bartolozzi, Heath, Sharp, Caldwell, &c. a new Edition, 1l. 12s. 6d. boards.

10. HOOLE's TASSO's JERUSALEM DELIVERED, 2 vol. Fool's-cap 8vo. with beautiful Frontispieces, boards, 7s.

The same Work in 8vo. boards, 12s.

11. SOLITUDE; or the Effects of occasional Retirement on the Mind, the Heart, general Society, in Exile, in Old Age, and on the Bed of Death.

ELEGANT PUBLICATIONS.

Translated from the German of Dr. Zimmerman. A new Edition, printed on fine Vellum Paper, and embellished with seven beautiful Copper Plates, from Designs of the late Mr. Kirk; besides elegant Tail-pieces: 12mo. 6s. 6d. boards; and Medium 8vo. 8s. 6d. boards.
Ditto, Vol. II. with four elegant Plates, 12mo. 6s. and 8vo. 7s. 6d. boards.

12. ZIMMERMAN's REFLECTIONS AND APHORISMS ON MAN, extracted from his Posthumous Papers, 3s. 6d. boards.

13. THE ODES AND POEMS OF WILLIAM COLLINS, elegantly printed, and ornamented with nineteen beautiful Plates, 8vo. boards, 8s.

14. THE ECONOMY OF HUMAN LIFE, in two Parts. By Robert Dodsley. A new Edit. with 49 elegant Plates by Harding, boards, 10s. 6d.

15. THE LETTERS OF MARCUS TULLIUS CICERO to several of his Friends; translated by William Melmoth, Esq. with Remarks and Notes: 3 vol. 8vo. 18s. boards.

16. ELEMENTS OF GEOGRAPHY, AND OF NATURAL AND CIVIL HISTORY, with thirty Plates and Maps, correctly engraved: a new Edition, greatly enlarged, boards, 8s.

17. THE UNIVERSAL GAZETTEER; being a concise Description, alphabetically arranged, of the Nations, Kingdoms, States, Towns, Empires, Provinces, Cities, Oceans, Seas, Harbours, Rivers, Lakes, Canals, Mountains, Capes, &c. in the known World; the Government, Manners, and Religion of the Inhabitants; with the Extent, Boundaries, and natural Productions, Manufactures, and Curiosities, of the different Countries: containing several Thousand Places not to be met with in any similar Gazetteer. By John Walker. A new Edition, carefully corrected, and considerably enlarged, with fourteen Maps, boards, 8s. or with coloured Maps, 9s. 6d. boards.——In this Edition, besides many other Improvements for Commercial Purposes, the Editor has pointed out the Post Towns of Great Britain and Ireland, not in any similar work.

18. A GENERAL PRONOUNCING AND EXPLANATORY DICTIONARY of the English Language; for the use of Schools, Foreigners learning English, &c. in which it has been attempted to improve on the Plan of Mr. Sheridan; the Discordancies of that celebrated Orthoëpist being avoided, and his Improprieties corrected. The fourth Edition, revised, and considerably enlarged by Selections from Ash, Bailey, Barclay, Buchanan, Dyche, Elphinston, Entick, Fry, Johnson, Johnston, Kenrick, Lemon, Marriott, Martin, Nares, Perry, Rider, Scot, and Walker. By Stephen Jones, Author of the " New Biographical Dictionary," and " The History of Poland," and Compiler of " Dr. Johnson's Table Talk," &c. In one vol. 8vo. a new Edition, enlarged with upwards of 2000 Words, boards, 8s. or on fine Royal Paper, in boards, 10s. 6d.

19. The same Work, printed on a fine Crown Paper for the Pocket, boards, 3s. 6d. or on fine Vellum Paper, hot-pressed, boards, 4s. 6d.

PRINTED BY THOMAS BENSLEY,
Bolt-Court, Fleet-Street, London.
Jan. 1, 1800.

RURAL TALES,

BALLADS, AND SONGS:

BY

ROBERT BLOOMFIELD,

AUTHOR OF

THE FARMER'S BOY.

———

LONDON:

PRINTED FOR VERNOR AND HOOD, POULTRY;
AND
LONGMAN AND REES, PATERNOSTER ROW.

1802.

T. Bensley, Printer, Bolt Court, Fleet Street.

PREFACE.

―――

THE Poems here offered to the public were chiefly written during the interval between the concluding, and the publishing of " the " Farmer's Boy," an interval of nearly two years. The pieces of a later date are, " *the* " *Widow to her Hour-Glass*," " *The Fakenham Ghost*," " *Walter and Jane*," &c. At the time of publishing the Farmer's Boy, circumstances occurred which rendered it necessary to submit these poems to the perusal of my Friends: under whose approbation I now give them, with some confidence as to their moral merit, to the judgment of the public. And as they treat of village manners, and rural scenes, it appears to me not ill-tim'd to avow, that I have hopes of meeting in some degree the approbation of my Country. I was not prepar'd for the decided, and I may surely say extraordinary attention which The Public has shewn towards the Farmer's Boy: the consequence has been such as my true friends will rejoice to hear; it has produc'd me many essential blessings. And I feel peculiarly gratified in finding that a poor man in England may assert the dignity of Virtue, and speak of the imperishable beauties of Nature, and be heard, and heard, perhaps, with greater attention for his being poor.

Whoever thinks of me or my concerns, must necessarily indulge the pleasing idea of gratitude, and join a thought of my first great friend Mr. Lofft. And on this head, I believe every reader, who has himself any feel-

PREFACE.

ing, will judge rightly of mine: if otherwife, I would much rather he would lay down this volume, and grafp hold of fuch fleeting pleafures as the world's bufinefs may afford him. I fpeak not of that gentleman as a public character, or as a fcholar. Of the former I know but little, and of the latter nothing. But I know from experience, and I glory in this fair opportunity of faying it, that his private life is a leffon of morality; his manners gentle, his heart fincere: and I regard it as one of the moft fortunate circumftances of my life, that my introduction to public notice fell to fo zealous and unwearied a friend *.

* I dare not take to myfelf a praife like this; and yet I was, perhaps, hardly at liberty to difclaim what fhould be mine and the endeavour of every one to deferve. This I can fay, that I have reafon to rejoice that Mr. *George Bloomfield* introduced *The Farmer's Boy* to me. C. L.

PREFACE.

I have received many honourable testimonies of esteem from strangers; letters without a name, but fill'd with the most cordial advice, and almost a parental anxiety, for my safety under so great a share of public applause. I beg to refer such friends to the great teacher Time: and hope that he will hereafter give me my deserts, and no more.

One piece in this collection will inform the reader of my most pleasing visit to *Wakefield Lodge:* books, solitude, and objects entirely new, brought pleasures which memory will always cherish. That noble and worthy Family, and all my immediate and unknown Friends, will, I hope, believe the sincerity of my thanks for all their numerous favours, and candidly judge the poems before them.

R. BLOOMFIELD.

Sept. 29, 1801.

P. S. Since affixing the above date, an event of much greater importance than any to which I have been witnefs, has taken place, to the univerfal joy (it is to be hoped) of every inhabitant of Europe. My portion of joy fhall be expreffed while it is warm. And the reader will do fufficient juftice, if he only believes it to be fincere.
OCTOBER 10.

PEACE.

I

HALT! ye Legions, fheathe your Steel:
Blood grows precious; fhed no more:
Ceafe your toils; your wounds to heal
Lo! beams of Mercy reach the fhore!
From Realms of everlafting light
The favour'd gueft of Heaven is come:
Proftrate your Banners at the fight,
And bear the glorious tidings home.

2

The plunging corpfe with half clos'd eyes,
No more fhall ftain th' unconfcious brine;
Yon pendant gay, that ftreaming flies,
Around its idle Staff fhall twine.
Behold! along th' etherial fky
Her beams o'er conquering Navies fpread;
Peace! Peace! the leaping Sailors cry,
With fhouts that might aroufe the dead.

3

Then forth Britannia's thunder pours;
A vaft reiterated found!
From Line to Line the Cannon roars,
And fpreads the blazing joy around.
Return, ye brave! your Country calls;
Return; return, your tafk is done:
While here the tear of tranfport falls,
To grace your Laurels nobly won.

4

Albion Cliffs—from age to age,

That bear the roaring ſtorms of Heav'n,

Did ever fiercer Warfare rage,

Was ever Peace more timely given?

Wake! ſounds of Joy: rouſe, generous Iſle;

Let every patriot boſom glow.

Beauty, reſume thy wonted ſmile,

And, Poverty, thy cheerful brow.

5

Boaſt, Britain, of thy glorious Gueſts;

Peace, Wealth, and Commerce, all thine own:

Still on contented Labour reſts

The baſis of a laſting Throne.

Shout, Poverty! 'tis Heaven that ſaves;

Protected Wealth, the chorus raiſe,

Ruler of War, of Winds, and Waves,

Accept a proſtrate Nation's praiſe *.

* A moſt animated and pleaſing Ode on an event moſt deſirable to Britain, France, and Mankind. C. L.

CONTENTS.

	Page
RICHARD and Kate: Ballad	1
Walter and Jane: A Tale	13
The Miller's Maid: A Tale	35
The Widow to her Hour-Glaſs	59
Market-Night: Ballad	63
The Fakenham Ghoſt: Ballad	70
The French Mariner: Ballad	78
Dolly: Ballad	83
A viſit to Whittlebury Foreſt	90
A Highland Drover: Song	97
A word to two Young Ladies	101
On hearing of the tranſlation of the Farmer's Boy	104
Nancy: Song	106
Roſy Hannah: Song	109
The Shepherd and his Dog Rover: Song	111
Hunting Song	113
Lucy: Song	115
Winter Song	117

RICHARD AND KATE:

OR,

FAIR-DAY.

A SUFFOLK BALLAD.

1

'Come, Goody, stop your humdrum wheel,
' Sweep up your orts, and get your Hat;
' Old joys reviv'd once more I feel,
' 'Tis Fair-day;—ay, *and more than that.*

2

' Have you forgot, Kate, prithee say,
' How many Seasons here we've tarry'd?
' 'Tis *Forty* years, this very day,
' Since you and I, old Girl, were *married!*

B

2   RICHARD AND KATE.

The Deliberation.

3

'Look out;—the Sun shines warm and bright,
'The Stiles are low, the paths all dry;
'I know you cut your corns laſt night:
'Come; be as free from care as I.

4

'For I'm refolv'd once more to fee
'That place where we fo often met;
'Though few have had more cares than we,
'We've none juſt now to make us fret.'

5

KATE fcorn'd to damp the generous flame
That warm'd her aged Partner's breaſt:
Yet, ere determination came,
She thus fome trifling doubts expreſs'd.

RICHARD AND KATE.

Difficulties—Consent.

6

' Night will come on; when seated snug,
' And you've perhaps begun some tale,
' Can you then leave your dear stone mug;
' Leave all the folks, and all the Ale ?'

7

' Ay KATE, I wool;—because I know,
' Though time has been we both could run,
' Such days are gone and over now;—
' I only mean to see the fun.'

8

She straight slipp'd off the Wall, and Band ⁑,
And laid aside her Lucks and Twitches ⁑:
And to the Hutch † she reach'd her hand,
And gave him out his Sunday Breeches.

⁑ ⁑ Terms used in spinning.   † Hutch, a chest.

RICHARD AND KATE.

The Walk to the Fair.

9

His Mattock he behind the door
And Hedging-gloves again replac'd;
And look'd acrofs the yellow Moor,
And urg'd his tott'ring Spoufe to hafte.

10

The day was up, the air ferene,
The Firmament without a cloud;
The Bee humm'd o'er the level green
Where knots of trembling Cowflips bow'd.

11

And RICHARD thus, with heart elate,
As paft things rufh'd acrofs his mind,
Over his fhoulder talk'd to KATE,
Who fnug tuckt up, walk'd flow behind.

RICHARD AND KATE.

Discourse on past Days.

12

' When once a gigling Mawther you,
' And I a redfac'd chubby Boy,
' Sly tricks you play'd me not a few;
' For mischief was your greatest joy.'

13

' Once, passing by this very Tree,
' A Gotch * of Milk I'd been to fill,
' You shoulder'd me; then laugh'd to see
' Me and my Gotch spin down the Hill.'

14

' 'Tis true,' she said;' ' But here behold,
' And marvel at the course of Time;
' Though you and I are both grown old,
' This Tree is only in its prime!'

* A pitcher.

RICHARD AND KATE.

The Arrival.

15

'Well, Goody, don't stand preaching now;
'Folks don't preach Sermons at a FAIR:
'We've rear'd Ten *Boys* and *Girls* you know;
'And I'll be bound they'll all be there.'

16

Now friendly nods and smiles had they,
From many a kind *Fair-going* face:
And many a pinch KATE gave away,
While RICHARD kept his usual pace.

17

At length arriv'd amidst the throng,
Grand-children bawling hem'd them round;
And dragg'd them by the skirts along
Where gingerbread bestrew'd the ground.

RICHARD AND KATE.

Country Sports.

18

And soon the aged couple spy'd
Their lusty *Sons*, and *Daughters* dear:—
When RICHARD thus exulting cried,
' Did'nt I tell you they'd be here?'

19

The cordial greetings of the soul
Were visible in every face;
Affection, void of all controul,
Govern'd with a resistless grace.

20

'Twas good to see the honest strife,
Which should contribute most to please;
And hear the long-recounted life,
Of infant tricks, and happy days.

Recollections.

21

But now, as at some nobler places,
Amongst the Leaders 'twas decreed
Time to begin the DICKY RACES;
More fam'd for laughter than for speed.

22

RICHARD look'd on with wond'rous glee,
And prais'd the Lad who chanc'd to win;
' KATE, wa'nt I such a one as he?
' As like him, ay, as pin to pin?'

23

' Full *Fifty* years are pass'd away
' Since I rode this same ground about:
' Lord! I was lively as the day!
' I won the High-lows out and out!'

RICHARD AND KATE.

The Departure.

24

' I'm furely growing young again ;
' I feel myfelf fo kedge and plump.
' From head to foot I've not one pain ;
' Nay, hang me if I cou'd 'nt jump.'

25

Thus fpoke the ALE in RICHARD's pate,
A very little made him mellow;
But ftill he lov'd his faithful KATE,
Who whifper'd thus, ' My good old fellow,'

26

' Remember what you promis'd me :
' And fee, the Sun is getting low ;
' The Children want an hour ye fee
' To talk a bit before we go.'

RICHARD AND KATE.

Parental and Filial Feelings.

27

Like youthful Lover moſt complying
He turn'd, and chuckt her by the chin:
Then all acroſs the green graſs hieing,
Right merry faces, all akin,

28

Their farewell quart, beneath a tree
That droop'd its branches from above;
Awak'd the pure felicity
That waits upon PARENTAL LOVE.

29

KATE view'd her blooming Daughters round,
And Sons, who ſhook her wither'd hand:
Her features ſpoke what joy ſhe found;
But utterance had made a ſtand.

RICHARD AND KATE.

An old Man's Joy.

30

The Children toppled on the green,
And bowl'd their *fairings* down the hill;
Richard with pride beheld the scene,
Nor could he for his life sit still.

31

A Father's uncheck'd feelings gave
A tenderness to all he said;
' My Boys, how proud am I to have
' My name thus round the Country spread!

32

' Through all my days I've labour'd hard,
' And could of pains and Crosses tell;
' But this is Labour's great reward,
' To meet ye thus, and see ye well.'

Old Man's Joy continued.

33

' My good old Partner, when at home,
' Sometimes with wishes mingles tears;
' Goody, says I, let what wool come,
' We've nothing for them but our pray'rs.

34

' May you be all as old as I,
' And see your Sons to manhood grow;
' And, many a time before you die,
' Be just as pleas'd as I am now.'

35

Then, (raising still his Mug and Voice,)
' An Old Man's weakness don't despise!
' I love you well, my Girls and Boys;
' God bless you all;' ... so said his eyes———

RICHARD AND KATE

The Return home.

36

For, as he spoke, a big round drop
Fell bounding on his ample sleeve;
A witness which he could not stop,
A witness which all hearts believe.

37

Thou, FILIAL PIETY, wert there;
And round the ring, benignly bright,
Dwelt in the luscious half-shed tear,
And in the parting word—*Good Night*.

38

With thankful Hearts and strengthen'd Love,
The poor old PAIR, supremely blest,
Saw the Sun sink behind the grove,
And gain'd once more their lowly rest.

14 RICHARD AND KATE.

I do not wonder that one of the firſt men of the age for ſtrength and compaſs of mind, for taſte, variety of information, high and amiable qualities, a man generally admir'd, reſpected, and belov'd, even in times like theſe, has expreſs'd the moſt particular ſatisfaction in this ſimple, characteriſtic, and moſt engaging Tale. C. L.
April 1800.

WALTER AND JANE:

OR,

THE POOR BLACKSMITH.

A COUNTRY TALE.

———◆———

Bright was the fummer fky, the Mornings gay,
And Jane was young and chearful as the Day.
Not yet to Love but Mirth fhe paid her vows;
And Echo mock'd her as fhe call'd her Cows.
Tufts of green Broom, that full in bloffom vied,
And grac'd with fpotted gold the upland fide,
The level fogs o'erlook'd; too high to fhare;
So lovely Jane o'erlook'd the clouds of Care;

WALTER AND JANE.

Jane. v. 9.

No meadow-flow'r rose fresher to the view,
That met her morning footsteps in the dew;
Where, if a nodding stranger ey'd her charms,
The blush of innocence was up in arms,
Love's random glances struck the unguarded mind,
And Beauty's magic made him look behind.

Duly as morning blush'd or twilight came,
Secure of greeting smiles and Village fame,
She pass'd the Straw-roof'd Shed, in ranges where
Hung many a well-turn'd Shoe and glitt'ring *Share*;
Where WALTER, as the charmer tripp'd along,
Would stop his roaring Bellows and his Song.—

Dawn of affection; Love's delicious sigh!
Caught from the lightnings of a speaking eye,
That leads the heart to rapture or to woe,
'Twas WALTER's fate thy mad'ning power to know;
And scarce to know, ere in its infant twine,
As the Blast shakes the tendrils of the Vine,

WALTER AND JANE.

v. 27.   The Separation.

The budding blifs that full of promife grew
The chilling blight of feparation knew.
Scarce had he told his heart's unquiet cafe,
And JANE to fhun him ceas'd to mend her pace,
And learnt to liften trembling as he fpoke,
And fondly judge his words beyond a joke;
When, at the Goal that bounds our profpects here,
Jane's widow'd Miftrefs ended her career:
Bleffings attended her divided ftore,
The Manfion fold, (Jane's peaceful home no more,)
A diftant Village own'd her for its Queen,
Another fervice, and another fcene;
But could another fcene fo pleafing prove,
Twelve weary miles from Walter and from Love?
The Maid grew thoughtful: Yet to Fate refign'd,
Knew not the worth of what fhe'd left behind.

  He, when at Eve releas'd from toil and heat,
Soon mifs'd the fmiles that taught his heart to beat,

The Lover's Journey. v. 35.

Each fabbath-day of late was wont to prove
Hope's liberal feaft, the holiday of Love:
But now, upon his fpirit's ebbing ftrength
Came each dull hour's intolerable length.
The next had fcarcely dawn'd when Walter hied
O'er hill and dale, Affection for his guide:
O'er the brown Heath his pathlefs journey lay,
Where fcreaming Lapwings hail'd the op'ning day.
High rofe the Sun, the anxious Lover figh'd;
His flipp'ry foles befpoke the dew was dried:
Her laft farewell hung fondly on his tongue
As o'er the tufted Furze elate he fprung;
Trifling impediments; his heart was light,
For Love and Beauty glow'd in fancy's fight;
And foon he gaz'd on Jane's enchanting face,
Renew'd his paffion,—but, deftroy'd his peace.
Truth, at whofe fhrine he bow'd, inflicted pain;
And Confcience whifper'd, " *never come again.*"

WALTER AND JANE.

v. 63.   Self-Denial.

For now, his tide of gladness to oppose,
A clay-cold damp of doubts and fears arose;
Clouds, which involve, midst Love and Reason's strife,
The poor man's prospect when he takes a wife.
Though gay his journeys in the Summer's prime,
Each seem'd the repetition of a crime;
He never left her but with many a sigh,
When tears stole down his face, she knew not why.
Severe his task those visits to forego,
And feed his heart with voluntary woe,
Yet this he did; the wan Moon circling found
His ovenings cheerless, and his rest unsound;
And saw th' unquenched flame his bosom swell:
What were his doubts, thus let the Story tell.

 A month's sharp conflict only serv'd to prove
The pow'r, as well as truth, of Walter's love.
Absence more stron on his mind portray'd
His own sweet, injur'd, unoffending Maid.

C 2

WALTER AND JANE.

The renew'd Journey.   v. 31.

Once more he'd go; full refolute awhile,
But heard his native Bells on every ftile;
The found recall'd him with a pow'rful charm,
The Heath wide open'd, and the day was warm;
There; where a bed of tempting green he found,
Increafing anguifh weigh'd him to the ground;
His well-grown limbs the fcatter'd Daifies prefs'd,
While his clinch'd hand fell heavy on his breaft.

    ' Why do I go in cruel fport to fay,
" I love thee Jane, appoint the happy day?"
' Why feek her fweet ingenuous reply,
' Then grafp her hand and proffer—poverty?
' Why, if I love her and adore her name,
' Why act like time and ficknefs on her frame?
' Why fhould my fcanty pittance nip her prime,
' And chace away the Rofe before its time?
' I'm young 'tis true; the world beholds me free;
' Labour ne'er fhow'd a frightful face to me;

WALTER AND JANE.

v. 99.   Love of Prudence.

' Nature's first wants hard labour *should* supply;
' But should it fail, 'twill be too late to fly.
' Some Summers hence, if nought our loves annoy,
' The image of my Jane may lisp her joy;
' Or, blooming boys with imitative swing
' May mock my arm, and make the Anvil ring;
' Then if in rags.—But, O my heart, forbear,—
' I love the Girl, and why should I despair?
' And that I love her all the village knows;
' Oft from my pain the mirth of others flows;
' As when a neighbour's Steed with glancing eye
' Saw his par'd hoof supported on my thigh:
' Jane pass'd that instant; mischief came of course;
' I drove the nail awry and lam'd the Horse;
' The poor beast limp'd: I bore a Master's frown,
' A thousand times I wish'd the wound my own.
' When to these tangling thoughts I've been resign'd,
' Fury or languor has possess'd my mind,

> Recollections. v. 117.

'All eyes have stared, I've blown a blast so strong;
'Forgot to smite at all, or smote too long.
'If at the Ale-house door, with careless glee
'One drinks to Jane, and darts a look on me;
'I feel that blush which her dear name will bring,
'I feel:—but, guilty Love, 'tis not thy sting!
'Yet what are jeers? the bubbles of an hour;
'Jane knows what Love can do, and feels its pow'r;
'In her mild eye fair Truth her meaning tells;
''Tis not in looks like her's that falsehood dwells.
'As water shed upon a dusty way
'I've seen midst downward pebbles devious stray;
'If kindred drops an adverse channel keep,
'The crystal friends toward each other creep;
'Near, and still nearer, rolls each little tide,
'Th' expanding mirror swells on either side:
'They touch—'tis done—receding bound'ries fly,
'An instantaneous union strikes the eye:

WALTER AND JANE.

v. 135.   The Interview.

' So 'tis with us; for Jane would be my bride;
' Shall coward fears then turn the bliss aside?'
 While thus he spoke he heard a gentle sound,
That seem'd a jarring footstep on the ground:
Asham'd of grief, he bade his eyes unclose,
And shook with agitation as he rose;
All unprepared the sweet surprise to bear,
His heart beat high, for Jane herself was there.—
 Flusht was her cheek; she seem'd the full-blown
  flower,
For warmth gave loveliness a double power;
Round her fair brow the deep confusion ran,
A waving handkerchief became her fan,
Her lips, where dwelt sweet love and smiling
  ease,
Puff'd gently back the warm assailing breeze.
' 'Ive travell'd all these weary miles with pain,
' To see my native village once again;

WALTER AND JANE.

Resentment and Tenderness.

'And show my true regard for neighbour *Hind*;
'Not like you, Walter, *she* was always kind.'
'Twas thus, each soft sensation laid aside,
She buoy'd her spirits up with maiden pride;
Disclaim'd her love, e'en while she felt the sting;
'What, come for Walter's sake!' 'Twas no such thing,
But when astonishment his tongue releas'd,
Pride's usurpation in an instant ceas'd:
By force he caught her hand as passing by,
And gaz'd upon her half averted eye;
His heart's distraction, and his boding fears
She heard, and answer'd with a flood of tears;
Precious relief; sure friends that forward press
To tell the mind's unspeakable distress.
Ye Youths, whom crimson'd health and genuine fire
Bear joyous on the wings of young desire,
Ye, who still bow to Love's almighty sway,
What could true passion, what could Walter say?

WALTER AND JANE.

v. 171.   Visit to a Friend.

Age, tell me true, nor shake your locks in vain,
Tread back your paths, and be in love again;
In your young days did such a favouring hour
Show you the littleness of wealth and pow'r,
Advent'rous climbers of the Mountain's brow,
While Love, their master, spreads his couch below.

" My dearest Jane," the untaught Walter cried,
As half repell'd he pleaded by her side;
" My dearest Jane, think of me as you may"——
Thus—still unutter'd what he strove to say,
They breath'd in sighs the anguish of their minds,
And took the path that led to neighbour *Hind's*.

A secret joy the well-known roof inspir'd,
Small was its store, and little they desir'd;
Jane dried her tears; while Walter forward flew
To aid the Dame; who to the brink updrew
The pond'rous Bucket as they reach'd the well,
And scarcely with exhausted breath could tell

The Expostulation. v. 189.

How welcome to her Cot the blooming Pair,
O'er whom she watch'd with a maternal care.
" What ails thee, Jane?" the wary Matron cried;
With heaving breast the modest Maid reply'd,
Now gently moving back her wooden Chair
To shun the current of the cooling air;
" Not much, good Dame; I'm weary by the way;
" Perhaps, anon, I've something else to say."
Now, while the Seed-cake crumbled on her knee,
And Snowy Jasmine peeped in to see;
And the transparent Lilac at the door,
Full to the Sun its purple honors bore,
The clam'rous Hen her fearless brood display'd,
And march'd around; while thus the Matron said:
' Jane has been weeping, Walter;—prithee why?
' I've seen her laugh, and dance, but never cry.
' But I can guess; with *her* you should have been,
' When late I saw you loit'ring on the green;

WALTER AND JANE.

v. 207. Pleadings of Experience for Love with extreme Prudence.

' I'm an old Woman, and the truth may tell:
' I say then, Boy, you have not us'd her well.'
Jane felt for Walter; felt his cruel pain,
While Pity's voice brought forth her tears again.
' Don't scold him Neighbour, he has much to say,
' Indeed he came and met me by the way.'
The Dame resum'd—' Why then, my Children, why
' Do such young bosoms heave the piteous sigh?
' The ills of Life to you are yet unknown;
' Death's fev'ring shaft, and Poverty's cold frown:
' I've felt them both, by turns:—but as they pass'd,
' Strong was my trust, and here I am at last.
' When I dwelt young and cheerful down the *Lane*
' (And, though I say it, I was much like Jane,)
' O'er flow'ry fields with *Hind*, I lov'd to stray,
' And talk, and laugh, and fool the time away:
' And Care defied; who not one pain could give,
' Till the thought came of how we were to live;

The Victory.	v. 22;.

' And then Love plied his arrows thicker still:
' And prov'd victorious;—as he always will.
' We brav'd Life's storm together; while that Drone,
' Your poor old Uncle, WALTER, liv'd alone.
' He died the other day: when round his bed
' No tender soothing tear Affection shed—
' Affection! 'twas a plant he never knew;—
' Why should he feast on fruits he never grew?'

WALTER caught fire: nor was *he* charm'd alone
With conscious Truth's firm elevated tone;
JANE from her seat sprang forward, half afraid,
Attesting with a blush what Goody said.
Her Lover took a more decided part:—
(O! 'twas the very Chord that touch'd his heart,)—
Alive to the best feelings man can prize,
A Bridegroom's transport sparkled in his eyes;
Love, conquering power, with unrestricted range
Silenc'd the arguments of Time and Change;

v. 243.	The Confeſſion.

And led his vot'ry on, and bade him view,
And prize the light-wing'd moments as they flew:
All doubts gave way, all retroſpective lore,
Whence cooler Reaſon tortur'd him before;
Compariſon of times, the Lab'rer's hire,
And many a truth Reflection might inſpire,
Sunk powerleſs. " Dame, I am a fool," he cried;
" Alone I might have reaſon'd till I died.
" I caus'd thoſe tears of Jane's:—but as they fell
" How much I felt none but ourſelves can tell.
" While daſtard fears withheld me from her ſight,
" Sighs reign'd by day and hideous dreams by night;
" 'Twas then the Soldier's plume and rolling Drum
" Seem'd for a while to ſtrike my ſorrows dumb;
" To fly from Care then half reſolv'd I ſtood,
" And without horror mus'd on fields of blood,
" But Hope prevail'd.—Be then the ſword reſign'd;
" And I'll make *Shares* for thoſe that ſtay behind,

| Unexpected Visit. | v. 261. |

" And you, sweet Girl,"——
He would have added more,
Had not a glancing shadow at the door
Announc'd a guest, who bore with winning grace
His well-tim'd errand pictur'd in his face.
Around with silent reverence they stood;
A blameless reverence—the man was good.
Wealth he had some, a match for his desires,
First on the list of active Country 'Squires.
Seeing the youthful pair with downcast eyes,
Unmov'd by Summer flowers and cloudless skies,
Pass slowly by his Gate; his book resign'd,
He watch'd their steps and follow'd far behind,
Bearing with inward joy, and honest pride,
A trust of WALTER's kinsman ere he died,
A hard-earn'd mite, deposited with care,
And with a miser's spirit worshipt there.

WALTER AND JANE.

v. 270.   The Difficulty remov'd.

He found what oft the generous bosom seeks,
In the Dame's court'seys and JANE's blushing
 cheeks,
That consciousness of Worth, that freeborn Grace,
Which waits on Virtue in the meanest place.
 ' Young Man, I'll not apologize to you,
' Nor name intrusion, for my news is true;
' 'Tis duty brings me here: your wants I've heard,
' And can relieve: yet be the dead rever'd.
' Here, in this Purse, (what should have cheer'd a
 Wife,)
' Lies, half the savings of your Uncle's life!
' I know your history, and your wishes know
' And love to see the seeds of Virtue grow.
' I've a spare Shed that fronts the public road:
' Make that your Shop; I'll make it your abode.
' Thus much from me,—the rest is but your due;
' That instant twenty pieces sprung to view.'

How little of outward Good suffices for Happiness.　v. 297.

Goody, her dim eyes wiping, rais'd her brow,
And saw the young pair look they knew not how;
Perils and Power while humble minds forego,
Who gives them half a Kingdom gives them woe;
Comforts may be procur'd and want defied,
Heav'ns! with how small a Sum, when right applied!
Give Love and honest Industry their way,
Clear but the Sun-rise of Life's little day,
Those we term poor shall oft that wealth obtain,
For which th' ambitious sigh, but sigh in vain:
Wealth that still brightens, as its stores increase;
The calm of Conscience, and the reign of Peace.

 Walter's enamour'd Soul, from news like this,
Now felt the dawnings of his future bliss;
E'en as the Red-breast shelt'ring in a bower,
Mourns the short darkness of a passing Shower,

v. 315.   Joy above Wealth.

Then, while the azure sky extends around,
Darts on a worm that breaks the moisten'd ground,
And mounts the dripping fence, with joy elate,
And shares the prize triumphant with his mate
So did the Youth;—the treasure straight became
An humble servant to Love's sacred flame;
Glorious subjection!—Thus his silence broke:
Joy gave him words; still quick'ning as he spoke.

'Want was my dread, my wishes were but few;
'Others might doubt, but JANE those wishes knew:
'This Gold may rid my heart of pains and sighs;
'But her true love is still my greatest prize.
'Long as I live, when this bright day comes round,
'Beneath my Roof your noble deeds shall sound;
'But, first, to make my gratitude appear,
'I'll shoe your Honour's Horses for a Year;
'If clouds should threaten when your Corn is down,
'I'll lend a hand, and summon half the town;

Grateful frankness. v. 333.

' If good betide, I'll found it in my songs,
' And be the first avenger of your wrongs:
' Though rude in manners, free I hope to live:
' This Ale's not mine, no Ale have I to give;
' Yet, Sir, though Fortune frown'd when I was born,
' Let's drink eternal friendship from this Horn.
' How much our present joy to you we owe,
' Soon our three Bells shall let the Neighbours know;
' The sound shall raise e'en stooping Age awhile,
' And every Maid shall meet you with a smile;
' Long may you *live*'—the wish like lightning flew;
By each repeated as the 'Squire withdrew.
' Long may *you* live,' his feeling heart rejoin'd;
Leaving well-pleas'd such happy Souls behind.
Hope promis'd fair to cheer them to the end;
With Love their guide, and Goody for their friend.

I think this tale, and especially the beginning and middle of it, has much of the clear, animated, easy narrative, the familiar but graceful diction, and the change of numbers so interesting in DRYDEN. In the following poem these excellencies are all greater. C. L.

THE MILLER'S MAID.

A TALE.

NEAR the High road upon a winding stream
An honest Miller rose to Wealth and Fame:
The noblest Virtues cheer'd his lengthen'd days,
And all the Country echo'd with his praise:
His Wife, the Doctress of the neighb'ring Poor *,
Drew constant pray'rs and blessings round his door.

One Summer's night, (the hour of rest was come)
Darkness unusual overspread their home;
A chilling blast was felt: the foremost cloud
Sprinkl'd the bubbling Pool; and thunder loud,

---

* This village and the poor of this neighbourhood know what it is to have possest such a blessing, and feel at this moment what it is to lose it by death. C. L.
Troston, 13th of September 1801.

THE MILLER'S MAID.

The Tempeſt.   v. 11.

Though diſtant yet, menac'd the country round,
And fill'd the Heavens with its ſolemn ſound.
Who can retire to reſt when tempeſts lour?
Nor wait the iſſue of the coming hour?
Meekly reſign'd ſhe ſat, in anxious pain;
He fill'd his pipe, and liſten'd to the rain
That batter'd furiouſly their ſtrong abode,
Roar'd in the Damm, and laſh'd the pebbled road:
When, mingling with the ſtorm, confus'd and wild,
They heard, or thought they heard, a ſcreaming
    Child:
The voice approach'd; and 'midſt the thunder's
    roar,
Now loudly begg'd for Mercy at the door.
    MERCY was *there:* the Miller heard the call;
His door he open'd; when a ſudden ſquall
Drove in a wretched Girl; who weeping ſtood,
Whilſt the cold rain dripp'd from her in a flood.

THE MILLER'S MAID.

v. 29.   The Young Stranger.

With kind officiousnefs the tender Dame
Rous'd up the dying embers to a flame;
Dry cloaths procur'd, and cheer'd her fhiv'ring gueft,
And footh'd the forrows of her infant breaft.
But as fhe ftript her fhoulders, lily-white,
What marks of cruel ufage fhock'd their fight!
Weals, and blue wounds, moft piteous to behold
Upon a Child yet fcarcely Ten years old.

 The *Miller* felt his indignation rife,
Yet, as the weary ftranger clos'd her eyes,
And feem'd fatigu'd beyond her ftrength and years,
" Sleep, Child, (he faid), and wipe away your tears."
They watch'd her flumbers till the ftorm was done;
When thus the generous Man again begun.
' See, flutt'ring fighs that rife againft her will,
' And agitating dreams difturb her ftill!
' Dame, we fhould know before we go to reft,
' Whence comes this Girl, and how fhe came diftreft.

'Wake her, and afk; for fhe is forely bruis'd:
'I long to know by whom fhe's thus mifus'd.
  'Child, what's your name? how came you in
      the ftorm?
'Have you no home to keep you dry and warm?
'Who gave you all thofe wounds your fhoulders
  'fhow?
'Where are your Parents? Whither would you go?
  The Stranger burfting into tears, look'd pale,
And this the purport of her artlefs tale.
  'I have no Parents; and no friends befide:
'I well remember when my Mother died:
'My Brother cried; and fo did I that day:
'We had no Father;—he was gone away;
'That night we left our home new cloaths to wear:
'The *Work-houfe* found them; we were carried there.
'We lov'd each other dearly; when we met
'We always fhar'd what trifles we could get.

THE MILLER'S MAID.

v. 5c. Rustic Hospitality and Protection of the friendless.

' But *George* was older by a year than me :—
' He parted from me and was sent to Sea.
" Good-bye, dear Phœbe," the poor fellow said !
' Perhaps he'll come again; perhaps he's dead.
' When I grew strong enough I went to place,
' My Mistress had a four ill-natur'd face;
' And though I've been so often beat and chid,
' I strove to please her, Sir; indeed, I did.
' Weary and spiritless to bed I crept,
' And always cried at night before I slept.
' This Morning I offended; and I bore
' A cruel beating, worse than all before.
' Unknown to all the House I ran away;
' And thus far travell'd through the sultry day;
' And, O don't send me back ! I dare not go—.'
' I send you back !' (the Miller cried) ' no, no.'
Th' appeals of Wretchedness had weight with him,
And Sympathy would warm him every limb;

THE MILLER'S MAID.

The Child becomes one of the Family. v. 73.

He mutter'd, glorying in the work begun,
' Well done, my little Wench; 'twas nobly done !'
Then said, with looks more cheering than the fire,
And feelings such as Pity can inspire,
' My house has childless been this many a year;
' While you deserve it you shall tarry here.'
The Orphan mark'd the ardor of his eye,
Blest his kind words, and thank'd him with a sigh.

Thus was the sacred compact doubly seal'd;
Thus were her spirits rais'd, her bruises heal'd:
Thankful, and cheerful too, no more afraid,
Thus little PHOEBE was the Miller's Maid.
Grateful they found her; patient of controul:
A most bewitching gentleness of soul
Made pleasure of what work she had to do:
She grew in stature, and in beauty too.

Five years she pass'd in this delightful home;
Five happy years: but, when the sixth was come,

THE MILLER'S MAID.

v. 91.   The New Comer.

The *Miller* from a Market Town hard by,
Brought home a sturdy Youth his strength to try,
To raise the sluice-gates early every morn,
To heave his powder'd sacks and grind his corn:
' And meeting *Phœbe*, whom he lov'd so dear,
' I've brought you home a Husband, Girl;—D'ye
  ' hear?
' He begg'd for work; his money seem'd but scant:
' Those that will work 'tis pity they should want. *
' So use him well, and we shall shortly see
' Whether he merits what I've done, like thee.'
  Now throbb'd her heart,—a new sensation
    quite,—
Whene'er the comely Stranger was in sight:
For he at once assiduously strove
To please so sweet a Maid, and win her love.
At every corner stopp'd her in her way;
And saw fresh beauties opening ev'ry day.

* A Maxim which all ought to remember.   C. L.

THE MILLER'S MAID.

Firſt Impreſſions. v. 101.

He took delight in tracing in her face
The mantling bluſh, and every nameleſs grace,
That Senſibility would bring to view,
When Love he mention'd;—Love, and Honour true.
But *Phœbe* ſtill was ſhy; and wiſh'd to know
More of the honeſt Youth, whoſe manly brow
She verily believ'd was Truth's own throne,
And all his words as artleſs as her own:
Moſt true ſhe judg'd; yet, long the Youth forbore
Divulging where, and how, he liv'd before;
And ſeem'd to ſtrive his Hiſtory to hide,
Till fair Eſteem enliſted on his ſide.
The *Miller* ſaw, and mention'd, in his praiſe,
The prompt fidelity of all his ways:
Till in a vacant hour, the Dinner done,
One day he joking cried, ' Come here, my Son!
' 'Tis pity that ſo good a Lad as you
' Beneath my roof ſhould bring diſorders new!

THE MILLER'S MAID.

v. 119.   Enquiry.   Ingenuous Explanation.

' But here's my *Phœbe*,—once so light and airy
' She'd trip along the passage like a Fairy,—
' Has lost her swiftness quite, since here you came:—
' And yet; ....I can't perceive the Girl is lame!
' The obstacles she meets with still fall thicker:
' Old as I am I'd turn a corner quicker.'——
The *Youth* blush'd deep; and *Phœbe* hung her
    head:
The *good Man* smil'd, and thus again he said:
' Not that I deem it matter of surprise,
' That you should love to gaze at *Phœbe's* eyes;
' But be explicit, Boy; and deal with honour:
' I feel my happiness depend upon her.
' When here you came you'd sorrow on your brow;
' And I've forborne to question you till now.
' First, then, say what thou art.' He instant
    bow'd,
And thus, in *Phœbe's* hearing, spoke aloud:

The little Hiftory.	v. 137.

' Thus far experienc'd, Sir, in you I find
' All that is generous, fatherly, and kind;
' And while you look for proofs of real worth,
' You'll not regard the meannefs of my birth.
' When, pennylefs and fad, you met with me,
' I'd juft efcap'd the dangers of the Sea;
' Refolv'd to try my fortune on the fhore:
' To get my bread; and truft the waves no more.
' Having no Home, nor Parents, left behind,
' I'd all my fortune, all my Friends, to find.
' Keen difappointment wounded me that morn:
' For, trav'lling near the fpot where I was born,
' I at the well-known door where I was bred,
' Inquir'd who ftill was living, who was dead:
' But firft, and moft, I fought with anxious fear
' Tidings to gain of her who once was dear;
' A Girl, with all the meeknefs of the dove,
' The conftant fharer of my childhood's love;

THE MILLER'S MAID.

v. 155.	The Recognition.

' She call'd me, *Brother :*—which I heard with pride,
' Though now fufpect we are not fo allied.
' Thus much I learnt; (no more the churls would
    fay;)
' She went to fervice, and fhe ran away,
' And fcandal added'——' Hold!' the *Miller* cried,
And, in an inftant, ftood at *Phœbe's* fide;
For he obferved, while lift'ning to the tale,
Her fpirits faulter'd, and her cheeks turn'd pale;
Whilft her clafp'd hands defcended to her knee
She finking whifper'd forth, " O *God,* 'tis *he!"*
The good Man, though he guefs'd the pleafing
    truth,
Was far too bufy to inform the Youth;
But ftirr'd himfelf amain to aid his Wife,
Who foon reftor'd the trembler back to life.
Awhile infenfible fhe ftill appear'd;
But, " O *my Brother,"* was diftinctly heard:

| Mutual Recollections. | v. 173. |

The aſtoniſht Youth now held her to his breaſt;
And tears and kiſſes ſoon explain'd the reſt.
 Paſt deeds now from each tongue alternate fell:
For news of deareſt import both could tell.
Fondly, from childhood's tears to youth's full prime,
They match'd the incidents of jogging time;
And prov'd, that when with Tyranny oppreſt,
Poor *Phœbe* groan'd with wounds and broken reſt,
George felt no leſs : was haraſs'd and forlorn ;
A rope's-end follow'd him both night and morn.
And in that very ſtorm when *Phœbe* fled,
When the rain drench'd her yet unſhelter'd head;
That very Storm he on the Ocean brav'd,
The Veſſel founder'd, and the Boy was ſav'd!
Myſterious Heaven!—and O with what delight—
She told the happy iſſue of her flight:
To his charm'd heart a living picture drew;
And gave to hoſpitality it's due!

THE MILLER'S MAID.

v. 191.   The Investigation.

The lift'ning Hoft obferv'd the gentle Pair;
And ponder'd on the means that brought them
    there:
Convinc'd, while unimpeach'd their Virtue ftood,
'Twas *Heav'n's* high Will that he fhould do them
    good.
But now the anxious Dame, impatient grown,
Demanded what the Youth had heard, or known,
Whereon to ground thofe doubts but juft expreft;—
Doubts, which muft intereft the feeling breaft;
' Her Brother wert thou, George?—how; prithee fay:
' Canft thou forego, or caft that name away?
  " No living proofs have I," the Youth reply'd,
" That we by clofeft ties are not allied;
" But in my memory live, and ever will,
" A mother's dying words..... I hear them ftill:
" She faid, to one who watch'd her parting breath,
" Don't feparate the Children at my death,"

| The Perplexity. | v. 209. |

"They're not both mine: But——" here the scene
    was clos'd,
"She died; and left us helpless and expos'd;
"Nor Time hath thrown, nor Reason's opening
    "power,
"One friendly ray on that benighted hour."
Ne'er did the Chieftains of a Warring State
Hear from the *Oracle* their half-told fate
With more religious fear, or more suspence,
Than *Phœbe* now endur'd:—for every sense
Became absorb'd in this unwelcome theme;
Nay every meditation, every dream,
Th' inexplicable sentence held to view,
"They're not both mine," was every morning new:
For, till this hour, the Maid had never prov'd
How far she was enthrall'd, how much she lov'd:
In that fond character he first appear'd;
His kindness charm'd her, and his smiles endear'd:

THE MILLER'S MAID.

v. 227.   Anxiety.   The Enquiry fuggefted.

This dubious myftery the paffion croft;
Her peace was wounded, and her Lover loft.
For *George*, with all his refolution ftrove
To check the progrefs of his growing love;
Or, if he e'er indulg'd a tender kifs,
Th' unravell'd fecret robb'd him of his blifs.
Health's foe, Sufpence, fo irkfome to be borne,
An ever-piercing and retreating thorn,
Hung on their Hearts, when Nature bade them rife,
And ftole Content's bright enfign from their eyes.

The good folks faw the change, and griev'd to find
Thefe troubles labouring in *Phœbe's* mind;
They lov'd them both; and with one voice propos'd
The only means whence *Truth* might be difclos'd;
That, when the Summer Months fhould fhrink the
    rill,
And fcarce its languid ftream wou'd turn the Mill,

E

THE MILLER'S MAID.

Eager Expectation.   v. 245.

When the Spring broods, and Pigs, and Lambs
    were rear'd,
(A time when *George* and *Phœbe* might be spar'd,)
Their birth place they should visit once again,
To try with joint endeavours to obtain
From Record, or Tradition, what might be
To chain, or set their chain'd affections free:
Affinity beyond all doubts to prove;
Or clear the road for Nature and for Love.

Never, till now, did PHŒBE count the hours,
Or think *May* long, or wish away its flowers;
With mutual sighs both fann'd the wings of Time;
As we climb Hills and gladden as we climb,
And reach at last the distant promis'd seat,
Casting the glowing landscape at our feet.
Oft had the Morning Rose with dew been wet,
And oft the journeying Sun in glory set,

THE MILLER'S MAID.

v. 263.   The Old Soldier.

Beyond the willow'd meads of vigorous grafs,
The fteep green hill, and woods they were to pafs;
When now the day arriv'd: Impatience reign'd;
And GEORGE,—by trifling obftacles detain'd,—
His bending Blackthorn on the threfhold preft,
Survey'd the windward clouds, and hop'd the beft.
PHŒBE, attir'd with every modeft grace,
While Health and Beauty revell'd in her face,
Came forth; but foon evinc'd an abfent mind,
For, back fhe turn'd for fomething left behind;
Again the fame, till George grew tir'd of home,
And peevifhly exclaim'd, " *Come, Phœbe, come.*"
Another hindrance yet he had to feel:
As from the door they tripp'd with nimble heel,
A poor old Man, foot-founder'd and alone,
Thus urgent fpoke, in Trouble's genuine tone:
" My pretty Maid, if happinefs you feek,
" May difappointment never fade your cheek!—

THE MILLER'S MAID.

The Soldier's Tale.

" Your's be the joy;—yet, feel another's woe:
" O leave some little gift before you go."
His words struck home; and back she turn'd again,
(The ready friend of indigence and pain,)
To banish hunger from his shatter'd frame;
And close behind her, Lo, the *Miller* came,
With Jug in hand, and cried, " GEORGE, why
  " such haste?
" Here; take a draught; and let that *Soldier* taste."
" Thanks for your bounty, Sir;" the *Veteran* said;
Threw down his Wallet, and made bare his head;
And straight began, though mix'd with doubts
  and fears,
Th' unprefac'd History of his latter years.
" I cross'd th' *Atlantic* with our Regiment brave,
" Where Sickness sweeps whole Regiments to the
  grave;

THE MILLER'S MAID.

v. 299.   The Surprize.

" Yet I've escap'd; and bear my arms no more;
" My age discharg'd me when I came on shore.
" My *Wife*, I've heard,"—and here he wip'd his
    eyes,—
" In the cold corner of the Church-yard lies.
" By her consent it was I left my home:
" Employment fail'd, and poverty was come;
" The Bounty tempted me;—she had it all:
" We parted; and I've seen my betters fall.
" Yet, as I'm spar'd, though in this piteous case,
" I'm trav'lling homeward to my native place;
" Though should I reach that dear remember'd spot,
" Perhaps OLD GRAINGER will be quite forgot."

All eyes beheld young *George* with wonder start:
Strong were the secret bodings of his heart;
Yet not indulg'd: for he with doubts survey'd
By turns the Stranger, and the lovely Maid.

THE MILLER'S MAID.

v. 317.   The Discovery.

" Had you no Children?"—" Yes, young Man;
     I'd two:
" A *Boy*, if still he lives, as old as you:
" Yet not my own; but likely so to prove;
" Though but the pledge of an unlawful Love:
" I cherish'd him, to hide a *Sister*'s shame:
" He shar'd my best affections, and my name.
" But why, young folks, should I detain you here?
" Go: and may blessings wait upon your cheer,
" I too will travel on;.... perhaps to find
" The only treasure that I left behind.
" Such kindly thoughts my fainting hopes revive!—
" *Phœbe*, my Cherub, ART *thou* still alive?"

    Could Nature hold!—Could youthful Love forbear!
George clasp'd the wond'ring *Maid*, and whisper'd,
    '*There!*

THE MILLER'S MAID.

v. 335.   The happy Relations now found.

' *You're mine for ever!*—O, fuſtain the reſt;
' And huſh the tumult of your throbbing breaſt.'
Then to the *Soldier* turn'd, with manly pride,
And fondly led his long-intended *Bride:*
' Here, ſee your *Child*; nor wiſh a ſweeter flow'r.
' 'Tis *George* that ſpeaks; thou'lt bleſs the happy
    hour!—
' Nay, be compos'd; for all will yet be well,
' Though here our hiſtory's too long to tell.'——
  A long-loſt Father found, the myſtery clear'd,
What mingled tranſports in *her* face appear'd!
The gazing *Veteran* ſtood with hands upraiſ'd—
' Art thou *indeed* my Child! then, GOD be
    prais'd.'
O'er his rough cheeks the tears profuſely ſpread:
Such as fools ſay become not Men to ſhed;
Paſt hours of bliſs, regenerated charms,
Roſe, when he felt his Daughter in his arms:

THE MILLER'S MAID.

The bliss of disinterested Benevolence. v. 353.

So tender was the scene, the generous DAME
Wept, as she told of *Phœbe's* virtuous fame,
And the good HOST, with gestures passing strange,
Abstracted seem'd through fields of joy to range:
Rejoicing that his favour'd Roof should prove
VIRTUE's asylum, and the nurse of LOVE;
Rejoicing that to him the task was given,
While his full Soul was mounting up to Heav'n.
But now, as from a dream his Reason sprung,
And heartiest greetings dwelt upon his tongue:
The sounding Kitchen floor at once receiv'd
The happy group, with all their fears reliev'd:
" Soldier," he cried, " you've found your Girl;
" 'tis true:
" But suffer *me* to be a Father too;
" For, never Child that blest a Parent's knee,
" Could show more duty than she has to me,

THE MILLER'S MAID.

v. 371.   The adopted Daughter.

" Strangely she came; Affliction chas'd her hard:
" I pitied her;—and this is my reward !
" Here sit you down; recount your perils o'er:
" Henceforth be this your home; and grieve no
    more:
" Plenty hath shower'd her dewdrops on my head;
" Care visits not my Table, nor my Bed.
" My heart's warm wishes thus then I fulfill:—
" My Dame and I can live without the Mill:
" *George*, take the whole; I'll near you still re-
    main,
" To guide your judgment in the choice of Grain :
" In Virtue's path commence your prosperous life;
" And from my hand receive your worthy Wife.
" Rise, *Phœbe*; rise, my Girl!—kneel not to me;
" But to THAT Pow'r who interpos'd for thee.
" Integrity hath mark'd your favourite Youth;
" Fair budding Honour, Constancy, and Truth:

THE MILLER'S MAID.

v. 389. Perfect Content: hopes and prospects of Goodness.

" Go to his arms;—and may unsullied joys
" Bring smiling round me, rosy Girls and Boys!
" I'll love them for thy sake. And may your days
" Glide on, as glides the Stream that never stays;
" Bright as whose shingled bed, till life's decline,
" May all your Worth, and all your Virtues shine!"

I believe there has been no such Poem in its kind as the MILLER's MAID, since the days of DRYDEN, for ease and beauty of language; concise, clear and interesting narrative; sweet and full flow of verse; happy choice of the subject, and delightful execution of it. C. L.

THE WIDOW

TO

HER HOUR-GLASS.

1

Come, friend, I'll turn thee up again:
Companion of the lonely hour!
Spring thirty times hath fed with rain
And cloath'd with leaves my humble bower,
 Since thou haſt ſtood
 In frame of wood,

On Cheſt or Window by my ſide:
At every Birth ſtill thou wert near,
Still ſpoke thine admonitions clear.—
 And, when my Huſband died,

2

I've often watch'd thy ſtreaming ſand
And ſeen the growing Mountain riſe,
And often found Life's hopes to ſtand
On props as weak in Wiſdom's eyes:
 Its conic crown
 Still ſliding down,
Again heap'd up, then down again;
The ſand above more hollow grew,
Like days and years ſtill filt'ring through,
 And mingling joy and pain.

HER HOUR-GLASS.

3

While thus I spin and sometimes sing,
(For now and then my heart will glow)
Thou measur'st Time's expanding wing:
By thee the noontide hour I know:
  Though silent thou,
  Still shalt thou flow,
And jog along thy destin'd way:
But when I glean the sultry fields,
When Earth her yellow Harvest yields,
  Thou get'st a Holiday.

4

Steady as Truth, on either end
Thy daily task performing well,
Thou'rt Meditation's constant friend,
And strik'st the Heart without a Bell:

THE WIDOW, &c.

Come, lovely May!

Thy lengthen'd day

Shall gild once more my native plain;

Curl inward here, sweet Woodbine flow'r;—

" Companion of the lonely hour,

" I'll turn thee up again."

There is something very pleasing in the lyric stanza here used. It is a very harmonious and characteristic form of versification: which, after having slept, if I mistake not, above a Century, is here happily reviv'd. The turn of thought is natural, affecting, and poetic. C. L.

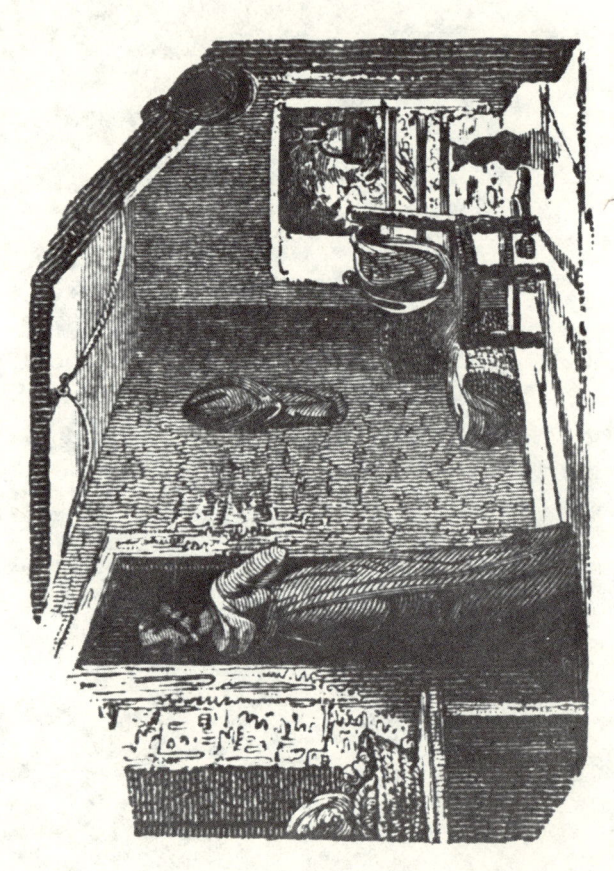

MARKET-NIGHT.

1

' O Winds, howl not so long and loud;
' Nor with your vengeance arm the snow:
' Bear hence each heavy-loaded cloud;
' And let the twinkling Star-beams glow.

2

' Now sweeping floods rush down the slope,
' Wide scattering ruin.—Stars, shine soon!
' No other light my Love can hope;
' Midnight will want the joyous *Moon*.

MARKET-NIGHT.

3

' O guardian Spirits!—Ye that dwell
' Where woods, and pits, and hollow ways,
' The lone night-trav'ller's fancy swell
' With fearful tales, of older days,—

4

' Press round him:—guide his willing steed
' Through darkness, dangers, currents, snows;
' Wait where, from shelt'ring thickets freed,
' The dreary Heath's rude whirlwind blows.

5

' From darkness rushing o'er his way,
' The Thorn's white load it bears on high!
' Where the short furze all shrouded lay,
' Mounts the dried grass;—Earth's bosom dry.

MARKET-NIGHT.

6

' Then o'er the Hill with furious sweep
' It rends the elevated tree——
' Sure-footed beast thy road thou'lt keep :
' Nor storm nor darkness startles thee !'

7

' O blest assurance, (trusty steed,)
' To thee the buried road is known ;
' *Home,* all the spur thy footsteps need,
' When loose the frozen rein is thrown.'

8

' Between the roaring blasts that shake
' The naked Elder at the door,
' Though not one prattler to me speak,
' Their sleeping sighs delight me more.'

F

9

'Sound is their rest:—they little know
'What pain, what cold, their Father feels;
'But dream, perhaps, they see him now,
'While each the promis'd Orange peels.'

10

'Would it were so!—the fire burns bright,
'And on the warming trencher gleams;
'In Expectation's raptur'd sight
'How precious his arrival seems!'

11

'I'll look abroad!—'tis piercing cold!—
'How the bleak wind assails his breast!
'Yet some faint light mine eyes behold:
'The storm is verging o'er the West.'

MARKET-NIGHT.

12

' There shines a *Star!*—O welcome Sight!—
' Through the thin vapours bright'ning still!
' Yet, 'twas beneath the fairest night
' The murd'rer stain'd yon lonely Hill.'

13

' Mercy, kind Heav'n! such thoughts dispel!
' No voice, no footstep can I hear!'
(Where Night and Silence brooding dwell,
Spreads thy cold reign, heart-chilling Fear.)

14

' Distressing hour! uncertain fate!
' O Mercy, Mercy, guide him home!—
' Hark!—then I heard the distant gate,——
' Repeat it, Echo; quickly, come!'

15

'One minute now will eafe my fears ....
' Or, ftill more wretched muft I be?
' No: furely Heaven has fpar'd our tears:
' I fee him, cloath'd in fnow; ... 'tis he.———'

16

' Where have you ftay'd? put down your load.
' How have you borne the ftorm, the cold?
' What horrors did I not forbode———
' That Beaft is worth his weight in gold.'

17

Thus fpoke the joyful Wife;—then ran
And hid in grateful fteams her head:
Dapple was hous'd, the hungry Man
With joy glanc'd o'er the Children's bed.

MARKET-NIGHT.

18

' What, all asleep !'—so best; he cried :
' O what a night I've travell'd through !
' Unseen, unheard, I might have died;
' But Heaven has brought me safe to you.

19

' Dear Partner of my nights and days,
' That smile becomes thee!—Let us then
' Learn, though mishap may cross our ways,
' It is not ours to reckon when.'

I judge not for other readers; and it is needless; but to me Market-Night is exquisitely and almost singularly pleasing, by the natural force and tenderness of the sweetness of the numbers, the easy yet animated and characteristic beauty of the style and manner. C. L.

Sept. 1801.

THE

FAKENHAM GHOST.

A BALLAD.

1

The Lawns were dry in Euston Park;
(Here Truth * infpires my Tale)
The lonely footpath, ftill and dark,
Led over Hill and Dale.

---

* This Ballad is founded on a fact. The circumftance occurred perhaps long before I was born: but is ftill related by my Mother, and fome of the oldeft inhabitants in that part of the country. R. B.

THE FAKENHAM GHOST.

2

Benighted was an ancient Dame,
And fearful haste she made
To gain the vale of Fakenham,
And hail its Willow shade.

3

Her footsteps knew no idle stops,
But follow'd faster still;
And echo'd to the darksome Copse
That whisper'd on the Hill;

4

Where clam'rous Rooks, yet scarcely hush'd
Bespoke a peopled shade;
And many a wing the foliage brush'd,
And hov'ring circuits made.

72 THE FAKENHAM GHOST.

5

The dappled herd of grazing Deer
That fought the Shades by day,
Now ſtarted from her path with fear,
And gave the Stranger way.

6

Darker it grew; and darker fears
Came o'er her troubled mind;
When now, a ſhort quick ſtep ſhe hears
Come patting cloſe behind.

7

She turn'd; it ſtopt!—nought could ſhe ſee
Upon the gloomy plain!
But, as ſhe ſtrove the Sprite to flee,
She heard the ſame again.

THE FAKENHAM GHOST.

8

Now terror feiz'd her quaking frame:
For, where the path was bare,
The trotting Ghoſt kept on the fame!
She mutter'd many a pray'r.

9

Yet once again, amidſt her fright
She tried what flight could do;
When through the cheating glooms of night,
A MONSTER ſtood in view.

10

Regardleſs of whate'er ſhe felt,
It follow'd down the plain!
She own'd her fins, and down ſhe knelt,
And ſaid her pray'rs again.

THE FAKENHAM GHOST.

11

Then on she sped: and Hope grew strong,
The white park gate in view;
Which pushing hard, so long it swung
That *Ghost* and all pass'd through.

12

Loud fell the gate against the post!
Her heart-strings like to crack:
For, much she fear'd the grisly Ghost
Would leap upon her back.

13

Still on, pat, pat, the Goblin went,
As it had done before:—
Her strength and resolution spent
She fainted at the door.

THE FAKENHAM GHOST.

14

Out came her Husband much surpris'd:
Out came her Daughter dear:
Good-natur'd Souls! all unadvis'd
Of what they had to fear.

15

The Candle's gleam pierc'd through the night,
Some short space o'er the green;
And there the little trotting Sprite
Distinctly might be seen.

16

An *Ass's Foal* had lost its Dam
Within the spacious Park;
And simple as the playful Lamb,
Had follow'd in the dark.

THE FAKENHAM GHOST.

17

No Goblin he; no imp of sin :
No crimes had ever known.
They took the shaggy stranger in,
And rear'd him as their own.

18

His little hoofs would rattle round
Upon the Cottage floor :
The Matron learn'd to love the sound
That frighten'd her before.

19

A favorite the Ghost became;
And, 'twas his fate to thrive :
And long he liv'd and spread his fame,
And kept the joke alive.

THE FAKENHAM GHOST.

20

For many a laugh went through the Vale;
And some conviction too:—
Each thought some other Goblin tale,
Perhaps, was just as true *.

---

  * A charming little story: excellently told: and most pleasingly and pointedly concluded.   C. L.
    Sept. 1801.

THE FRENCH MARINER.

A BALLAD.

An Old *French Mariner* am I,
Whom Time hath render'd poor and gray;
Hear, conquering *Britons*, ere I die,
What anguish prompts me thus to say.

2

I've rode o'er many a dreadful wave,
I've seen the reeking blood descend:
I've heard the last groans of the brave;—
The shipmate dear, the steady Friend.

3

'Twas when *De Graffe* the battle join'd
And ſtruck, on *April's* fatal morn:
I left three ſmiling boys behind,
And ſaw my Country's Lillie torn.

4

There, as I brav'd the ſtorms of Fate,
Dead in my arms my Brother fell;
Here ſits forlorn his widow'd Mate,
Who weeps whene'er the tale I tell.

5

Thy reign, ſweet Peace, was o'er too ſoon;
War, piecemeal, robs me of my joy:
For, on the bloodſtain'd *firſt* of *June*
Death took my *eldeſt* favorite Boy.

6

The other two enrag'd arofe,
' Our Country claims our lives,' they faid.
With them I loft my Soul's repofe,
That fatal hour my laft hope fled.

7

With Bruey's the proud Nile they fought:
Where one in ling'ring wounds expir'd;
While yet the other bravely fought
The Orient's magazine was fir'd.

8

And muft I mourn my Country's fhame?
And envious curfe the conquering Foe?
No more I feel that thirft of Fame;—
All I can feel is private woe.

THE FRENCH MARINER.

9

E'en all the joy that Vict'ry brings,
(Her bellowing Guns, and flaming pride)
Cold, momentary comfort flings
Around where weeping Friends reside.

10

Whose blighted bud no Sun shall cheer,
Whose Lamp of Life no longer shine:
Some Parent, Brother, Child, most dear,
Who ventur'd, and who died like mine.

11

Proud crested Fiend, the World's worst foe,
Ambition; canst thou boast one deed,
Whence no unsightly horrors flow,
Nor private peace is seen to bleed.

12

Ah! why do these Old Eyes remain
To see succeeding mornings rise!
My Wife is dead, my Children slain,
And Poverty is all my prize.

13

Yet shall not poor enfeebled Age
Breathe forth revenge;... but rather say,
O God, who seest the Battle's rage,
Take from men's Hearts that rage away.

14

From the vindictive tongue of strife,
Bid Hatred and false Glory flee;
That babes may meet advancing life,
Nor feel the woes that light on me.

I can hardly imagine any thing more great, generous, and pathetic, than the subject, sentiment, and expression of this Ballad. C. L.

DOLLY.

"*Ingenuous trust, and confidence of Love.*"

1

The Bat began with giddy wing
His circuit round the Shed, the Tree;
And clouds of dancing Gnats to sing
A summer-night's serenity.

2

Darkness crept slowly o'er the East!
Upon the Barn-roof watch'd the Cat;
Sweet breath'd the ruminating Beast
At rest where DOLLY musing sat.

3

A simple Maid, who could employ
The silent lapse of Evening mild,
And lov'd its solitary joy:
For Dolly was Reflection's child.

4

He who had pledg'd his word to be
Her life's dear guardian, far away,
The flow'r of Yeoman Cavalry,
Bestrode a Steed with trappings gay.

5

And thus from memory's treasur'd sweets,
And thus from Love's pure fount she drew
That peace, which busy care defeats,
And bids our pleasures bloom anew.

DOLLY.

6

Six weeks of abfence have I borne
Since Henry took his fond farewell:
The charms of that delightful morn
My tongue could thus for ever tell.

7

He at my Window whiftling loud,
Arous'd my lightfome heart to go:
Day, conqu'ring climb'd from cloud to cloud;
The fields all wore a purple glow.

8

We ftroll'd the bordering flow'rs among;
One hand the Bridle held behind;
The other round my waift was flung:
Sure never Youth fpoke half fo kind!

DOLLY.

9

The rising Lark I could but hear;
And jocund seem'd the song to be:
But sweeter sounded in my ear,
" Will *Dolly* still be true to me!"

10

From the rude Dock my skirt had swept
A fringe of clinging burrs so green;
Like them our hearts still closer crept,
And hook'd a thousand holds unseen.

11

High o'er the road each branching bough
Its globes of silent dew had shed;
And on the pure-wash'd sand below
The dimpling drops around had spread.

12

The sweet-brier op'd its pink-ey'd rose,
And gave its fragrance to the gale;
Though modest flow'rs may sweets disclose,
More sweet was HENRY's earnest tale.

13

He seem'd, methought, on that dear morn,
To pour out all his heart to me;
As if, the separation borne,
The coming hours would joyless be.

14

A bank rose high beside the way,
And full against the Morning Sun;
Of heav'nly blue there Violets gay
His hand invited one by one.

15

The pofy with a fmile he gave;
I faw his meaning in his eyes:
The wither'd treafure ftill I have;
My bofom holds the fragrant prize.

16

With his laft kifs he would have vow'd;
But bleffings crouding forc'd their way:
Then mounted he his Courfer proud;
His time elaps'd he could not ftay.

17

Then firft I felt the parting pang;—
Sure the worft pang the Lover feels!
His Horfe unruly from me fprang,
The pebbles flew beneath his heels;

18

Then down the road his vigour tried,
His rider gazing, gazing ſtill;
"*My deareſt, I'll be true,*" he cried:—
And, if he lives, I'm ſure he will.

19

Then haſte, ye hours, haſte, Eve and Morn,
Yet ſtrew your bleſſings round my home:
Ere Winter's blaſts ſhall ſtrip the thorn
My promis'd joy, my love, will come.

 Highly animated, natural, and engaging. **C. L.**

LINES,

OCCASIONED BY

A VISIT TO WHITTLEBURY FOREST,

NORTHAMPTONSHIRE,

IN AUGUST, 1800.

ADDRESSED TO MY CHILDREN.

I

Genius of the Forest Shades!
Lend thy pow'r, and lend thine ear!
A Stranger trod thy lonely glades,
Amidst thy dark and bounding Deer;
Inquiring Childhood claims the verse,
O let them not inquire in vain;
Be with me while I thus rehearse
The glories of thy Sylvan Reign.

A VISIT, &c.

2

Thy Dells by wint'ry currents worn,
Secluded haunts, how dear to me!
From all but Nature's converse borne,
No ear to hear, no eye to see.
Their honour'd leaves the green Oaks rear'd,
And crown'd the upland's graceful swell;
While answering through the vale was heard
Each distant Heifer's tinkling bell.

3

Hail, Greenwood shades, that stretching far,
Defy e'en Summer's noontide pow'r,
When August in his burning Car
Withholds the Cloud, withholds the Show'r.
The deep-ton'd Low from either Hill,
Down hazel aisles and arches green;
(The Herd's rude tracks from rill to rill)
Roar'd echoing through the solemn scene.

4

From my charm'd heart the numbers sprung,
Though Birds had ceas'd the choral lay:
I pour'd wild raptures from my tongue,
And gave delicious tears their way.
Then, darker shadows seeking still,
Where Human foot had seldom stray'd,
I read aloud to every Hill
Sweet Emma's Love, " the Nut-brown Maid."

5

Shaking his matted mane on high
The gazing Colt would raise his head;
Or, tim'rous Doe would rushing fly,
And leave to me her grassy bed:
Where, as the azure sky appear'd
Through Bow'rs of every varying form,
'Midst the deep gloom methought I heard
The daring progress of the storm.

WHITTLEBURY FOREST.

6

How would each sweeping pond'rous bough
Resist, when straight the Whirlwind cleaves,
Dashing in strength'ning eddies through
A roaring wilderness of leaves!
How would the prone descending show'r
From the green Canopy rebound!
How would the lowland torrents pour!
How deep the pealing thunder sound!

7

But Peace was there: no lightnings blaz'd:—
No clouds obscur'd the face of Heav'n:
Down each green op'ning while I gaz'd
My thoughts to home, and you, were giv'n.
O tender minds! in life's gay morn
Some clouds must dim your coming day;
Yet, bootless pride and falsehood scorn,
And peace like this shall cheer your way.

8

Now, at the dark Wood's stately side,
Well pleas'd I met the Sun again;
Here fleeting Fancy travell'd wide!
My seat was destin'd to the Main:
For, many an Oak lay stretch'd at length,
Whose trunks (with bark no longer sheath'd)
Had reach'd their full meridian strength
Before your Father's Father breath'd!

9

Perhaps they'll many a conflict brave,
And many a dreadful storm defy;
Then groaning o'er the adverse wave
Bring home the flag of victory.
Go, then, proud Oaks; we meet no more!
Go, grace the scenes to me denied,
The white Cliffs round my native shore,
And the loud Ocean's swelling tide.

WHITTLEBURY FOREST.

10

' Genius of the Foreſt Shades,'
Sweet, from the heights of thy domain,
When the grey ev'ning ſhadow fades,
To view the Country's golden grain!
To view the gleaming Village Spire
'Midſt diſtant groves unknown to me;
Groves, that grown bright in borrow'd fire,
Bow o'er the peopled Vales to thee!

11

Where was thy Elfin train that play
Round *Wake's* huge Oak, their favourite tree?
May a poor ſon of Song thus ſay,
Why were they not reveal'd to me!
Yet, ſmiling Fairies left behind,
Affection brought you to my view;
To love and tenderneſs reſign'd,
I ſat me down and thought of you.

12

When Morning still unclouded rose,
Refresh'd with sleep and joyous dreams,
Where fruitful fields with woodlands close,
I trac'd the births of various streams.
From beds of Clay, here creeping rills
Unseen to parent *Ouse* would steal;
Or, gushing from the northward Hills,
Would glitter through *Toves*' winding dale.

13

But ah! ye cooling springs, farewell!
Herds, I no more your freedom share;
But long my grateful tongue shall tell
What brought your gazing stranger there.
' Genius of the Forest Shades,'
' Lend thy power, and lend thine ear;'
Let dreams still lengthen thy long glades,
And bring thy peace and silence here.

These lyric stanzas have much of the solemn picturesque, and pathetic. And the address to the author's children gives a new and peculiar interest to the description. C. L.
Sept. 25. 1801.

SONG

FOR

A HIGHLAND DROVER

RETURNING FROM ENGLAND.

Now fare-thee-well, England; no further I'll roam;
But follow my shadow that points the way home:
Your gay southern Shores shall not tempt me to stay;
For my Maggy's at Home, and my Children at play!
'Tis this makes my Bonnet set light on my brow,
Gives my sinews their strength and my bosom its glow.

H

HIGHLAND DROVER.

2

Farewell, Mountaineers! my companions, adieu;
Soon, many long miles when I'm fever'd from you,
I shall miss your white Horns on the brink of the Bourne,
And o'er the rough Heaths, where you'll never return:
But in brave English pastures you cannot complain,
While your Drover speeds back to his Maggy again.

3

O Tweed! gentle Tweed, as I pass your green vales,
More than life, more than Love my tir'd Spirit inhales;
There Scotland, my darling, lies full in my view,
With her bare footed Lasses and Mountains so blue:
To the Mountains away; my heart bounds like the Hind;
For home is so sweet, and my Maggy so kind.

HIGHLAND DROVER.

4

As day after day I still follow my course,
And in fancy trace back every Stream to its source,
Hope cheers me up hills, where the road lies before
O'er hills just as high, and o'er tracks of wild Moor;
The keen polar Star nightly rising to view;
But Maggy's my Star, just as steady and true.

5

O Ghosts of my Fathers! O heroes, look down!
Fix my wandering thoughts on your deeds of renown,
For the glory of Scotland reigns warm in my breast,
And fortitude grows both from toil and from rest;
May your deeds and your worth be for ever in view,
And may Maggy bear sons not unworthy of you.

6

Love, why do you urge me, so weary and poor?
I cannot step faster, I cannot do more;
I've pass'd silver Tweed; e'en the Tay flows behind:
Yet fatigue I'll disdain;—my reward I shall find;
Thou, sweet smile of innocence, thou art my prize;
And the joy that will sparkle in Maggy's blue eyes.

7

She'll watch to the southward; ... perhaps she
    will sigh,
That the way is so long, and the Mountains so high;
Perhaps some huge Rock in the dusk she may see,
And will say in her fondness, " that surely is he?"
Good Wife you're deceiv'd; I'm still far from my
    home;
Go, sleep, my dear Maggy,—to-morrow I'll come.

Natural, affectionate, spirited, and poetical. C. L.

A WORD

TO

TWO YOUNG LADIES.

When tender Rose-trees first receive
On half-expanded Leaves, the Shower;
Hope's gayest pictures we believe,
And anxious watch each coming flower.

2

Then, if beneath the genial Sun
That spreads abroad the full-blown May,
Two infant Stems the rest out-run,
Their buds the first to meet the day

3

With joy their op'ning tints we view,
While morning's precious moments fly:
My pretty Maids, 'tis thus with *you*,
The fond admiring gazer, *I.*

4

Preserve, sweet Buds, where'er you be,
The richest gem that decks a Wife;
The charm of *female modesty:*
And let sweet Music give it life.

5

Still may the favouring Muse be found:
Still circumspect the paths ye tread:
Plant moral truths in Fancy's ground;
And meet old Age without a dread.

TWO YOUNG LADIES.

6

Yet, ere that comes, while yet ye quaff
The cup of Health without a pain,
I'll shake my grey hairs when you laugh,
And, when you sing, be young again.

Partial and interesting in all respects. C. L.

Both the young Ladies had addressed to me a few complimentary lines, (and I am sorry that those of the elder sister were never in my possession;) in return for which I sent the above. It was received on the day on which the younger completed her ninth year. Surely it cannot be ascribed to vanity, if, in gratitude to a most amiable family, I here preserve verbatim an effort of a child nine years old. I have the more pleasure in doing it, because *I know* them to be her own. R. B.

"Accept, dear Bard, the Muse's genuine thought,
"And take not ill the tribute of my heart:——
"For thee the laureat wreath of praise I'll bind;
"None that have read thy commendable mind
"Can let it pass unnotic'd—nor can I—
"For by thy lays I know thy sympathy." F. P.

ON HEARING OF THE TRANSLATION

OF PART OF

THE FARMER'S BOY

INTO LATIN;

By the Rev. Mr. C————.

Hey Giles! in what new garb art drefst?
For Lads like you methinks a bold one;
I'm glad to fee thee fo carefst;
But, hark ye'—don't defpife your old one.

Thou'rt not the firſt by many a Boy
Who've found abroad good friends to own 'em;
Then, in ſuch Coats have ſhown their joy,
E'en their *own Fathers* have not known 'em.

Lively and pointed.   C. L.

NANCY:
A SONG.

1.

You aſk me, dear Nancy, what makes me preſume
That you cheriſh a ſecret affection for me?
When we ſee the Flow'rs bud, don't we look for
    the Bloom?
Then, ſweeteſt, attend, while I anſwer to thee.

2.

When we Young Men with paſtimes the Twilight
    beguile,
I watch your plump cheek till it dimples with joy:
And obſerve, that whatever occaſions the ſmile,
You give me a glance; but provokingly coy.

3

Laſt Month, when wild Strawberries pluckt in the Grove,
Like beads on the tall ſeeded graſs you had ſtrung;
You gave me the choiceſt; I hop'd 'twas for Love;
And I told you my hopes while the Nightingale ſung.

4

Remember the Viper:—'twas cloſe at your feet,
How you ſtarted, and threw yourſelf into my arms;
Not a Strawberry there was ſo ripe nor ſo ſweet
As the lips which I kiſs'd to ſubdue your alarms.

5

As I pull'd down the cluſters of Nuts for my Fair,
What a blow I receiv'd from a ſtrong bending bough;
Though Lucy and other gay laſſes were there,
Not one of them ſhow'd ſuch compaſſion as you.

6

And was it compaſſion?—by Heaven 'twas more!
A telltale betrays you;—that bluſh on your cheek.
Then come, deareſt Maid, all your trifling give o'er,
And whiſper what Candour will teach you to ſpeak.

7

Can you ſtain my fair Honour with one broken vow?
Can you ſay that I've ever occaſion'd a pain?
On Truth's honeſt baſe let your tenderneſs grow:
I ſwear to be faithful, again and again.

Simply pleaſing.   C. L.

ROSY HANNAH.

A Spring o'erhung with many a flow'r,
The grey sand dancing in its bed,
Embank'd beneath a Hawthorn bower,
Sent forth its waters near my head:
A rosy Lass approach'd my view;
I caught her blue eye's modest beam:
The stranger nodded " how d'ye do!"
And leap'd across the infant stream.

2

The water heedless pass'd away:
With me her glowing image stay'd,
I strove, from that auspicious day,
To meet and bless the lovely Maid.

3

I met her where beneath our feet
Through downy Mofs the wild-Thyme grew;
Nor Mofs elaftic, flow'rs though fweet,
Match'd Hannah's cheek of rofy hue.

4

I met her where the dark Woods wave,
And fhaded verdure fkirts the plain;
And when the pale Moon rifing gave
New glories to her cloudy train.
From her fweet Cot upon the Moor
Our plighted vows to Heaven are flown;
Truth made me welcome at her door,
And rofy Hannah is my own.

This delightful little fong is charmingly fet to *mufic* by Mr. ISAAC BLOOMFIELD, the brother to the author. In thus fpeaking my opinion of the mufic, I fpeak, not only my own fentimen's, but thofe of a lady diftinguifhed by ner voice, fkill, tafte, and expreffion. C. L.

SONG.

THE SHEPHERD AND HIS DOG ROVER.

Rover, awake! the grey Cock crows!
Come, shake your coat and go with me!
High in the East the green Hill glows;
And glory crowns our shelt'ring Tree.
The Sheep expect us at the fold:
My faithful Dog, let's haste away,
And in his earliest beams behold,
And hail, the source of cheerful day.

2

Half his broad orb o'erlooks the Hill,
And, darting down the Valley flies:
At every casement welcome still;
The golden summons of the skies.

SONG.

Go, fetch my Staff; and o'er the dews
Let Echo waft thy gladsome voice.
Shall we a cheerful note refuse
When rising Morn proclaims, " rejoice."

3

Now then we'll start; and thus I'll fling
Our store, a trivial load to bear:
Yet, ere night comes, should hunger sting,
I'll not encroach on *Rover's* share.
The fresh breeze bears its sweets along;
The Lark but chides us while we stay:
Soon shall the Vale repeat my song;
Go brush before, away, away.

This story is indeed, " full of life and vivifying soul." I hear this also is set to music by the author's brother. And I am sure that it is highly suited to musical expression. C. L.
29th Sept. 1801.

HUNTING SONG

1

Ye darksome Woods where Echo dwells,
Where every bud with freedom swells
    To meet the glorious day:
The morning breaks; again rejoice;
And with old Ringwood's well-known voice
    Bid tuneful Echo play.

2

We come, ye Groves, ye Hills, we come:
The vagrant Fox shall hear his doom,
    And dread our jovial train.
The shrill Horn sounds, the courser flies,
While every Sportsman joyful cries,
    "There's Ringwood's voice again."

HUNTING-SONG.

3

Ye Meadows, hail the coming throng;
Ye peaceful Streams that wind along,
 Repeat the Hark-away:
Far o'er the Downs, ye Gales that sweep,
The daring Oak that crowns the steep,
 The roaring peal convey.

4

The chiming notes of chearful Hounds,
Hark! how the hollow Dale resounds;
 The sunny Hills how gay.
But where's the note, brave Dog, like thine?
Then urge the Steed, the chorus join,
 'Tis Ringwood leads the way.

LUCY:
A SONG.

1

Thy favourite Bird is foaring ſtill:
My Lucy, haſte thee o'er the dale;
The Stream's let looſe, and from the Mill
All ſilent comes the balmy gale;
    Yet, ſo lightly on its way,
    Seems to whiſper, " Holiday."

2

The pathway flowers that bending meet
And give the Meads their yellow hue,
The May-buſh and the Meadow-ſweet
Reſerve their fragrance all for you.
    Why then, Lucy, why delay?
    Let us ſhare the Holiday.

SONG.

3

Since there thy smiles, my charming Maid,
Are with unfeigned rapture seen,
To Beauty be the homage paid;
Come, claim the triumph of the Green.
    Here's my hand, come, come away;
    Share the merry Holiday.

4

A promise too my Lucy made,
(And shall my heart its claim resign?)
That ere May-flowers again should fade,
Her heart and hand should both be mine.
    Hark 'ye, Lucy, this is May;
    Love shall crown our Holiday.

Lively and interesting. C. L.

WINTER SONG.

1

Dear Boy, throw that Icicle down,
And sweep this deep Snow from the door:
Old Winter comes on with a frown;
A terrible frown for the poor.
In a Season so rude and forlorn
How can age, how can infancy bear
The silent neglect and the scorn
Of those who have plenty to spare?

2

Fresh broach'd is my Cask of old Ale,
Well-tim'd now the frost is set in;
Here's Job come to tell us a tale,
We'll make him at home to a pin.

WINTER SONG.

While my Wife and I bask o'er the fire,
The roll of the Seasons will prove,
That Time may diminish desire,
But cannot extinguish true love.

3

O the pleasures of neighbourly chat,
If you can but keep scandal away,
To learn what the world has been at,
And what the great Orators say;
Though the Wind through the crevices sing,
And Hail down the chimney rebound;
I'm happier than many a king
While the Bellows blow Bass to the sound.

4

Abundance was never my lot:
But out of the trifle that's given,
That no curse may alight on my Cot,
I'll distribute the bounty of Heaven;

WINTER SONG.

The fool and the slave gather wealth:
But if I add nought to my store,
Yet while I keep conscience in health,
I've a Mine that will never grow poor.

This song pleases by natural and virtuous sentiment, and all the free emanation of a good heart: though in diction it might have been a little more select, without injuring simplicity. C. L.

Oct. 8th, 1801.

THE END.

Page 5.

WILD FLOWERS;

OR,

PASTORAL AND LOCAL POETRY.

BY

ROBERT BLOOMFIELD,

Author of the Farmer's Boy & Rural Tales.

LONDON:

PRINTED FOR VERNOR, HOOD, AND SHARPE, POULTRY;
AND LONGMAN, HURST, REES, AND ORME,
PATERNOSTER-ROW.

1806.

WRIGHT, Printer,
No. 38, St. John's Square, Clerkenwell.

DEDICATION.

TO

MY ONLY SON.

My Dear Boy,

IN thus addressing myself to you, and in expressing my regard for your person, my anxiety for your health, and my devotion to your welfare, I enjoy an advantage over those dedicators who indulge in adulation;—I shall at least be believed.

Should you arrive at that period when reason shall be mature, and affection or curiosity induce you to look back on your father's poetical progress through life, you may con-

clude that he had many to boast as friends, whose names, in a dedication, would have honoured both him and his children; but you must also reflect, that to particularize such friends was a point of peculiar delicacy. The earliest patron of my unprotected strains has the warm thanks which are his due, for the introduction of blessings which have been diffused through our whole family, and nothing will ever change this sentiment. But amidst a general feeling of gratitude, which those who know me will never dispute, I feel for you, Charles, what none but parents can conceive; and on your account, my dear boy, there can be no harm in telling the world that I hope these "Wild Flowers" will be productive of sweets of the worldly kind; for your unfortunate lameness (should it never be removed) may preclude you from the means of procur-

DEDICATION.

ing comforts and advantages which might otherwise have fallen to your share.

What a lasting, what an unspeakable satisfaction would it be to know that the Ballads, the Plowman Stories, and the "Broken Crutch" of your father would eventually contribute to lighten your steps to manhood, and make your own crutch, through life, rather a memorial of affection than an object of sorrow.

With a parent's feelings, and a parent's cares and hopes,

I am, Charles, yours,

R. B.

CORRECTIONS.

IN THE ADVERTISEMENT TO THE HORKEY
For Baund read *Bawnd.*
Thurk ——- *Thurck.*
Sibret ——— *Sibrit.*

PAGE 81, LINE 3d.
Angra's ——— *Angria's.*

PREFACE.

A MAN of the first eminence, in whose day (fortunately perhaps for me) I was not destined to appear before the public, or to abide the Herculean crab-tree of his criticism, Dr. Johnson, has said, in his preface to Shakspeare, that—"Nothing can please many, and please long, but just representations of general nature." My representations of nature, whatever may be said of their *justness*, are not *general*, unless we admit, what I suspect to be the case, that nature in a village is very much like nature every where else. It will be observed that all my pictures are from humble life, and most of my heroines servant maids. Such I would have them: being fully persuaded that, in no other way would my endeavours, either to please or to instruct, have an equal chance of success.

PREFACE.

The path I have thus taken, from necessity, as well as from choice, is well understood and approved by hundreds, who are capable of ranging in the higher walks of literature.— But with due deference to their superior claim, I confess, that no recompense has been half so grateful or half so agreeable to me as female approbation. To be readily and generally understood, to have my simple Tales almost instinctively relished by those who have so decided an influence over the lives, hearts, and manners of us all, is the utmost stretch of my ambition.

I here venture, before the public eye, a selection from the various pieces which have been the source of much pleasure, and the solace of my leisure hours during the last four years, and since the publication of the " Rural Tales." Perhaps, in some of them, more of mirth is intermingled than many who know me would expect, or than the severe will be

PREFACE.

inclined to approve. But surely what I can say, or can be expected to say, on subjects of country life, would gain little by the seriousness of a preacher, or by exhibiting fallacious representations of what has long been termed *Rural Innocence.*

The Poem of " Good Tidings " is partially known to the world, but, as it was originally intended to assume its present appearance and size, I have gladly availed myself of an endeavour to improve it; and, from its present extended circulation, I trust it will be new to thousands.

I anticipate some approbation from such readers as have been pleased with the " Rural Tales;" yet, though I will not falsify my own feelings by assuming a diffidence which I do not conceive to be either manly or becoming, the conviction that some reputation is hazarded in "a third attempt," is impressed deeply on my mind.

PREFACE.

With such sentiments, and with a lively sense of the high honour, and a hope of the bright recompence, of applause from the good, when heightened by the self-approving voice of my own conscience, I commit the book to its fate.

ROBERT BLOOMFIELD.

CONTENTS.

	Page
Abner and the Widow Jones, a Familiar Ballad	1
To my Old Oak Table	21
The Horkey, a Provincial Ballad	33
The Broken Crutch, a Tale	51
Shooter's Hill	75
A Visit to Ranelagh	83
Love of the Country	89
The Woodland Hallò	93
Barnham Water	95
Mary's Evening Sigh	101
Good Tidings; or, News from the Farm	105

IN A FEW DAYS WILL BE PUBLISHED,

AN

ILLUSTRATION

OF THE

POEMS

OF

R. BLOOMFIELD,

By Views in Norfolk, Suffolk, and Northamptonshire.

Including all the LOCAL SCENERY noticed in his POEMS.
Accompanied with Descriptions,
By JAMES STORER and JOHN GREIG.
Interspersed with a number of Interesting Anecdotes,
By R. BLOOMFIELD.

―――

Printed for VERNOR, HOOD, and SHARP, POULTRY;

OF WHOM MAY BE HAD, AN

ILLUSTRATION of the WRITINGS

OF

W. COWPER and of R. BURNS.

―――

Charles Storer, Printer, 10, Little-Carter-Lane.

ABNER

AND

THE WIDOW JONES,

A FAMILIAR BALLAD.

W<small>ELL</small>! I'm determin'd; that's enough:—
 Gee, Bayard! move your poor old bones,
I'll take to-morrow, smooth or rough,
 To go and court the Widow Jones.

Our master talks of stable-room,
 And younger horses on his grounds;
'Tis easy to foresee thy doom,
 Bayard, thou'lt go to feed the hounds.

The first Determination.

But could I win the widow's hand,
    I'd make a truce 'twixt death and thee;
For thou upon the best of land
    Should'st feed, and live, and die with me.

And must the pole-axe lay thee low?
    And will they pick thy poor old bones?
No—hang me if it shall be so,——
    If I can win the Widow Jones.

Twirl went his stick; his curly pate
    A bran-new hat uplifted bore;
And Abner, as he leapt the gate,
    Had never look'd so gay before.

THE WIDOW JONES.

Old Love revived.

And every spark of love reviv'd
   That had perplex'd him long ago,
When busy folks and fools contriv'd
   To make his Mary answer—*no*.

But whether, freed from recent vows,
   Her heart had back to Abner flown,
And mark'd him for a second spouse,
   In truth is not exactly known.

Howbeit, as he came in sight,
   She turn'd her from the garden stile,
And downward look'd with pure delight,
   With half a sigh and half a smile.

Rustic Salutation.

She heard his sounding step behind,
    The blush of joy crept up her cheek,
As cheerly floated on the wind,
    " Hoi! Mary Jones—what wont you speak?"

Then, with a look that ne'er deceives,
    She turn'd, but found her courage fled;
And scolding sparrows from the eaves
    Peep'd forth upon the stranger's head.

Down Abner sat, with glowing heart,
    Resolv'd, whatever might betide,
To speak his mind, no other art
    He ever knew, or ever tried.

THE WIDOW JONES.

A close Question.

And gently twitching Mary's hand,
 The bench had ample room for two,
His first word made her understand
 The plowman's errand was to woo.

" My Mary—may I call thee so?
 " For many a happy day we've seen,
" And if not mine, aye, years ago,
 " Whose was the fault? you might have been!

" All that's gone by: but I've been musing,
 " And vow'd, and hope to keep it true,
" That she shall be my own heart's choosing
 " Whom I call, wife.—Hey, what say you?

ABNER AND

Past Thoughts stated.

" And as I drove my plough along,
   " And felt the strength that's in my arm,
" Ten years, thought I, amidst my song,
   " I've been head-man at Harewood farm.

" And now, my own dear Mary's free,
   " Whom I have lov'd this many a day,
" Who knows but she may think on *me?*
   " I'll go hear what she has to say.

" Perhaps that little stock of land
   " She holds, but knows not how to till,
" Will suffer in the widow's hand,
   " And make poor Mary poorer still

THE WIDOW JONES.

The Avowal.

" That scrap of land, with one like her,

" How we might live! and be so blest!

" And who should Mary Jones prefer?

" Why, surely, him who loves her best!

" Therefore I'm come to-night, sweet wench,

" I would not idly thus intrude,"——

Mary look'd downward on the bench,

O'erpower'd by love and gratitude.

And lean'd her head against the vine,

With quick'ning sobs of silent bliss,

Till Abner cried, " You must be mine,

" You must,"—and seal'd it with a kiss.

ABNER AND

The Interest of an old Horse asserted.

She talk'd of shame, and wip'd her cheek,
But what had shame with them to do,
Who nothing meant but truth to speak,
And downright honour to pursue?

His eloquence improv'd apace,
As manly pity fill'd his mind;
" You know poor Bayard; here's the case,—
" He's past his labour, old, and blind:

" If you and I should but agree
" To settle here for good and all,
" Could you give all your heart to me,
" And grudge that poor old rogue a stall?

His Character.

" I'll buy him, for the dogs shall never
  " Set tooth upon a friend so true;
" He'll not live long, but I for ever
  " Shall know I gave the beast his due.

" 'Mongst all I've known of plows and carts,
  " And ever since I learn'd to drive,
" He was not match'd in all these parts;
  " There was not such a horse alive!

" Ready, as birds to meet the morn,
  " Were all his efforts at the plough;
" Then, the mill-brook with hay or corn,
  " Good creature! how he'd spatter through!

ABNER AND

Character continued.

" He was a horse of mighty pow'r,

" Compact in frame, and strong of limb;

" Went with a chirp from hour to hour;

" Whip-cord! 'twas never made for him.

" I left him in the shafts behind,

" His fellows all unhook'd and gone,

" He neigh'd, and deem'd the thing unkind,

" Then, starting, drew the load alone!

" But I might talk till pitch-dark night,

" And then have something left to say;

" But, Mary, am I wrong or right,

" Or, do I throw my words away?

Something like Consent.

" Leave me, or take me and my horse;

" I've told thee truth, and all I know:

" Truth *should* breed truth; that comes of course;

" If I sow wheat, why wheat will grow."

" Yes, Abner, but thus soon to yield,

" Neighbours would fleer, and look behind 'em;

" Though, with a husband in the field,

" Perhaps, indeed, I should not mind 'em.

" I've known your generous nature well,

" My first denial cost me dear;

" How this may end we cannot tell,

" But, as for Bayard, bring him here.

Parting of the Lovers.---Sad News.

"Bless thee for that," the plowman cried,
  At once both starting from the seat,
He stood a guardian by her side,
  But talk'd of home,—'twas growing late.

Then step for step within his arm,
  She cheer'd him down the dewy way;
And no two birds upon the farm
  E'er prated with more joy than they.

What news at home? The smile he wore
  One little sentence turn'd to sorrow;
An order met him at the door,
  "Take Bayard to the dogs to-morrow."

THE WIDOW JONES.

The Journey renewed.

Yes, yes, thought he; and heav'd a sigh,
    Die when he will he's not your debtor:
I must obey, and he *must* die,—
    That's if I can't contrive it better.

He left his Mary late at night,
    And had succeeded in the main,
No sooner peep'd the morning light
    But he was on the road again!

Suppose she should refuse her hand?
    Such thoughts will come, I know not why;
Shall I, without a wife or land,
    Want an old horse? then wherefore buy?

Perplexity.

From bush to bush, from stile to stile,
   Perplex'd he trod the fallow ground,
And told his money all the while
   And weigh'd the matter round and round.

" I'll borrow," that's the best thought yet;
   Mary shall save the horse's life.—
Kind-hearted wench! what, run in debt
   Before I know she'll be my wife?

These women wo'nt speak plain and free.—
   Well, well, I'll keep my service still;
She has not *said* she'd marry me,
   But yet I dare to say she will.

THE WIDOW JONES.

A fresh Thought---Turns back.

But while I take this shay brain'd course,
    And like a fool run to and fro,
Master, perhaps, may sell the horse!
    Therefore this instant home I'll go.

The nightly rains had drench'd the grove,
    He plung'd right on with headlong pace;
A man but half as much in love
    Perhaps had found a cleaner place.

The day rose fair; with team a-field,
    He watch'd the farmer's cheerful brow;
And in a lucky hour reveal'd
    His secret at his post, the plough.

ABNER AND

Coming to the Point.---Generosity.

And there without a whine began,
    " Master, you'll give me your advice;
I'm going to marry—if I can—
    " And want old Bayard; what's his price?

" For Mary Jones last night agreed,
    " Or near upon't, to be my wife:
" The horse's value I don't heed,
    " I only want to save his life."

" Buy him, hey! Abner! trust me I
    " Have not the thought of gain in view;
" Bayard's best days we've seen go by;
    " He shall be cheap enough to you."

THE WIDOW JONES.

Symptoms of good Feelings.

The wages paid, the horse brought out,
    The hour of separation come;
The farmer turn'd his chair about,
    " Good fellow, take him, take him home.

" You're welcome, Abner, to the beast,
    " For you've a faithful servant been;
" They'll thrive I doubt not in the least,
    " Who know what work and service mean."

The maids at parting, one and all,
    From different windows different tones;
Bade him farewel with many a bawl,
    And sent their love to Mary Jones.

Victory!

He wav'd his hat, and turn'd away,
 When loud the cry of children rose;
"Abner, good bye!" they stopt their play;
 "There goes poor Bayard! there he goes!"

Half choak'd with joy, with love, and pride,
 He now with dainty clover fed him,
Now took a short triumphant ride,
 And then again got down and led him.

And hobbling onward up the hill,
 The widow's house was full in sight,
He pull'd the bridle harder still,
 "Come on, we shan't be there to-night."

THE WIDOW JONES.

Victory!

She met them with a smile so sweet,
    The stable-door was open thrown;
The blind horse lifted high his feet,
    And loudly snorting, laid him down.

O Victory! from that stock of laurels
    You keep so snug for camps and thrones,
Spare us *one twig* from all their quarrels
    For Abner and the Widow Jones.

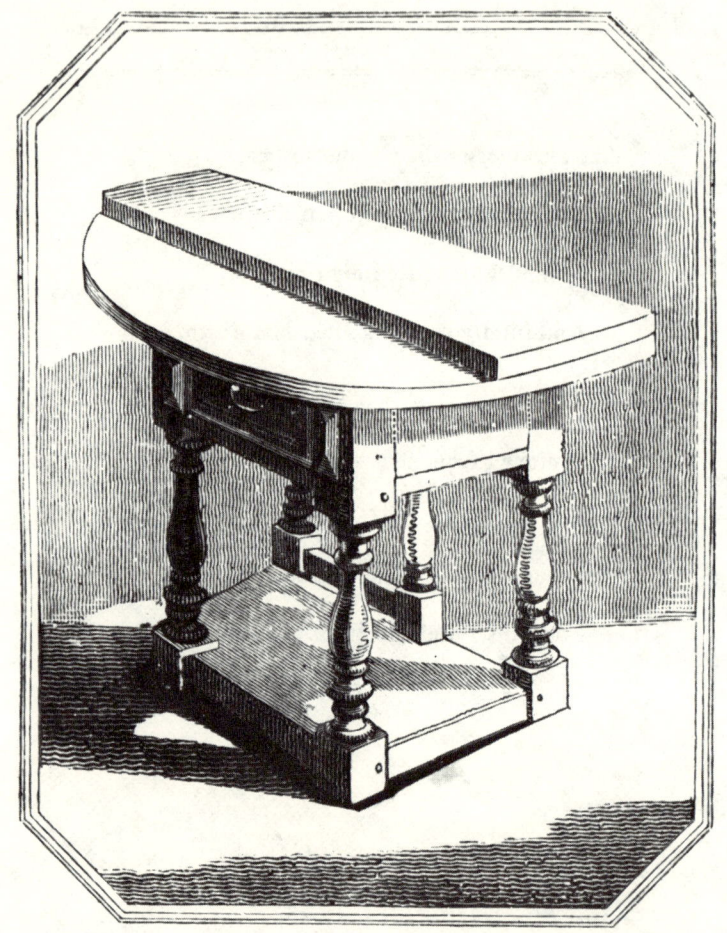

Page 21.

TO

MY OLD OAK TABLE.

Friend of my peaceful days! substantial friend,
Whom wealth can never change, nor int'rest bend,
I love thee like a child. Thou wert to me
The dumb companion of my misery,
And oftner of my joys;—then as I spoke,
I shar'd thy sympathy, Old Heart of Oak!
For surely when my labour ceas'd at night,
With trembling, feverish hands, and aching sight,
The draught that cheer'd me and subdu'd my care,
On thy broad shoulders thou wert proud to bear

TO MY OLD OAK TABLE.

O'er thee, with expectation's fire elate,
I've sat and ponder'd on my future fate:
On thee, with winter muffins for thy store,
I've lean'd, and quite forgot that I was poor.

   Where dropp'd the acorn that gave birth to thee?
Can'st thou trace back thy line of ancestry?
We're match'd, old friend, and let us not repine,
Darkness o'erhangs thy origin and mine;
Both may be truly honourable: yet,
We'll date our honours from the day we met;
When, of my worldly wealth the parent stock,
Right welcome up the Thames from Woolwich Dock
Thou cam'st, when hopes ran high and love was young;
But soon our olive-branches round thee sprung;
Soon came the days that tried a faithful wife,
The noise of children, and the cares of life.

Then, midst the threat'nings of a wintry sky,
That cough which blights the bud of infancy,
The dread of parents, Rest's inveterate foe,
Came like a plague, and turn'd my songs to woe.
  Rest! without thee what strength can long survive,
What spirit keep the flame of Hope alive?
The midnight murmur of the cradle gave
Sounds of despair; and chilly as the grave
We felt its undulating blast arise,
Midst whisper'd sorrows and ten thousand sighs.
Expiring embers warn'd us each to sleep,
By turns to watch alone, by turns to weep,
By turns to hear, and keep from starting wild,
The sad, faint wailings of a dying child.
But Death, obedient to Heav'n's high command,
Withdrew his jav'lin, and unclench'd his hand;

TO MY OLD OAK TABLE.

The little sufferers triumph'd over pain,
Their mother smil'd, and bade me hope again.
Yet Care gain'd ground, Exertion triumph'd less,
Thick fell the gathering terrors of Distress;
Anxiety, and Griefs without a name,
Had made their dreadful inroads on my frame;
The creeping Dropsy, cold as cold could be,
Unnerv'd my arm, and bow'd my head to thee.
Thou to thy trust, old friend, hast not been true;
These eyes the bitterest tears they ever knew
Let fall upon thee; now all wip'd away;
But what from memory shall wipe out that day?
The great, the wealthy of my native land,
To whom a guinea is a grain of sand,
I thought upon them, for my *thoughts* were free,
But all unknown were then my woes and me.

TO MY OLD OAK TABLE.

Still, Resignation was my dearest friend,
And Reason pointed to a glorious end;
With anxious sighs, a parent's hopes and pride,
I wish'd to live——I trust I could have died!
But winter's clouds pursu'd their stormy way,
And March brought sunshine with the length'ning day,
And bade my heart arise, that morn and night
Now throbb'd with irresistible delight.
Delightful 'twas to leave disease behind,
And feel the renovation of the mind!
To lead abroad upborne on Pleasure's wing,
Our children, midst the glories of the spring;
Our fellow sufferers, our only wealth,
To gather daisies in the breeze of health!
  'Twas then, too, when our prospects grew so fair,
And Sabbath bells announc'd the morning pray'r;

TO MY OLD OAK TABLE.

Beneath that vast gigantic dome we bow'd,
That lifts its flaming cross above the cloud;
Had gain'd the centre of the checquer'd floor;—
That instant, with reverberating roar
Burst forth the pealing organ——mute we stood;—
The strong sensation boiling through my blood,
Rose in a storm of joy, allied to pain,
I wept, and worshipp'd GOD, and wept again;
And felt, amidst the fervor of my praise,
The sweet assurances of better days.

In that gay season, honest friend of mine,
I mark'd the brilliant sun upon thee shine;
Imagination took her flights so free,
Home was delicious with my book and thee,
The purchas'd nosegay, or brown ears of corn,
Were thy gay plumes upon a summer's morn,

TO MY OLD OAK TABLE.

Awakening memory, that disdains control,
They spoke the darling language of my soul:
They whisper'd tales of joy, of peace, of truth,
And conjur'd back the sunshine of my youth:
Fancy presided at the joyful birth,
I pour'd the torrent of my feelings forth;
Conscious of *truth* in Nature's humble track,
And wrote "The Farmer's Boy" upon thy back!
Enough, old friend:—thou'rt mine; and shalt partake,
While I have pen to write, or tongue to speak,
Whatever fortune deals me.—Part with thee!
No, not till death shall set my spirit free;
For know, should plenty crown my life's decline,
A most important duty may be thine:
Then, guard me from Temptation's base control,
From apathy and littleness of soul

TO MY OLD OAK TABLE.

The sight of thy old frame, so rough, so rude,
Shall twitch the sleeve of nodding Gratitude;
Shall teach me but to venerate the more
Honest Oak Tables and their guests—the poor:
Teach me unjust distinctions to deride,
And falshoods gender'd in the brain of Pride;
Shall give to Fancy still the cheerful hour,
To Intellect, its freedom and its power;
To Hospitality's enchanting ring
A charm, which nothing but thyself can bring.
The man who would not look with honest pride
On the tight bark that stemm'd the roaring tide,
And bore him, when he bow'd the trembling knee,
Home, through the mighty perils of the sea,
I love him not.—He ne'er shall be my guest;
Nor sip my cup, nor witness how I'm blest;

TO MY OLD OAK TABLE.

Nor lean, to bring my honest friend to shame,
A sacrilegious elbow on thy frame;
But thou through life a monitor shalt prove,
Sacred to Truth, to Poetry, and Love.

Dec. 1803.

Page 33.

THE HORKEY.

A PROVINCIAL BALLAD.

ADVERTISEMENT.

In the descriptive ballad which follows, it will be evident that I have endeavoured to preserve the style of a gossip, and to transmit the memorial of a custom, the extent or antiquity of which I am not acquainted with, and pretend not to enquire.

In Suffolk husbandry the man who (whether by merit or by sufferance I know not) goes foremost through the harvest with the scythe or the sickle, is honoured with the title of "*Lord*," and at the Horkey, or harvest-home feast, collects what he can, for himself and brethren, from the farmers and visitors, to make a "frolick" afterwards, called "the largess spending." By way of returning thanks, though perhaps formerly of much more, or of different signification, they immediately leave the seat of festivity, and with a very long and repeated shout of "a largess," the number of shouts being regulated by the sums given, seem to wish to make themselves heard by the people of the surrounding farms. And before they rejoin the company within, the pranks and the jollity I have endeavoured to describe, usually take place. These customs, I believe, are going fast out of use; which is one great reason for my trying to tell the rising race of mankind that such were the customs when I was a boy.

ADVERTISEMENT.

I have annexed a glossary of such words as may be found by general readers to require explanation. And will add a short extract from Sir Thomas Brown, of Norwich, M. D. who was born three years before Milton, and outlived him eight years.

"It were not impossible to make an original reduction of many words of no general reception in *England*, but of common use in *Norfolk*, or peculiar to the *East-Angle* counties; as, Baund, Bunny, Thurk, Enemis, Matchly, Sammodithee, Mawther, Kedge, Seele, Straft, Clever, Dere, Nicked, Stingy, Noneare, Feft, Thepes, Gosgood, Kamp, Sibret, Fangast, Sap, Cothish, Thokish, Bide-owe, Paxwax. Of these, and some others, of no easy originals, when time will permit, the resolution shall be attempted; which to effect, the Danish language, new, and more ancient, may prove of good advantage: which nation remained here fifty years upon agreement, and have left many families in it, and the language of these parts had surely been more commixed and perplex, if the fleet of *Hugo de Bones* had not been cast away, wherein threescore thousand souldiers, out of Britany and Flanders, were to be wafted over, and were, by King *John's* appointment, to have a settled habitation in the counties of *Norfolk* and *Suffolk*." Tract the viii. on Languages, particularly the Saxon. Folio, 1686, page 48.

THE HORKEY.

A PROVINCIAL BALLAD.

W<small>HAT</small> gossips prattled in the sun,
   Who talk'd him fairly down,
Up, memory! tell; 'tis Suffolk fun,
   And lingo of their own.

Ah! *Judie Twitchet!** though thou'rt dead,
   With thee the tale begins;
For still seems thrumming in my head
   The rattling of thy pins.

---

* Judie Twitchet was a real person, who lived many years with my mother's cousin Bannock, at Honington.

THE HORKEY.

Silence commanded.

Thou Queen of knitters! for a ball
  Of worsted was thy pride;
With dangling stockings great and small,
  And world of clack beside!

" We did so laugh; the moon shone bright;
  " More fun you never knew;
" 'Twas Farmer Cheerum's *Horkey night*,
  " And I, and Grace, and Sue——

" But bring a stool, sit round about,
  " And boys, be quiet, pray;
" And let me tell my story out;
  " 'Twas *sitch* a merry day!

THE HORKEY.

The Story begun.

" The butcher whistled at the door,

" And brought a load of meat;

" Boys rubb'd their hands, and cried,' there's more,'

" Dogs wagg'd their tails to see't.

" On went the boilers till the *hake**

" Had much ado to bear 'em;

" The magpie talk'd for talking sake,

" Birds sung;—but who could hear 'em?

" Creak went the jack; the cats were *scar'd*,

" We had not time to heed 'em,

" The *owd hins* cackled in the yard,

" For we forgot to feed 'om!

* A sliding pot-hook.

Judie sure to be right.

" Yet 'twas not I, as I may say,
  " Because as how, d'ye see ;
" I only help'd there for the day ;
  " They cou'dn't lay't to me.

" Now Mrs. Cheerum's best lace cap
  " Was mounted on her head ;
" Guests at the door began to rap,
  " And now the cloth was spread.

" Then clatter went the earthen plates—
  " ' Mind Judie,' was the cry ;
" I could have *cop't** them at their pates ;
  " ' Trenchers for me,' said I.

* Thrown.

THE HORKEY

The Horkey Load.

  " ' That look so clean upon the ledge,
     " ' And never mind a fall;
  " ' Nor never turn a sharp knife's edge;—
     " ' But fashion rules us all.'

  " Home came the jovial *Horkey load,*
     " Last of the whole year's crop;
  " And Grace amongst the green boughs rode
     " Right plump upon the top.

  " This way and that the waggon reel'd,
     " And never queen rode higher;
  " *Her* cheeks were colour'd in the field,
     " And ours before the fire.

THE HORKEY.

The Harvest Supper.

" The laughing harvest-folks, and John,
" Came in and look'd askew;
" 'Twas my red face that set them on,
" And then they leer'd at Sue.

" And Farmer Cheerum went, good man,
" And broach'd the *Horkey beer;*
" And *sitch a mort** of folks began
" To eat up our good cheer.

" Says he, ' Thank God for what's before us;
" ' That thus we meet agen,'
" The mingling voices, like a chorus,
" Join'd cheerfully, ' Amen.'—

* Such a number.

THE HORKEY.

An old Kind of Contest.

" Welcome and plenty, there they found 'em,

" The ribs of beef grew light;

" And puddings—till the boys got round 'em,

" And then they vanish'd quite!

" Now all the guests, with Farmer Crouder,

" Began to prate of corn;

" And we found out they talk'd the louder,

" The oftner pass'd the Horn.

" Out came the nuts; we set a cracking;

" The ale came round our way;

" *By gom*, we women fell a clacking

" As loud again as they.

Something very true.

" John sung ' Old Benbow' loud and strong,
 " And I, ' The Constant Swain,'
" ' Cheer up my Lads,' was Simon's song,
 " ' We'll conquer them again.'

" Now twelve o'clock was drawing nigh,
 " And all in merry cue;
" I knock'd the cask, ' O, ho !' said I,
 " ' We've almost conquer'd you.'

" *My Lord** begg'd round, and held his hat,
 " Says Farmer Gruff, says he,
" ' There's many a Lord, Sam, I know that,
 " ' Has begg'd as well as thee.'

* The leader of the reapers.

THE HORKEY.

Rustic Wit.

" Bump in his hat the shillings tumbl'd
" All round among the folks ;
" ' Laugh if you wool,' said Sam, and mumbl'd,
" ' You pay for all your jokes.'

" Joint stock you know among the men,
" To drink at their own charges ;
" So up they got full drive, and then
" Went out to *halloo largess*.*

" And sure enough the noise they made !!—
—" But let me mind my tale ;
" We follow'd them, we wor'nt afraid,
" We'ad all been drinking ale.

* See advertisement.

THE HORKEY.

A bit of Fun.

" As they stood hallooing back to back,
   " We, lightly as a feather,
" Went sideling round, and in a crack
   " Had pinn'd their coats together.

" 'Twas near upon't as light as noon;
   " ' *A largess*,' on the hill,
" They shouted to the full round moon,
   " I think I hear 'em still!

" But when they found the trick, my stars!
   " They well knew who to blame,
" Our giggles turn'd to ha, ha, ha's,
   " And *arter* us they came.

The Chace.

" Grace by the tumbril made a squat,
　" Then ran as Sam came by,
" They said she could not run for fat;
　" *I know* she did not try.

" Sue round the *neathouse** squalling ran,
　" Where Simon scarcely dare;
" He stopt,—for he's a fearful man——
　" ' *By gom* there's *suffen*† there !'

" And off set John, with all his might,
　" To chase me down the yard,
" Till I was nearly *gran'd*‡ outright;
　" He hugg'd so woundly hard.

* Cow-house.　　† Something.　　‡ Strangled.

A Mistake.

" Still they kept up the race and laugh,
   " And round the house we flew;
" But hark ye! the best fun by half
   " Was Simon *arter* Sue.

" She car'd not, dark nor light, not she,
   " So, near the dairy door
" She pass'd a clean white hog, you see,
   " They'd *kilt* the day before.

" High on the *spirket** there it hung,—
   " ' Now Susie—what can save ye?'
" Round the cold pig his arms he flung,
   " And cried, ' Ah! here I have ye!'

* An iron hook.

Something like Mischief.

"The farmers heard what Simon said,
  "And what a noise! good lack!
"Some almost laugh'd themselves *to dead,*
  "And others clapt his back.

"We all at once began to tell
  "What fun we had abroad;
"But Simon stood our jeers right well;
  —"He fell asleep and snor'd.

"Then in his button-hole upright,
  "Did Farmer Crouder put,
"A slip of paper twisted tight,
  "And held the candle *to't.*

Reserve thrown off.

"It smok'd, and smok'd, beneath his nose,
  "The harmless blaze crept higher;
"Till with a vengeance up he rose,
  "Grace, Judie, Sue! fire, fire!

"The clock struck one—some talk'd of parting,
  "Some said it was a sin,
"And *hitch'd* their chairs;—but those for starting
  "Now let the moonlight in.

"*Owd* women, loitering *for the nonce*,*
  "Stood praising the fine weather;
"The menfolks took the hint at once
  "To kiss them altogether.

* For the purpose.

THE HORKEY.

Mirth without Mischief.

"And out ran every soul beside,
  "A *shanny-pated** crew ;
"*Owd* folks could neither run nor hide,
  "So some *ketch'd* one, some *tew*.

"They *skriggl'd*† and began to scold,
  "But laughing got the master ;
"Some *quack'ling*‡ cried, 'let go your hold;
  "The farmers held the faster.

"All innocent, that I'll be sworn,
  "There wor'nt a bit of sorrow,
"And women, if their gowns *are* torn,
  "Can mend them on the morrow.

* Giddy, thoughtless. † To struggle quick. ‡ Choaking.

The Separation.

" Our shadows helter skelter danc'd
  " About the moonlight ground ;
" The wondering sheep, as on we pranc'd,
  " Got up and gaz'd around,

" And well they might—till Farmer Cheerum,
  " Now with a hearty glee,
" Bade all good morn as he came near 'em,
  " And then to bed went he.

" Then off we stroll'd this way and that,
  " With merry voices ringing ;
" And Echo answered us right pat,
  " As home we rambl'd singing.

THE HORKEY.

Conclusion.

" For, when we laugh'd, it laugh'd again,
" And to our own doors follow'd!
" ' Yo, ho!' we cried; ' Yo, ho!' so plain
" The misty meadow halloo'd.

" That's all my tale, and all the fun,
" Come, turn your wheels about;
" My worsted, see!—that's nicely done,
" Just held my story out!!"

Poor Judie!—Thus Time knits or spins
The worsted from Life's ball!
Death stopt thy tales, and stopt thy pins,
—And so he'll serve us all.

THE BROKEN CRUTCH.

A TALE.

" I TELL you, Peggy," said a voice behind
A hawthorn hedge, with wild briars thick entwin'd,
Where unseen trav'llers down a shady way
Journey'd beside the swaths of new-mown hay,
" I tell you, Peggy, 'tis a time to prove
" Your fortitude, your virtue, and your love.
" From honest poverty our lineage sprung,
" Your mother was a servant quite as young;—
" You weep; perhaps *she* wept at leaving home,
" Courage, my girl, nor fear the days to come.

THE BROKEN CRUTCH.

A Father's Advice and Blessing.

" Go still to church, my Peggy, plainly drest,
" And keep a living conscience in your breast ;
" Look to yourself, my lass, the maid's best fame,
" Beware, nor bring the Meldrums into shame :
" Be modest, to the voice of age attend,
" Be honest, and you'll always find a friend :
" Your uncle Gilbert, stronger far than I,
" Will see you safe ; on him you must rely ;
" I've walk'd too far ; this lameness, oh ! the pain ;
" Heav'n bless thee, child ! I'll halt me back again ;
" But when your first fair holiday may be,
" Rise with the lark, and spend your hours with me."

Young Herbert Brooks, in strength and manhood bold,
Who, round the meads, his own possessions, stroll'd,
O'erheard the charge, and with a heart so gay,
Whistled his spaniel and pursu'd his way.

THE BROKEN CRUTCH.

A Hint for a Libertine.

Soon cross'd his path, and short obeisance paid,
Stout Gilbert Meldrum and a country maid;
A box upon his shoulder held full well
Her worldly riches, but the truth to tell
She bore the chief herself; that nobler part,
That beauteous gem, an uncorrupted heart.
And then that native loveliness! that cheek!
It bore the very tints her betters seek;
At such a sight the libertine would glow,
With all the warmth that *he* can ever know;
Would send his thoughts abroad without control,
The glimmering moon-shine of his little soul.
" Above the reach of justice I shall soar,
" Her friends may weep, not punish; they're too poor:
" That very thought the rapture will enhance,
" Poor, young, and friendless; what a glorious chance!

THE BROKEN CRUTCH.

Herbert's Character.

" A few spare guineas may the conquest make,—
" I love the treachery for treachery's sake,
" And when her wounded honour jealous grows,
" I'll cut away ten thousand oaths and vows,
" And tell my comrades, with a manly stride,
" How I, *a girl out-witted and out-lied.*"
Such was not Herbert—he had never known
Love's genuine smiles, nor suffer'd from his frown;
And as to that most honourable part
Of planting daggers in a parent's heart,
A novice quite:—he past his hours away,
Free as a bird and buxom as the day;
Yet, should a lovely girl by chance arise,
Think not that Herbert Brooks would shut his eyes.

 On thy calm joys with what delight I dream,
Thou dear green valley of my native stream!

THE BROKEN CRUTCH.

Regret for Devastation by Enclosures.

Fancy o'er thee still waves th' enchanting wand,
And every nook of thine is fairy land,
And ever will be, though the axe should smite
In Gain's rude service, and in Pity's spite,
Thy clustering alders, and at length invade
The last, last poplars, that compose thy shade:
Thy stream shall then in native freedom stray,
And undermine the willows in its way,
These, nearly worthless, may survive this storm,
This scythe of desolation call'd "Reform."
No army past that way! yet are they fled,
The boughs that, when a school-boy, screen'd my head:
I hate the murderous axe; estranging more
The winding vale from what it was of yore,
Than e'en mortality in all its rage,
And all the change of faces in an age.

THE BROKEN CRUTCH.

The Tale pursued.

"Warmth," will they term it, that I speak so free?
They strip thy shades,—thy shades so dear to me!
In Herbert's days woods cloth'd both hill and dale;
But peace, Remembrance! let us tell the tale.

His home was in the valley, elms grew round
His moated mansion, and the pleasant sound
Of woodland birds that loud at day-break sing,
With the first cuckoos that proclaim the spring,
Flock'd round his dwelling; and his kitchen smoke,
That from the towering rookery upward broke,
Of joyful import to the poor hard by,
Stream'd a glad sign of hospitality;
So fancy pictures; but its day is o'er;
The moat remains, the dwelling is no more!
Its name denotes its melancholy fall,
For village children call the spot "Burnt-Hall."

Page 57.

Page 62.

THE BROKEN CRUTCH.

The Church.

But where's the maid, who in the meadow-way
Met Herbert Brooks amongst the new-mown hay?
  Th' adventure charm'd him, and next morning rose
The Sabbath, with its silence and repose,
The bells ceas'd chiming, and the broad blue sky
Smil'd on his peace, and met his tranquil eye
Inverted, from the foot-bridge on his way
To that still house where all his fathers lay;
There in his seat, each neighbour's face he knew—
The stranger girl was just before his pew!
He saw her kneel, with meek, but cheerful air,
And whisper the response to every prayer;
And, when the humble roof with praises rung,
He caught the Hallelujah from her tongue,
Rememb'ring with delight the tears that fell
When the poor father bade his child farewell;

THE BROKEN CRUTCH.

Love strengthen'd by Reflection.

And now, by kindling tenderness beguil'd,
He blest the prompt obedience of that child,
And link'd his fate with hers :—for, from that day,
Whether the weeks past cheerily away,
Or deep revolving doubts procur'd him pain,
The same bells chim'd—and there she was again!
What could be done? they came not there to woo,
On holy ground,—though love is holy too.

   They met upon the foot-bridge one clear morn,
She in the garb by village lasses worn;
He, with unbutton'd frock that careless flew,
And buskin'd to resist the morning dew;
With downcast look she courtsied to the ground,
Just in his path—no room to sidle round.

   " Well, pretty girl, this early rising yields
" The best enjoyment of the groves and fields,

THE BROKEN CRUTCH.

An Interview.

" And makes the heart susceptible and meek,
" And keeps alive that rose upon your cheek.
" I long'd to meet you, Peggy, though so shy,
" I've watch'd your steps and learn'd your history;
" You love your poor lame father, let that be
" A happy presage of your love for me.
" Come then, I'll stroll these meadows by your side,
" I've seen enough to wish you for my bride,
" And plainly tell you so.—Nay, let me hold
" This guiltless hand, I prize it more than gold;
" Of that I have my share, but now pursue
" Such lasting wealth as I behold in you.
" My lands are fruitful and my gardens gay,
" My houshold cheerful as the summer's day;
" One blessing more will crown my happy life,
" Like Adam, pretty girl, I want a wife."

Frequent Meetings.—Family Pride.

Need it be told his suit was not denied,
With youth, and wealth, and candour on his side
Honour took charge of love so well begun,
And accidental meetings, one by one,
Increas'd so fast midst time's unheeded flight,
That village rumour married them outright;
Though wiser matrons, doubtful in debate,
Pitied deluded Peggy's hapless fate.
Friends took th' alarm, "And will he then disgrace
"The name of Brooks with this plebeian race?"
Others, more lax in virtue, not in pride,
Sported the wink of cunning on one side;
"He'll buy, no doubt, what Peggy has to sell,
"A little gallantry becomes him well."
Meanwhile the youth with self-determin'd aim,
Disdaining fraud, and pride's unfeeling claim,

THE BROKEN CRUTCH.

Marriage proposed

Above control pursued his generous way,
And talk'd to Peggy of the marriage day.
Poor girl! she heard, with anguish and with doubt,
What her too knowing neighbours preach'd about,
That Herbert would some nobler match prefer,
And surely never, never marry her;
Yet, with what trembling and delight she bore
The kiss, and heard the vow, "I'll doubt no more;"
"Protect me Herbert, for your honour's sake
"You will," she cried, "nor leave my heart to break.
Then wrote to uncle Gilbert, joys, and fears,
And hope, and trust, and sprinkled all with tears.

Rous'd was the dormant spirit of the brave,
E'en lameness rose to succour and to save;
For, though they both rever'd young Herbert's name,
And knew his unexceptionable fame;

THE BROKEN CRUTCH.

Doubts.---Parental Feelings.

And though the girl had honestly declar'd
Love's first approaches, and their counsel shar'd,
Yet, that he truly meant to take for life
The poor and lowly Peggy for a wife ;
Or, that she was not doom'd to be deceiv'd,
Was out of bounds :—it *could not* be believ'd.
" Go, Gilbert ; save her ; I, you know, am lame ;
" Go, brother, go ; and save my child from shame.
" Haste, and I'll pray for your success the while,
" Go, go ;"—then bang'd his crutch upon the stile :—
It snapt.—E'en Gilbert trembled while he smote,
Then whipt the broken end beneath his coat ;
" Aye, aye, I'll settle them ; I'll let them see
" Who's to be conqu'ror this time, I or he !"
　　Then off he set, and with enormous strides,
Rebellious mutterings and oaths besides,

THE BROKEN CRUTCH.

Gilbert on the Road.---An Adventure.

O'er clover-field and fallow, bank and brier,
Pursu'd the nearest cut, and fann'd the fire
That burnt within him.—Soon the Hall he spied,
And the grey willows by the water side;
Nature cried "halt!" nor could he well refuse;
Stop, Gilbert, breathe awhile, and ask *the news.*
" News ?" cried a stooping grandame of the vale,
" Aye, rare news too; I ll tell you such a tale;
" But let me rest; this bank is dry and warm;
" Do you know Peggy Meldrum at the farm ?
" Young Herbert's girl ? He's as cloath'd her all in white,
" You never saw so beautiful a sight!
" Ah! he's a fine young man, and such a face!
" I knew his grandfather and all his race;
" He rode a tall white horse, and look'd so big,
" But how shall I describe his hat and wig ?"

THE BROKEN CRUTCH.

A promising Story cut short.

" Plague take his wig," cried Gilbert, " and his hat,
" Where's Peggy Meldrum ? can you tell me *that ?*"
" Aye ; but have patience man, you'll hear anon,
" For I shall come to her as I go on,
" So hark'ye friend ; his grandfather I say,"—
" Poh, poh,"—cried Gilbert, as he turn'd away.
Her eyes were fix'd, her story at a stand,
The snuff-box lay half open'd in her hand;
" You great ill-manner'd clown ! but I must bear it;
" You oaf; to ask the news, and then won't hear it !"
But Gilbert had gain'd forty paces clear,
When the reproof came murmuring on his ear.

Again he ask'd the first that past him by ;
A cow-boy stopt his whistle to reply.
" Why, I've a mistress coming home, that's all,
" They're playing Meg's diversion at the Hall ;

THE BROKEN CRUTCH.

A Cow-Boy's Brevity.

" For master's gone, with Peggy, and his cousin,
" And all the lady-folks, about a dozen,
" To church, down there; he'll marry *one* no doubt,
" For that it seems is what they're gone about;
" I know it by their laughing and their jokes,
" Tho' they *wor'nt* ask'd at church like other folks."
Gilbert kept on, and at the Hall-door found
The winking servants, where the jest went round:
All expectation; aye, and so was he,
But not with heart so merry and so free.
The kitchen table, never clear from beef,
Where hunger found its solace and relief,
Free to all strangers, had no charms for him,
For agitation worried every limb;
Ale he partook, but appetite had none,
And grey-hounds watch'd in vain to catch the bone

Sitting upon Thorns.

All sounds alarm'd him, and all thoughts perplex'd,
With dogs, and beef, himself, and all things vex'd,
Till with one mingled caw above his head,
Their gliding shadows o'er the court-yard spread,
The rooks by thousands rose: the bells struck up;
He guess'd the cause, and down he set the cup,
And listening, heard, amidst the general hum,
A joyful exclamation, "Here they come!"—
Soon Herbert's cheerful voice was heard above,
Amidst the rustling hand-maids of his love,
And Gilbert follow'd without thought or dread,
The broad oak stair-case thunder'd with his tread;
Light tript the party, gay as gay could be,
Amidst their bridal dresses—there came he!
And with a look that guilt could ne'er withstand,
Approach'd his niece and caught her by the hand,

Anger disarmed.

" Now are you married, Peggy, yes or no ?
" Tell me at once, before I let you go !"
Abrupt he spoke, and gave her arm a swing,
But the same moment felt the wedding ring,
And stood confus'd.—She wip'd th' empassion'd tear,
" I am, I am ; but is my father here ?"
Herbert stood by, and sharing with his bride,
That perturbation which she strove to hide ;
" Come, honest Gilbert, you're too rough this time,
" Indeed here's not the shadow of a crime ;
" But where's your brother ? When did you arrive ?
" We waited long, for Nathan went at five !"

All this was Greek to Gilbert, downright Greek ;
He knew not what to think, nor how to speak.
The case was this ; that Nathan with a cart
To fetch them both at day-break was to start,

THE BROKEN CRUTCH.

An Explanation.

And so he did—but ere he could proceed,
He suck'd a charming portion with a reed,
Of that same wedding-ale, which was that day
To make the hearts of all the village gay;
Brim full of glee he trundled from the Hall,
And as for sky-larks, he out-sung them all;
Till growing giddy with his morning cup,
He, stretch'd beneath a hedge, the reins gave up;
The horse graz'd soberly without mishap,
And Nathan had a most delightful nap
For three good hours—Then, doubting, when he woke,
Whether his conduct would be deem'd a joke,
With double haste perform'd just half his part,
And brought the lame John Meldrum in his cart:
And at the moment Gilbert's wrath was high,
And while young Herbert waited his reply,

THE BROKEN CRUTCH.

A general Meeting.

The sound of rattling wheels was at the door;
" There's my dear father now,"—they heard no more,
The bridegroom glided like an arrow down,
And Gilbert ran, though something of a clown,
With his best step; and cheer'd with smiles and pray'rs
They bore old John in triumph up the stairs:
Poor Peggy, who her joy no more could check,
Clung like a dewy woodbine round his neck,
And all stood silent——Gilbert, off his guard,
And marvelling at virtue's rich reward,
Loos'd the one loop that held his coat before,
Down thumpt the broken crutch upon the floor!
They started, half alarm'd, scarce knowing why,
But through the glist'ning rapture of his eye
The bridegroom smil'd, then chid their simple fears,
And rous'd the blushing Peggy from her tears;

THE BROKEN CRUTCH.

Gilbert put upon his Defence.

Around the uncle in a ring they came,

And mark'd his look of mingled pride and shame.

" Now honestly, good Gilbert, tell us true

" What meant this cudgel? What was it to do?

" I know your heart suspected me of wrong,

" And that most true affection urg'd along

" Your feelings and your wrath; you were beside

" Till now the rightful guardian of the bride.

" But why this cudgel?"—" Guardian! that's the case,

" Or else to day you had not seen my face,

" But John about the girl was so perplex'd,

" And I, to tell the truth, so mortal vex'd,

" That when he broke *this crutch,* and stampt and cried,

" For John and Peggy, Sir, I could have died,

" I know I could; for she was such a child,

" So tractable, so sensible, and mild,

The plain Truth.

" That if between you roguery had grown,
" (Begging your pardon,) 'twould have been your own;
" She would not hurt a fly.—So off I came
" And had you only sought to blast her fame,
" Been base enough to act as hundreds would,
" And ruin a poor maid—because you *could*,
" With this same cudgel, (you may smile or frown)
" An' please you, Sir, I meant to knock you down."

A burst of laughter rang throughout the hall,
And Peggy's tongue, though overborne by all,
Pour'd its warm blessings, for, without control
The sweet unbridled transport of her soul
Was obviously seen, till Herbert's kiss
Stole, as it were, the eloquence of bliss.
" Welcome, my friends; good Gilbert, here's my hand;
" Eat, drink, or rest, they're all at your command:

THE BROKEN CRUTCH.

Mirth and Reconciliation.

" And whatsoever pranks the rest may play,

" Still you shall be the hero of to-day,

" Doubts might torment, and blunders may have teaz'd,

" But ale can cure them ; let us all be pleas'd.

" Thou, venerable man, let me defend

" The father of my new dear bosom friend ;

" You broke your crutch, well, well, worse luck might be,

" I'll be your crutch, John Meldrum, lean on me,

" And when your lovely daughter shall complain,

" Send Gilbert's wooden argument again.

" If still you wonder that I take a wife

" From the unpolish'd walks of humble life,

" I'll tell you on what ground my love began,

" And let the wise confute it if they can.

" I saw a girl, with nature's untaught grace,

" Turn from my gaze a most engaging face ;

THE BROKEN CRUTCH.

Herbert's Apology.

" I saw her drop the tear, I knew full well
" She felt for *you* much more than she could tell.
" I found her understanding, bright as day,
" Through all impediments still forc'd its way;
" On that foundation shall my soul rely,
" The rock of genuine humility.
" Call'd as she is to act a nobler part,
" To rule my houshold, and to share my heart,
" I trust her prudence, confident to prove
" Days of delight, and still unfading love;
" For, while her inborn tenderness survives,
" That heav'nly charm of mothers and of wives,
" I'll look for joy:—Here come the neighbours all;
" Broach the old barrel, feast them great and small,
" For I'm determin'd while the sun's so bright,
" That this shall be a wedding-day outright:

John Meldrum's Wish.---Conclusion.

" How cheerly sound the bells! my charmer, come,
" Expand your heart, and know yourself at home.
" Sit down, good John;"—" I will," the old man cried,
" And let me drink to you, Sir, and the bride;
" My blessing on you: I am lame and old,
" I can't make speeches, and I wo'nt be bold;
" But from my soul I wish, and wish with pain,
" *That brave good gentlemen would not disdain*
" *The poor, because they're poor:* for, if they live
" Midst crimes that parents *never can* forgive,
" If, like the forest beast they wander wild,
" To rob a father, or to crush a child,
" Nature *will* speak, aye, just as Nature feels,
" And wish—a Gilbert Meldrum at their heels."

SHOOTER'S HILL.*

H̲ealth! I seek thee;—dost thou love
  The mountain top or quiet vale,
Or deign o'er humbler hills to rove
  On showery June's dark south-west gale?
If so, I'll meet all blasts that blow,
  With silent step, but not forlorn;
Though, goddess, at thy shrine I bow,
  And woo thee each returning morn.

---

* Sickness may be often an incentive to poetical composition; I found it so; and I esteem the following lines only because they remind me of past feelings which I would not willingly forget.

SHOOTER'S HILL.

I seek thee where, with all his might,
    The joyous bird his rapture tells,
Amidst the half-excluded light,
    That gilds the fox-glove's pendant bells;
Where, cheerly up this bold hill's side
    The deep'ning groves triumphant climb;
In groves Delight and Peace abide,
    And Wisdom marks the lapse of time.

To hide me from the public eye,
    To keep the throne of Reason clear,
Amidst fresh air to breathe or die,
    I took my staff and wander'd here.
Suppressing every sigh that heaves,
    And coveting no wealth but thee,
I nestle in the honied leaves,
    And hug my stolen liberty.

SHOOTER'S HILL.

O'er eastward uplands, gay or rude,
    Along to Erith's ivied spire,
I start, with strength and hope renew'd,
    And cherish life's rekindling fire.
Now measure vales with straining eyes,
    Now trace the church-yard's humble names;
Or, climb brown heaths, abrupt that rise,
    And overlook the winding Thames.

I love to mark the flow'ret's eye,
    To rest where pebbles form my bed,
Where shapes and colours scatter'd lie
    In varying millions round my head.
The soul rejoices when alone,
    And feels her glorious empire free;
Sees GOD in every shining stone,
    And revels in variety.

SHOOTER'S HILL.

Ah me! perhaps within my sight,
    Deep in the smiling dales below,
Gigantic talents, Heav'n's pure light,
    And all the rays of genius glow
In some lone soul, whom no one sees
    With *power* and *will* to say "Arise,"
Or chase away the slow disease,
    And Want's foul picture from his eyes.

A worthier man by far than I,
    With more of industry and fire,
Shall see fair Virtue's meed pass by,
    Without one spark of fame expire!
Bleed not my heart, it will be so,
    The throb of care was thine full long;
Rise, like the Psalmist from his woe,
    And pour abroad the joyful song.

SHOOTER'S HILL.

Sweet Health, I seek thee! hither bring
    Thy balm that softens human ills;
Come, on the long-drawn clouds that fling
    Their shadows o'er the Surry-Hills.
Yon green-topt hills, and far away
    Where late as now I freedom stole,
And spent one dear delicious day
    On thy wild banks, romantic *Mole*.

Aye, there's the scene!* beyond the sweep
    Of London's congregated cloud,
The dark-brow'd wood, the headlong steep,
    And valley-paths without a crowd!
Here, Thames, I watch thy flowing tides,
    Thy thousand sails am proud to see;
But where the *Mole* all silent glides
    Dwells Peace—and Peace is wealth to me.

* Box-Hill, and the beautiful neighbourhood of Dorking, in Surry.

SHOOTER'S HILL.

Of Cambrian mountains still I dream,
   And mouldering vestiges of war;
By time-worn cliff or classic stream
   Would rove,—but prudence holds a bar.
Come then, O Health, I'll strive to bound
   My wishes to this airy stand;
'Tis not for *me* to trace around
   The wonders of my native land.

Yet, the loud torrent's dark retreat,
   Yet Grampian hills shall Fancy give,
And, towering in her giddy seat,
   Amidst her own creation live,
Live, if thou'lt urge my climbing feet,
   Give strength of nerve and vigorous breath,
If not, with dauntless soul I meet
   The deep solemnity of death.

SHOOTER'S HILL.

This far-seen monumental tower
　Records th' achievements of the brave,
And Angra's subjugated power,
　Who plunder'd on the eastern wave.
I would not that such turrets rise
　To point out where my bones are laid;
Save that some wandering bard might prize
　The comforts of its broad cool shade.

O Vanity! since thou'rt decreed
　Companion of our lives to be,
I'll seek the moral songster's meed,
　An earthly immortality;
Most vain!—O let me, from the past
　Remembering what to man is given,
Lay Virtue's broad foundations fast,
　Whose glorious turrets reach to Heav'n.

A

VISIT TO RANELAGH.

To Ranelagh, once in my life,
    By good-natur'd force I was driv'n;
The nations had ceas'd their long strife,
    And PEACE* beam'd her radiance from Heav'n.
What wonders were there to be found
    That a clown might enjoy or disdain?
First we trac'd the gay ring all around,
    Aye—and then we went round it again.

    * A grand Fete, in honour of the peace of 1802.

A VISIT TO RANELAGH.

A thousand feet rustled on mats,
    A carpet that once had been green;
Men bow'd with their outlandish hats,
    With corners so fearfully keen!
Fair maids, who at home in their haste
    Had left all clothing else but a train,
Swept the floor clean, as slowly they pac'd,
    And then—walk'd round and swept it again.

The music was truly enchanting!
    Right glad was I when I came near it;
But in fashion I found I was wanting:—
    'Twas the fashion to walk and not hear it!
A fine youth, as beauty beset him,
    Look'd smilingly round on the train;
"The king's nephew," they cried, as they met him;
    Then—we went round and met him again.

A VISIT TO RANELAGH.

Huge paintings of Heroes and Peace
    Seem'd to smile at the sound of the fiddle,
Proud to fill up each tall shining space
    Round the lanthorn* that stood in the middle.
And GEORGE's head too; Heav'n screen him!
    May he finish in peace his long reign!
And what did we when we had seen him?
    Why—went round and saw him again.

A bell rang, announcing new pleasures,
    A crowd in an instant prest hard,
Feathers nodded, perfumes shed their treasures,
    Round a door that led into the yard.
'Twas peopled all o'er in a minute,
    As a white flock would cover a plain!
We had seen every soul that was in it,
    Then we went round and saw them again.

* The intervals between the pillars in the centre of the Rotunda were filled up by transparent paintings.

A VISIT TO RANELAGH.

But now came a scene worth the showing,
    The fireworks! midst laughs and huzzas,
With explosions the sky was all glowing,
    Then down stream'd a million of stars;
With a rush the bright rockets ascended,
    Wheels spurted blue fires like a rain;
We turn'd with regret when 'twas ended,
    Then—star'd at each other again.

There thousands of gay lamps aspir'd
    To the tops of the trees and beyond;
And, what was most hugely admir'd,
    They look'd all up-side-down in a pond!
The blaze scarce an eagle could bear;
    And an owl had most surely been slain;
We return'd to the circle, and there——
    And there we went round it again.

A VISIT TO RANELAGH.

'Tis not wisdom to love without reason,
  Or to censure without knowing why:
I had witness'd no crime, nor no treason,
  " O Life, 'tis thy picture," said I.
'Tis just thus we saunter along,
  Months and years bring their pleasures or pain;
We sigh midst the *right* and the *wrong;*
  —And then *we go round them again!*

LOVE OF THE COUNTRY.

WRITTEN AT CLARE-HALL, HERTS.

June 1804.

Welcome silence! welcome peace!
   O most welcome, holy shade!
Thus I prove as years increase,
   My heart and soul for quiet made.
Thus I fix my firm belief
   While rapture's gushing tears descend;
That every flower and every leaf
   Is moral Truth's unerring friend.

LOVE OF THE COUNTRY.

I would not for a world of gold
   That Nature's lovely face should tire;
Fountain of blessings yet untold;
   Pure source of intellectual fire!
Fancy's fair buds, the germs of song,
   Unquicken'd midst the world's rude strife,
Shall sweet retirement render strong,
   And morning silence bring to life.

Then tell me not that I shall grow
   Forlorn, that fields and woods will cloy;
From Nature and her changes flow
   An everlasting tide of joy.
I grant that summer heats will burn,
   That keen will come the frosty night;
But both shall please: and each in turn
   Yield Reason's most supreme delight.

LOVE OF THE COUNTRY.

Build me a shrine, and I could kneel
    To Rural Gods, or prostrate fall;
Did I not see, did I not feel,
    That one GREAT SPIRIT governs all.
O heav'n permit that I may lie
    Where o'er my corse green branches wave;
And those who from life's tumult fly
    With kindred feelings press my grave.

Page 94.

THE

WOODLAND HALLO.

(Perhaps) adapted for Music.

In our cottage, that peeps from the skirts of the wood,
   I am mistress, no mother have I;
Yet blithe are my days, for my father is good,
   And kind is my lover hard by;
They both work together beneath the green shade,
   Both woodmen, my father and Joe.
Where I've listen'd whole hours to the echo that made
   So much of a laugh or—Halló.

94 THE WOODLAND HALLO.

From my basket at noon they expect their supply,
    And with joy from my threshold I spring;
For the woodlands I love, and the oaks waving high,
    And Echo that sings as I sing.
Though deep shades delight me, yet love is my food,
    As I call the dear name of my Joe;
His musical shout is the pride of the wood,
    And my heart leaps to hear the—Halló.

Simple flowers of the grove, little birds live at ease,
    I wish not to wander from you;
I'll still dwell beneath the deep roar of your trees,
    For I know that my Joe will be true.
The trill of the robin, the coo of the dove,
    Are charms that I'll never forego;
But resting through life on the bosom of love,
    Will remember the Woodland Halló.

BARNHAM WATER.

F<small>RESH</small> from the Hall of Bounty sprung,*
   With glowing heart and ardent eye,
With song and rhyme upon my tongue,
   And fairy visions dancing by,
The mid-day sun in all his pow'r
   The backward valley painted gay;
Mine was a road without a flower,
   Where one small streamlet cross'd the way.

* On a sultry afternoon, late in the summer of 1802, Euston-Hall lay in my way to Thetford, which place I did not reach until the evening, on a visit to my sister: the lines lose much of their interest except they could be read on the spot, or at least at a corresponding season of the year.

BARNHAM WATER.

What was it rous'd my soul to love?
    What made the simple brook so dear?
It glided like the weary dove,
    And never brook seem'd half so clear.
Cool pass'd the current o'er my feet,
    Its shelving brink for rest was made,
But every charm was incomplete,
    For Barnham Water wants a shade.

There, faint beneath the fervid sun,
    I gaz'd in ruminating mood;
For who can see the current run
    And snatch no feast of mental food?
" Keep pure thy soul," it seem'd to say,
    " Keep that fair path by wisdom trod,
" That thou may'st hope to wind thy way
    " To fame worth boasting, and to God."

BARNHAM WATER.

Long and delightful was the dream,
    A waking dream that Fancy yields,
Till with regret I left the stream
    And plung'd across the barren fields;
To where of old rich abbeys smil'd
    In all the pomp of gothic taste,
By fond tradition proudly styl'd,
    The mighty " City in the East."

Near, on a slope of burning sand,
    The shepherd boys had met to play,
To hold the plains at their command,
    And mark the trav'ller's leafless way.
The trav'ller with a cheerful look
    Would every pining thought forbear,
If boughs but shelter'd Barnham brook
    He'd stop and leave his blessing there.

BARNHAM WATER.

The Danish mounds of partial green,
    Still, as each mouldering tower decays,
Far o'er the bleak unwooded scene
    Proclaim their wond'rous length of days.
My burning feet, my aching sight,
    Demanded rest,—why did I weep?
The moon arose, and such a night!
    Good Heav'n! it was a sin to sleep.

All rushing came thy hallow'd sighs,
    Sweet Melancholy, from my breast;
" 'Tis here that eastern greatness lies,
    " That Might, Renown, and Wisdom rest!
" Here funeral rites the priesthood gave
    " To chiefs who sway'd prodigious powers,
" The Bigods and the Mowbrays brave,
    " From Framlingham's imperial towers.

BARNHAM WATER.

Full of the mighty deeds of yore,
    I bade good night the trembling beam;
Fancy e'en heard the battle's roar,
    Of what but slaughter could I dream?
Bless'd be that night, that trembling beam,
    Peaceful excursions Fancy made;
All night I heard the bubbling stream,
    Yet, Barnham Water wants a shade.

Whatever hurts my country's fame,
    When wits and mountaineers deride,
To me grows serious, for I name
    My native plains and streams with pride.
No mountain charms have I to sing,
    No loftier minstrel's rights invade;
From trifles oft *my* raptures spring;
    —Sweet Barnham Water wants a shade.

MARY'S EVENING SIGH.

How bright with pearl the western sky!
   How glorious far and wide,
Yon lines of golden clouds that lie
   So peaceful side by side!
Their deep'ning tints, the arch of light,
   All eyes with rapture see;
E'en while I sigh I bless the sight
   That lures my love from me

MARY'S EVENING SIGH.

Green hill, that shad'st the valley here,
    Thou bear'st upon thy brow
The only wealth to Mary dear,
    And all she'll ever know.
There, in the crimson light I see,
    Above thy summit rise,
My Edward's form, he looks to me
    A statue in the skies.

Descend my love, the hour is come,
    Why linger on the hill?
The sun hath left my quiet home,
    But thou canst see him still;
Yet why a lonely wanderer stray,
    Alone the joy pursue?
The glories of the closing day
    Can charm thy Mary too.

MARY'S EVENING SIGH.

Dear Edward, when we stroll'd along
    Beneath the waving corn,
And both confess'd the power of song,
    And bless'd the dewy morn;
Your eye o'erflow'd, " How sweet," you cried,
    (My presence then could move)
" How sweet, with Mary by my side,
    " To gaze and talk of love!"

Thou art not false! that cannot be;
    Yet I my rivals deem
Each woodland charm, the moss, the tree,
    The silence, and the stream;
Whate'er my love, detains thee now,
    I'll yet forgive thy stay;
But with to-morrow's dawn come thou,
    We'll brush the dews away.

Page 109.

GOOD TIDINGS;

OR,

NEWS FROM THE FARM.

———◆———

> How vain this tribute; vain, this lowly lay;
> Yet nought is vain which gratitude inspires!
> The Muse, besides, her duty thus approves
> To virtue, to her country, to mankind!
> *Thomson.*

ADVERTISEMENT.

To the few who know that I have employed my thoughts on the importance of Dr. JENNER's discovery, it has generally and almost unexceptionably appeared a subject of little promise; peculiarly unfit indeed for poetry. My method of treating it has endeared it to myself, for it indulges in domestic anecdote. The account given of my infancy and of my father's burial, is not only poetically, but strictly true, and with me it has its weight accordingly. I have witnessed the destruction described in my brother's family; and I have, in my own, insured the lives of four children by Vaccine Inoculation, who, I trust, are destined to look back upon the Small-pox as the scourge of days gone by.—My hopes are high, and my prayers sincere, for its universal adoption.

The few notes subjoined are chiefly from " Woodville on Inoculation;" and if I may escape the appearance of affectation of research, or a scientific treatment of the subject, I think the egotism, so conspicuous in the poem, (as facts give force to argument,) ought to be forgiven.

GOOD TIDINGS;

OR,

NEWS FROM THE FARM.

Where's the Blind Child, so admirably fair,
With guileless dimples, and with flaxen hair
That waves in ev'ry breeze? he's often seen
Beside yon cottage wall, or on the green,
With others match'd in spirit and in size,
Health on their cheeks and rapture in their eyes;
That full expanse of voice, to childhood dear,
Soul of their sports, is duly cherish'd here:

GOOD TIDINGS.

And, hark! that laugh is his, that jovial cry;
He hears the ball and trundling hoop brush by,
And runs the giddy course with all his might,
A very child in every thing but sight;
With circumscrib'd but not abated pow'rs,—
Play! the great object of his infant hours;—
In many a game he takes a noisy part,
And shows the native gladness of his heart;
But soon he hears, on pleasure all intent,
The new suggestion and the quick assent;
The grove invites, delight thrills every breast—
To leap the ditch and seek the downy nest
Away they start, leave balls and hoops behind,
And one companion leave——the boy is blind!
His fancy paints their distant paths so gay,
That childish fortitude awhile gives way,

GOOD TIDINGS.

He feels his dreadful loss—yet short the pain,
Soon he resumes his cheerfulness again;
Pond'ring how best his moments to employ,
He sings his little songs of nameless joy,
Creeps on the warm green turf for many an hour,
And plucks by chance the white and yellow flow'r;
Smoothing their stems, while resting on his knees,
He binds a nosegay which he never sees;
Along the homeward path then feels his way,
Lifting his brow against the shining day,
And, with a playful rapture round his eyes,
Presents a sighing parent with the prize.

She blest *that* day, which he remembers too,
When he could gaze on heav'n's ethereal blue,
See the green Spring, and Summer's countless dies,
And all the colours of the morning rise.—

GOOD TIDINGS.

' When was this work of bitterness begun?
' How came the blindness of your only son?'
Thus pity prompts full many a tongue to say,
But never, till she slowly wipes away
Th' obtruding tear that trembles in her eye,
This dagger of a question meets reply:—
" My boy was healthy, and my rest was sound,
" When last year's corn was green upon the ground:
" From yonder town infection found its way;
" Around me putrid dead and dying lay,
" I trembled for his fate: but all my care
" Avail'd not, for he breath'd the tainted air;
" Sickness ensu'd—in terror and dismay
" I nurs'd him in my arms both night and day,
" When his soft skin from head to foot became
" One swelling purple sore, unfit to name:

" Hour after hour, when all was still beside,
" When the pale night-light in its socket died,
" Alone I sat; the thought still sooths my heart,
" That surely I perform'd a mother's part,
" Watching with such anxiety and pain
" Till he might smile and look on me again;
" But that was not to be—ask me no more:
" GOD keep small-pox and blindness from your door!"

 Now, ye who think, whose souls abroad take wing,
And trace out human troubles to their spring,
Say, should Heav'n grant us, in some hallow'd hour,
Means to divest this demon of his power,
To loose his horrid grasp from early worth,
To spread a saving conquest round the earth,
Till ev'ry land shall bow the grateful knee,
Would it not be a glorious day to see?—

GOOD TIDINGS.

That day is come! my soul, in strength arise,
Invoke no muse, no power below the skies;
To Heav'n the energies of verse belong,
Truth is the theme, and truth shall be the song;
Arm with conviction ev'ry joyful line,
Source of all mercies, for the praise is thine!

Sweet beam'd the star of peace upon those days
When Virtue watch'd my childhood's quiet ways,
Whence a warm spark of Nature's holy flame
Gave the farm-yard an honourable name,
But left one theme unsung: then, who had seen
In herds that feast upon the vernal green,
Or dreamt that in the blood of kine there ran
Blessings beyond the sustenance of man?
We tread the meadow, and we scent the thorn,
We hail the day-spring of a summer's morn

GOOD TIDINGS.

Nor mead at dawning day, nor thymy heath,
Transcends the fragrance of the heifer's breath:
May that dear fragrance, as it floats along
O'er ev'ry flow'r that lives in rustic song;
May all the sweets of meadows and of kine
Embalm, O Health! this offering at thy shrine.
   Dear must that moment be when first the mind,
Ranging the paths of science unconfin'd,
Strikes a new light; when, obvious to the sense,
Springs the fresh spark of bright intelligence.
So felt the towering soul of MONTAGU,
Her sex's glory, and her country's too;
Who gave the spotted plague one deadly blow,
And bade its mitigated poison flow
With half its terrors; yet, with loathing still,
We hous'd a visitant with pow'r to kill.

Then when the healthful blood, though often tried,
Foil'd the keen lancet by the Severn side,
Resisting, uncontaminated still,
The purple pest and unremitting skill;
When the plain truth tradition seem'd to know,
By simply pointing to the harmless Cow,
Though wise distrust to reason might appeal;
What, when hope triumph'd, what did JENNER feel!
Where even hope itself could scarcely rise
To scan the vast, inestimable prize?
Perhaps supreme, alone, triumphant stood
The great, the conscious power of doing good,
The power to will, and wishes to embrace
Th' emancipation of the human race;
A joy that must all mortal praise outlive,
A wealth that grateful nations cannot give.

GOOD TIDINGS.

Forth sped the truth immediate from his hand,
And confirmations sprung in ev'ry land;
In ev'ry land, on beauty's lily arm,
On infant softness, like a magic charm,
Appear'd the gift that conquers as it goes;
The dairy's boast, the simple, saving *Rose!*
Momentous triumph—fiend! thy reign is o'er;
Thou, whose blind rage hath ravag'd ev'ry shore,
Whose name denotes destruction, whose foul breath
For ever hov'ring round the dart of death,
Fells, mercilessly fells, the brave and base,
Through all the kindreds of the human race.

Who has not heard, in warm, poetic tales,
Of eastern fragrance and Arabian gales?
Bowers of delight, of languor, and repose,
Where beauty triumph'd as the song arose?

GOOD TIDINGS.

Fancy may revel, fiction boldly dare,

But truth shall not forget that *thou* wert there,

Scourge of the world! who, borne on ev'ry wind,

From bow'rs of roses* sprang to curse mankind.

The Indian palm thy devastation knows:

Thou sweep'st the regions of eternal snows †:

Climbing the mighty period of his years,

The British oak his giant bulk uprears;

He, in his strength, while toll'd the passing bell,

Rejoic'd whole centuries as thy victims fell:

Armies have bled, and shouts of vict'ry rung,

Fame crown'd *their* deaths, *thy* deaths are all unsung:

---

* The first medical account of the small-pox is given by the Arabian physicians, and is traced no farther back than the siege of Alexandria, about the year of Christ, 640.—WOODVILLE.

† First introduced into Greenland in 1733, and almost depopulated the country.—IBID.

GOOD TIDINGS.

'Twas thine, while victories claim'd th' immortal lay,

Through private life to cut thy desperate way;

And when full power the wondrous magnet gave

Ambition's sons to dare the ocean wave,

Thee, in their train of horrid ills, they drew

Beneath the blessed sunshine of Peru*.

But why unskill'd th' historic page explore?

Why thus pursue thee to a foreign shore?

A homely narrative of days gone by,

Familiar griefs, and kindred's tender sigh

Shall still survive; for thou on ev'ry mind

Hast left some traces of thy wrath behind.

---

* In 1520, says Mr. Woodville, when the small-pox visited New Spain, it proved fatal to one half of the people in the provinces to which the infection extended; being carried thither by a negro slave, who attended Narvaez in his expedition against Cortes. He adds, about fifty years after the discovery of Peru, the small-pox was carried over from Europe to America by way of Carthagena, when it overran the Continent of the New World, and destroyed upwards of 100,000 Indians in the single province of Quito.—*Hist. of Inoculation.*

GOOD TIDINGS.

There dwelt, beside a brook that creeps along
Midst infant hills and meads unknown to song,
One to whom poverty and faith were giv'n,
Calm village silence, and the hope of heav'n:
Alone she dwelt; and while each morn brought peace
And health was smiling on her years' increase,
Sudden and fearful, rushing through her frame,
Unusual pains and feverish symptoms came.
Then, when debilitated, faint, and poor,
How sweet to hear a footstep at her door!
To see a neighbour watch life's silent sand,
To hear the sigh, and feel the helping hand!
Soon woe o'erspread the interdicted ground,
And consternation seiz'd the hamlets round:
Uprose the pest—its widow'd victim died;
And foul contagion spread on ev'ry side;

GOOD TIDINGS.

The helping neighbour for her kind regard,
Bore home *that* dreadful tribute of reward,
Home, where six children, yielding to its pow'r,
Gave hope and patience a most trying hour;
One at her breast still drew the living stream,
And, sense of danger never marr'd his dream;
Yet all exclaim'd, and with a pitying eye,
" Whoe'er survives the shock, *that child will die!*"
But vain the fiat,—Heav'n restor'd them all,
And destin'd one of riper years to fall.
Midnight beheld the close of all his pain,
His grave was clos'd when midnight came again;
No bell was heard to toll, no funeral pray'r,
No kindred bow'd, no wife, no children there;
Its horrid nature could inspire a dread
That cut the bonds of custom like a thread

GOOD TIDINGS.

The humble church-tow'r higher seem'd to shew,
Illumin'd by their trembling light below;
The solemn night-breeze struck each shiv'ring cheek;
Religious reverence forbade to speak:
The starting Sexton his short sorrow chid
When the earth murmur'd on the coffin lid,
And falling bones and sighs of holy dread
Sounded a requiem to the silent dead!

' Why tell us tales of woe, thou who didst give
' Thy soul to rural themes, and bade them live?
' What means this zeal of thine, this kindling fire?
' The rescu'd infant and the dying sire?'
Kind heart, who o'er the pictur'd Seasons glow'd,
When smiles approv'd the verse, or tears have flow'd,
Was then the lowly minstrel dear to thee?
Himself appeals—What, if *that child* were he!

Page 120.

GOOD TIDINGS.

What, if those midnight sighs a farewel gave,
While hands, all trembling, clos'd his father's grave
Though love enjoin'd not infant eyes to weep,
In manhood's zenith shall his feelings sleep?
Sleep not my soul! indulge a nobler flame;
Still the destroyer persecutes thy name.

Seven winter's cannot pluck from memory's store
That mark'd affliction which a brother bore;
That storm of trouble bursting on his head,
When the fiend came, and left *two children* dead!
Yet, still superior to domestic woes,
The native vigour of his mind arose,
And, as new summers teem'd with brighter views,
He trac'd the wand'rings of his darling Muse,
And all was joy—this instant all is pain,
The foe implacable returns again,

And claims a sacrifice; the deed is done—
Another child has fall'n, another son*!
His young cheek even now is scarcely cold,
And shall his early doom remain untold?
No! let the tide of passion roll along,
Truth *will* be heard, and GOD will bless the song
Indignant Reason, Pity, Joy, arise,
And speak in thunder to the heart that sighs:
Speak loud to parents;—know ye not the time
When age itself, and manhood's hardy prime,
With horror saw their short-liv'd friendships end,
Yet dar'd not visit e'en the dying friend?
Contagion, a foul serpent lurking near,
Mock'd Nature's sigh and Friendship's holy tear.

* I had proceeded thus far with the Poem, when the above fact became a powerful stimulus to my feelings, and to the earnestness of my exhortations.

GOOD TIDINGS.

Love ye your children?—let that love arise,
Pronounce the sentence, and the serpent dies;
Bid welcome a mild stranger at your door,
Distress shall cease, those terrors reign no more.
Love ye your neighbours?—let that love be shown;
Risk not *their* children while you guard your own;
Give not a foe dominion o'er your blood,
Plant not a poison, e'en to bring forth good;
For, woo the pest discreetly as you will,
Deadly infection must attend him still.
Then, let the serpent die! this glorious prize
Sets more than life and health before our eyes,
For beauty triumphs too! Beauty! sweet name,
The mother's feelings kindling into flame!
For, where dwells she, who, while the virtues grow,
With cold indifference marks the arching brow?

Or, with a lifeless heart and recreant blood,
Sighs not for daughters fair as well as good?
That sigh is nature, and cannot decay,
'Tis universal as the beams of day;
Man knows and feels its truth; for, Beauty's call
Rouses the coldest mortal of us all;
A glance warms age itself, and gives the boy
The pulse of rapture and the sigh of joy.
And is it then no conquest to insure
Our lilies spotless and our roses pure?
Is it no triumph that the lovely face
Inherits every line of Nature's grace?
That the sweet precincts of the laughing eye
Dread no rude scars, no foul deformity?
Our boast, old Time himself shall not impair,
Of British maids pre-eminently fair;

GOOD TIDINGS.

But, as he rolls his years on years along,
Shall keep the record of immortal song;
For song shall rise with ampler power to speak
The new-born influence of Beauty's cheek,
Shall catch new fires in every sacred grove,
Fresh inspiration from the lips of Love,
And write for ever on the rising mind—
DEAD IS ONE MORTAL FOE OF HUMAN KIND!

Yes, we have conquer'd! and the thought should raise
A spirit in our prayers as well as praise,
For who will say, in Nature's wide domain
There lurk not remedies for every pain?
Who will assert, where Turkish banners fly,
Woe still shall reign—the plague shall never die?
Or who predict, with bosom all unblest,
An everlasting fever in the West?

GOOD TIDINGS.

Forbid it Heav'n!—Hope cheers us with a smile,
The sun of Mercy's risen on our isle:
Its beams already, o'er th' Atlantic wave,
Pierce the dark forests of the suffering brave:
There, e'en th' abandon'd sick imbib'd a glow,
When warrior nations, resting on the bow,
Astonish'd heard the joyful rumour rise,
And call'd the council of their great and wise:
The truth by female pray'rs was urg'd along,
Youth ceas'd the chorus of the warrior song,
And present ills bade present feelings press
With all the eloquence of deep distress;
Till forth their chiefs* o'er dying thousands trod
To seek the white man and his bounteous God:

* The chiefs of the Cherokee Indians, in North America, have applied to the government of the United States for information on the subject of Vaccine Inoculation, and have spread the practice in the Woods.

GOOD TIDINGS.

Well sped their errand ; with a patriot zeal
They spread the blessing for their country's weal.

Where India's swarthy millions crowd the strand,
And round that isle, which crowns their pointed land,
Speeds the good angel with the balmy breath,
And checks the dreadful tyranny of death :
Whate'er we hear to hurt the peace of life,
Of Candian treachery and British strife,
The sword of commerce, nations bought and sold,
They owe to England more than mines of gold ;
England has sent a balm for private woe ;
England strikes down the nations' bitterest foe.

Europe, amidst the clangor of her arms,
While life was threaten'd with a thousand harms,
And Charity was freezing to its source,
Still saw fair Science keep her steady course ;

GOOD TIDINGS.

And, while whole legions fell, by friends deplor'd,
New germs of life sprung up beneath the sword,
And spread amain.—Then, in our bosoms, why
Must exultation mingle with a sigh?

Thought takes the retrospect of years just fled,
And, conjuring up the spirits of the dead,
Whispers each dear and venerated name
Of the last victims ere the blessing came,
Worthies, who through the lands that gave them birth
Breath'd the strong evidence of growing worth;
Parents, cut down in life's meridian day,
And childhood's thousand thousand swept away;
Life's luckless mariners! ye, we deplore
Who sunk within a boat's length of the shore*.

* So lately as the year 1793, the small-pox was carried to the Isle of France by a Dutch ship, and there destroyed five thousand four hundred persons in six weeks.---WOODVILLE.

GOOD TIDINGS.

A stranger youth, from his meridian sky,
Buoyant with hopes, came here—but came to *die!*
O'er his sad fate I've ponder'd hours away,
It suits the languor of a gloomy day:
He left his bamboo groves, his pleasant shore,
He left his friends to hear new oceans roar,
All confident, ingenuous, and bold,
He heard the wonders by the white men told;
With firm assurance trod the rolling deck,
And saw his isle diminish to a speck,
Plough'd the rough waves, and gain'd our northern clime,
In manhood's ripening sense and nature's prime.
Oh! had the fiend been vanquish'd ere he came,
The gen'rous youth had spread my country's fame,
Had known that honour dwells among the brave,
And England had not prov'd the stranger's grave:

GOOD TIDINGS.

Then, ere his waning sand of life had run,

Poor ABBA THULE might have seen his son!*

   Rise, exultation! spirit, louder speak !

Pity, dislodge thy dewdrops from my cheek :

Sleep sound, forefathers ; sleep, brave stranger boy,

While truth impels the current of my joy :

To all mankind, to all the earth 'tis giv'n,

Conviction travels like the light of heav'n :

Go, blessing, from thy birth-place still expand,

For that dear birth-place is my native land !

A nation consecrates th' auspicious day,

And wealth, and rank, and talents lead the way !

Time, with triumphant hand, shall truth diffuse,

Nor ask the unbought efforts of the Muse.

   * Lee Boo, second son of the King of the Pelew Islands, was brought to England by Capt. Wilson, and died of the Small-pox at Rotherhithe, in 1784.

GOOD TIDINGS.

Mothers! the pledges of your loves caress,
And heave no sighs but sighs of tenderness.
Fathers, be firm! keep down the fallen foe,
And on the memory of domestic woe
Build resolution,—Victory shall increase
Th' incalculable wealth of private peace;
And such a victory, unstain'd with gore,
That strews its laurels at the cottage door,
Sprung from the farm, and from the yellow mead,
Should be the glory of the pastoral reed.
In village paths, hence, may we never find
Their youth on crutches, and their children blind;
Nor, when the milk-maid, early from her bed,
Beneath the may-bush that embow'rs her head,
Sings like a bird, e'er grieve to meet again
The fair cheek injur'd by the scars of pain;

GOOD TIDINGS.

Pure, in her morning path, whero'er she treads,
Like April sunshine and the flow'rs it feeds,
She'll boast new conquests; Love, new shafts to fling
And Life, an uncontaminated spring.
In pure delight didst thou, my soul, pursue
A task to conscience and to kindred due,
And, true to feeling and to Nature, deem
The dairy's boast thy own appropriate theme;
Hail now the meed of pleasurable hours,
And, at the foot of Science, strew thy flow'rs!

THE END.

J. WRIGHT, Printer,
No. 38, St. John's Square, Clerkenwell.

THE
BANKS OF WYE;
A POEM.

FRONTISPIECE *page 93.*

VIEW of the WYE through a GATEWAY at CRICKHOWEL.

THE

BANKS OF WYE;

A POEM.

In Four Books.

BY ROBERT BLOOMFIELD,

AUTHOR OF THE FARMER'S BOY.

LONDON:

PRINTED FOR THE AUTHOR; VERNOR, HOOD, AND SHARPE, POULTRY; AND LONGMAN, HURST, REES, ORME, AND BROWN, PATERNOSTER ROW;

1811.

Printed by T. Hood and Co. St. John's Square, London.

TO
THOMAS LLOYD BAKER, ESQ.
OF STOUT'S HILL, ULEY,

AND HIS EXCELLENT LADY;

AND

ROBERT BRANSBY COOPER, ESQ.
OF FERNEY HILL, DURSLEY,

IN THE COUNTY OF GLOUCESTER,

AND ALL THE MEMBERS OF HIS FAMILY.

THIS JOURNAL
IS DEDICATED,

WITH SENTIMENTS OF HIGH ESTEEM,

AND A LIVELY RECOLLECTION OF PAST PLEASURES,

BY THEIR HUMBLE SERVANT,

THE AUTHOR.

PREFACE.

In the summer of 1807, a party of my good friends in Gloucestershire proposed to themselves a short excursion down the Wye, and through part of South Wales.

While this plan was in agitation, the lines which I had composed on " Shooter's Hill," during ill health, and inserted in my last volume, obtained their particular attention. A spirit of prediction, as well as sorrow, is there indulged; and it was now in the power of this happy party to falsify such predictions, and to render a pleasure to the writer of no common kind. An invitation to accompany

PREFACE.

them was the consequence; and the following Journal is the result of that invitation.

Should the reader, from being a resident, or frequent visitor, be well acquainted with the route, and able to discover inaccuracies in distances, succession of objects, or local particulars, he is requested to recollect, that the party was out but ten days; a period much too short for correct and laborious description, but quite sufficient for all the powers of poetry which I feel capable of exerting. The whole exhibits the language and feelings of a man who had never before seen a mountainous country; and of this it is highly necessary that the reader should be apprized.

A Swiss, or perhaps a Scottish Highlander, may smile at supposed or real exaggerations; but they will be excellent critics, when they call to mind that they themselves judge, in these cases, as I do, by comparison.

Perhaps it may be said, that because much of public approbation has fallen to my lot, it was unwise to venture again. I confess that the journey left such powerful, such unconquerable impressions on my mind, that embodying my thoughts in rhyme became a matter almost of necessity. To the parties concerned I know it will be an acceptable little volume: to whom, and to the public, it is submitted with due respect.

ROBERT BLOOMFIELD.

City Road, London,
June 30, 1811.

THE BANKS OF WYE.

BOOK I.

CONTENTS OF BOOK I.

The Vale of Uley.—Forest of Dean.—Ross.—Wilton Castle.—Goodrich Castle.—Courtfield, Welch Bicknor, Coldwell.—Gleaner's Song.—Coldwell Rocks.—Symmon's Yat.—Great Doward.—New Wier.—Arthur's Hall.—Martin's Well.—The Coricle.—Arrival at Monmouth.

THE BANKS OF WYE.

BOOK I.

" Rouse from thy slumber, pleasure calls, arise,
Quit thy half-rural bower, awhile despise
The thraldom that consumes thee. We who dwell
Far from thy land of smoke, advise thee well.
Here Nature's bounteous hand around shall fling,
Scenes that thy Muse hath never dar'd to sing.
When sickness weigh'd thee down, and strength declin'd;
When dread eternity absorb'd thy mind,

Flow'd the predicting verse, by gloom o'erspread, 9
That 'Cambrian mountains' thou should'st never
    tread,
That 'time-worn cliff, and classic stream to see,'
Was wealth's prerogative, despair for thee.
Come to the proof; with us the breeze inhale,
Renounce despair, and come to Severn's vale;
And where the COTSWOLD HILLS are stretch'd
    along,
Seek our green dell, as yet unknown to song:
Start hence with us, and trace, with raptur'd eye,
The wild meanderings of the beauteous WYE;
Thy ten days leisure ten days joy shall prove,
And rock and stream breathe amity and love."

  Such was the call; with instant ardour hail'd,
The syren Pleasure caroll'd and prevail'd:

Soon the deep dell appear'd, and the clear brow 23
Of ULEY BURY * smil'd o'er all below,
Mansion, and flock, and circling woods that hung
Round the sweet pastures where the sky-lark sung.
O for the fancy, vigorous and sublime,
Chaste as the theme, to triumph over time!
Bright as the rising day, and firm as truth,
To speak new transports to the lowland youth,
That bosoms still might throb, and still adore,
When his who strives to charm them beats no more!

ONE August morn, with spirits high,
Sound health, bright hopes, and cloudless sky,

---

* Bury, or Burg, the Saxon name for a hill, particularly for one wholly or partially formed by art.

A cheerful group their farewell bade   35
To DURSLEY tower, to ULEY's shade;
And where bold STINCHCOMB's greenwood side,
Heaves in the van of highland pride,
Scour'd the broad vale of Severn; there
The foes of verse shall never dare
Genius to scorn, or bound its power,
There blood-stain'd BERKLEY's turrets low'r,
A name that cannot pass away,
Till time forgets " the Bard" of GRAY.

    Quitting fair Glo'ster's northern road.
To gain the pass of FRAMELODE,
Before us DEAN's black forest spread,
And MAY HILL, with his tufted head,
Beyond the ebbing tide appear'd;
And Cambria's distant mountains rear'd

Their dark blue summits far away; 51
And SEVERN, 'midst the burning day,
Curv'd his bright line, and bore along
The mingled *Avon,* pride of song.

The trembling steeds soon ferry'd o'er,
Neigh'd loud upon the forest shore;
Domains that once, at early morn,
Rang to the hunter's bugle horn,
When barons proud would bound away;
When even kings would hail the day,
And swell with pomp more glorious shows,
Than ant-hill population knows.
Here crested chiefs their bright-arm'd train
Of javelin'd horsemen rous'd amain,
And chasing wide the wolf or boar,
Bade the deep woodland vallies roar.

Harmless we past, and unassail'd,   67
Nor once at roads or turnpikes rail'd:
Through depths of shade oft sun-beams broke,
Midst noble FLAXLEY's bowers of oak;
And many a cottage trim and gay,
Whisper'd delight through all the way;
On hills expos'd, in dells unseen,
To patriarchal MITCHEL DEAN.
Rose-cheek'd *Pomona* there was seen,
And *Ceres* edg'd her fields between,
And on each hill-top mounted high,
Her sickle wav'd in extasy;
Till Ross, thy charms all hearts confess'd,
Thy peaceful walks, thy hours of rest
And contemplation. Here the mind,
With all its luggage left behind,

Dame Affectation's leaden wares, 83
Spleen, envy, pride, life's thousand cares,
Feels all its dormant fires revive,
And sees " the *Man of Ross*" alive;
And hears the Twick'nham Bard again,
To KYRL's high virtues lift his strain;
Whose own hand cloth'd this far-fam'd hill
With rev'rend elms, that shade us still;
Whose mem'ry shall survive the day,
When elms and empires feel decay.
KYRL die, by bard ennobled? Never;
" *The Man of Ross*" shall live for ever;
Ross, that exalts its spire on high,
Above the flow'ry-margin'd WYE,
Scene of the morrow's joy, that prest
Its unseen beauties on our rest

In dreams; but who of dreams would tell,   99
Where truth sustains the song so well?

   The morrow came, and Beauty's eye
Ne'er beam'd upon a lovelier sky;
Imagination instant brought,
And dash'd amidst the train of thought,
Tints of the bow. The boatman strips;
Glee at the helm exulting tript,
And wav'd her flower-encircled wand,
" Away, away, to Fairy Land."
Light dipt the oars; but who can name
The various objects dear to fame,
That changing, doubting, wild, and strong,
Demand the noblest powers of song?
Then, O forgive the vagrant Muse,
Ye who the sweets of Nature choose;

And thou whom destiny hast tied
To this romantic river's side,
Down gazing from each close retreat,
On boats that glide beneath thy feet,
Forgive the stranger's meagre line,
That seems to slight that spot of thine:
For he, alas! could only glean
The changeful outlines of the scene;
A momentary bliss; and here
Links memory's power with rapture's tear.

Who curb'd the barons' kingly power *?
Let hist'ry tell that fateful hour

---

* Henry the Seventh gave an irrevocable blow to the dangerous privileges assumed by the barons, in abolishing liveries and retainers, by which every malefactor could shel-

At home, when surly winds shall roar,   127
And prudence shut the study door.
DE WILTON's here of mighty name,
The whelming flood, the summer stream,
Mark'd from their towers —The fabric falls,
The rubbish of their splendid halls,
Time in his march hath scatter'd wide,
And blank oblivion strives to hide.

  Awhile the grazing herd was seen,
And trembling willow's silver green,

---

ter himself from the law, on assuming a nobleman's livery, and attending his person. And as a finishing stroke to the feudal tenures, an act was passed, by which the barons and gentlemen of landed interest were at liberty to sell and mortgage their lands, without fines or licences for the alienation.

Till the fantastic current stood, 137
In line direct for PENCRAIG WOOD;
Whose bold green summit welcome bade,
Then rear'd behind his nodding shade.
Here, as the light boat skimm'd along,
The clarionet, and chosen song,
That mellow, wild, Eolian lay,
" Sweet in the Woodlands," roll'd away,
In echoes down the stream, that bore
Each dying close to every shore,
And forward Cape, and woody range,
That form the never-ceasing change,
To him who floating, void of care,
Twirls with the stream, he knows not where:
Till bold, impressive, and sublime,
Gleam'd all that's left by storms and time

Of GOODRICH TOWERS. The mould'ring pile 153
Tells noble truths,—but dies the while;
O'er the steep path, through brake and briar,
His batter'd turrets still aspire,
In rude magnificence. 'Twas here
LANCASTRIAN HENRY spread his cheer,
When came the news that HAL was born,
And MONMOUTH hail'd th' auspicious morn;
A boy in sports, a prince in war,
Wisdom and valour crown'd his car;
Of France the terror, England's glory,
As Stratford's bard has told the story.

No butler's proxies snore supine,
Where the old monarch kept his wine;
No Welch ox roasting, horns and all,
Adorns his throng'd and laughing hall;

But where he pray'd, and told his beads, 169
A thriving ash luxuriant spreads.

  No wheels by piecemeal brought the pile;
No barks embowel'd Portland Isle;
Dig, cried experience, dig away,
Bring the firm quarry into day,
The excavation still shall save
Those ramparts which its entrails gave.
" Here kings shall dwell," the builders cried;
" Here England's foes shall low'r their pride;
Hither shall suppliant nobles come,
And this be England's royal home."
Vain hope! for on the Gwentian shore,
The regal banner streams no more!
Nettles, and vilest weeds that grow,
To mock poor grandeur's head laid low,

Creep round the turrets valour rais'd, 185
And flaunt where youth and beauty gaz'd.
 Here fain would strangers loiter long,
And muse as Fancy's woof grows strong;
Yet cold the heart that could complain,
Where POLLETT * struck his oars again;
For lovely as the sleeping child,
The stream glides on sublimely wild,
In perfect beauty, perfect ease;
The awning trembled in the breeze,
And scarcely trembled, as we stood
For RUERDEAN Spire, and BISHOP's WOOD.
The fair domains of COURTFIELD † made
A paradise of mingled shade

---

* The boatman.
† A seat belonging to the family of Vaughan, which is not

Round BICKNOR's tiny church, that cowers   199
Beneath his host of woodland bowers.
  But who the charm of words shall fling,
O'er RAVEN CLIFF and COLDWELL Spring,
To brighten the unconscious eye,
And wake the soul to extasy?
  Noon scorch'd the fields; the boat lay to;
The dripping oars had nought to do,

---

unnoticed in the pages of history. According to tradition, it is the place where Henry the Fifth was nursed, under the care of the Countess of Salisbury, from which circumstance the original name of Grayfield is said to have been changed to Courtfield [*].

[*] This is probably an erroneous tradition; for *Court* was a common name for a manor-house, where the lord of the manor held his court.——*Coxe's Monmouth*.

Where round us rose a scene that might
Enchant an ideot—glorious sight!
Here, in one gay according mind,
Upon the sparkling stream we din'd;
As shepherds free on mountain heath,
Free as the fish that watch'd beneath
For falling crumbs, where cooling lay
The wine that cheer'd us on our way.

Th' unruffled bosom of the stream,
Gave every tint and every gleam;
Gave shadowy rocks, and clear blue sky,
And double clouds of various dye;
Gave dark green woods, or russet brown,
And pendant corn-fields, upside down.

 A troop of gleaners chang'd their shade,
And 'twas a change by music made;

For slowly to the brink they drew,   223
To mark our joy, and share it too.
How oft, in childhood's flow'ry days,
I've heard the wild impassion'd lays
Of such a group, lays strange and new,
And thought, was ever song so true?
When from the hazel's cool retreat,
They watch'd the summer's trembling heat;
And through the boughs rude urchins play'd,
Where matrons, round the laughing maid,
Prest the long grass beneath! And here
They doubtless shar'd an equal cheer;
Enjoy'd the feast with equal glee,
And rais'd the song of revelry:
Yet half abash'd reserv'd, and shy,
Watch'd till the strangers glided by.

Gleaner's Song.

Dear Ellen, your tales are all plenteously stor'd,
With the joys of some bride, and the wealth of her
    lord;   240
    Of her chariots and dresses,
    And worldly caresses,
And servants that fly when she's waited upon:
But what can she boast if she weds unbelov'd?
Can she e'er feel the joy that one morning I prov'd,
When I put on my new gown and waited for John?

These fields, my dear Ellen, I knew them of yore,
Yet to me they ne'er look'd so enchanting before;
    The distant bells ringing,
    The birds round us singing,

For pleasure is pure when affection is won; 251
They told me the troubles and cares of a wife;
But I lov'd him; and that was the pride of my life,
When I put on my new gown and waited for John.

He shouted and ran, as he leapt from the stile;
And what in my bosom was passing the while?
  For love knows the blessing
  Of ardent caressing,
When virtue inspires us, and doubts are all gone.
The sunshine of Fortune you say is divine;
True love and the sunshine of Nature were mine,
When I put on my new gown and waited for John.

 Never could spot be suited less
 To bear memorials of distress;

None, cries the sage, more fit is found,   265
They strike at once a double wound;
Humiliation bids you sigh,
And think of immortality.

   Close on the bank, and half o'ergrown,
Beneath a dark wood's sombrous frown,
A monumental stone appears,
Of one who in his blooming years,
While bathing spurn'd the grassy shore,
And sunk, midst friends, to rise no more;
By parents witness'd.—Hark! their shrieks!
The dreadful language horror speaks!
But why in verse attempt to tell
That tale the stone records so well *?

---

   * *Inscription on the side towards the water.*
   " Sacred to the memory of JOHN WHITEHEAD WARRE,

Nothing could damp th' awaken'd joy, 279
Not e'en thy fate, ingenuous boy;
The great, the grand of Nature strove,
To lift our hearts to life and love.

---

who perished near this spot, whilst bathing in the river Wye, in sight of his afflicted parents, brother, and sisters, on the 14th of September, 1804, in the sixteenth year of his age.

GOD'S WILL BE DONE,

" Who, in his mercy, hath granted consolation to the parents of the dear departed, in the reflection, that he possessed truth, innocence, filial piety, and fraternal affection, in the highest degree. That, but a few moments before he was called to a better life, he had (with a never to be forgotten piety) joined his family in joyful thanks to his Maker, for the restoration of his mother's health. His parents, in justice to his amiable virtue, and excellent disposition, declare, that he was void of offence towards them. With humbled hearts they bow to the Almighty's dispensation; trusting, through

HAIL! COLDWELL ROCKS; frown, frown away;
Thrust from your woods your shafts of gray: 284
Fall not, to crush our mortal pride,
Or stop the stream on which we glide.

---

the mediation of his blessed Son, he will mercifully receive their child he so suddenly took to himself.

"This monument is here erected to warn parents and others how they trust the deceitful stream; and particularly to exhort them to learn and observe the directions of the Humane Society, for the recovery of persons apparently drowned. Alas! it is with the extremest sorrow here commemorated, what anguish is felt from a want of this knowledge. The lamented swam very well; was endowed with great bodily strength and activity; and possibly, had proper application been used, might have been saved from his untimely fate. He was born at Oporto, in the kingdom of Portugal, on the 14th of February, 1789; third son of James Warre, of London, and of the county of Somerset, merchant, and Elinor, daughter of Thomas Gregg, of Belfast, Esq.

Our lives are short, our joys are few; 287
But, giants, what is time to you?
Ye who erect, in many a mass,
Rise from the scarcely dimpled glass,

"Passenger, whoever thou art, spare this tomb! It is erected for the benefit of the surviving, being but a poor record of the grief of those who witnessed the sad occasion of it. God preserve you and yours from such calamity! May you not require their assistance; but if you should, the apparatus, with directions for the application by the Humane Society, for the saving of persons apparently drowned, are lodged at the church of Coldwell."

On the opposite side is inscribed

"It is with gratitude acknowledged by the parents of the deceased, that permission was gratuitously, and most obligingly, granted for the erection of this monument, by William Vaughan, Esq. of Courtfield."

That with distinct and mellow glow, 291
Reflect your monstrous forms below;
Or in clear shoals, in breeze or sun,
Shake all your shadows into one;
Boast ye o'er man in proud disdain,
An everlasting silent reign?
Bear ye your heads so high in scorn
Of names that puny man hath borne?
Would that the Cambrian bards had here
Their names carv'd deep, so deep, so clear,
That such as gaily wind along,
Might shout and cheer them with a song;
Might rush on wings of bliss away,
Through Fancy's boundless blaze of day!

 Not nameless quite ye lift your brows,
For each the navigator knows;

Not by King Arthur, or his knights, 307
Bard fam'd in lays, or chief in fights;
But former tourists, just as free,
(Tho' surely not so blest as we,)
Mark'd towering BEARCROFT's ivy crown,
And grey VANSITTART's waving gown;
And who's that giant by his side?
" SERGEANT ADAIR," the boatman cried.
Strange may it seem, however true,
That here, where law has nought to do,
Where rules and bonds are set aside,
By wood, by rock, by stream defy'd;
That here, where nature seems at strife
With all that tells of busy life,
Man should by *names* be carried still,
To Babylon against his will.

But how shall memory rehearse, 323
Or dictate the untoward verse
That truth demands? Could he refuse
Thy unsought honours, darling Muse,
He who in idle, happy trim,
Rode just where friends would carry him?
Truth, I obey.—The generous band,
That spread his board and grasp'd his hand,
In native mirth, as here they came,
Gave a bluff rock *his* humble name:
A yew-tree clasps its rugged base;
The boatman knows its reverend face;
And with his *memory* and his *fee*,
Rests the result that time shall see.
Yet e'en if time shall sweep away
The fragile whimsies of a day;

Or travellers rest the dashing oar, 339
To hear the mingled echoes roar;
A stranger's triumph—he will feel
A joy that death alone can steal.
And should he cold indifference feign,
And treat such honours with disdain,
Pretending pride shall not deceive him,
Good people all, pray don't believe him;
In such a spot to leave a name,
At least is no opprobrious fame;
This rock perhaps uprear'd his brow,
Ere human blood began to flow.

And let not wandering strangers fear
That WYE is ended there or here;
Though foliage close, though hills may seem
To bar all access to a stream,

Some airy height he climbs amain,   355
And finds the silver eel again.

  No fears we form'd, no labours counted,
Yet SYMMON'S YAT must be surmounted;
A tower of rock that seems to cry,
  Go round about me, neighbour WYE *.'
On went the boat, and up the steep
Her straggling crew began to creep,

---

* This rocky isthmus, perforated at the base, would measure not more than six hundred yards, and its highest point is two thousand feet above the water. If this statement, taken from Coxe's History of Monmouthshire, and an Excursion down the Wye, by C. Heath, of Monmouth, is correct, its elevation is greater than that of the "Pen y Vale," or the "Sugar-Loaf Hill," near Abergavenny. Yet it has less the appearance of a mountain, than the river has that of an excavation.

To gain the ridge, enjoy the view, 363
Where the the pure gales of summer blew.
The gleaming WYE, that circles round
Her four-mile course, again is found;
And crouching to the conqueror's pride,
Bathes his huge cliffs on either side;
Seen at one glance, when from his brow,
The eye surveys twin gulphs below.

Whence comes thy name? What *Symon* he,
Who gain'd a monument in thee?
Perhaps a rude woodhunter, born
Peril, and toil, and death, to scorn;
Or warrior, with his powerful lance,
Who scal'd the cliff to gain a glance;
Or shepherd lad, or humble swain,
Who sought for pasture here in vain;

Or venerable bard, who strove 879
To tune his harp to themes of love;
Or with a poet's ardent flame,
Sung to the winds his country's fame?
 Westward GREAT DOWARD, stretching wide,
Upheaves his iron-bowel'd side;
And by his everlasting mound,
Prescribes th' imprison'd river's bound,
And strikes the eye with mountain force:
But stranger mark thy rugged course
From crag to crag, unwilling, slow,
To NEW WIER forge that smokes below.
Here rush'd the keel like lightning by;
The helmsman watch'd with anxious eye;
And oars alternate touch'd the brim,
To keep the flying boat in trim.

NEW WEAR on the WYE.

Forward quick changing, changing still,   395
Again rose cliff, and wood, and hill,
Where mingling foliage seem'd to strive,
With dark-brown saplings, flay'd alive * ;
Down to the gulph beneath, where oft
The toiling wood-boy dragg'd aloft
His stubborn faggot from the brim,
And gaz'd, and tugg'd with sturdy limb ;
And where the mind repose would seek,
A barren, storm-defying peak,
The Little DOWARD lifted high
His rocky crown of royalty.

* The custom is here alluded to, of stripping the bark from oaks while growing, which gives an almost undescribable, though not the most agreeable, effect to the landscape.

THE BANKS OF WYE.

Hush! not a whisper! Oars, be still!   407
Comes that soft sound from yonder hill?
Or is it close at hand, so near
It scarcely strikes the list'ning ear?
E'en so; for down the green bank fell,
An ice-cold stream from MARTIN'S WELL,
Bright as young beauty's azure eye,
And pure as infant chastity,
Each limpid draught, suffus'd with dew,
The dipping glass's crystal hue;
And as it trembling reach'd the lip,
Delight sprung up at every sip.

   Pure, temperate joys, and calm, were these;
We tost upon no Indian seas;
No savage chiefs, of various hue,
Came jabbering in the bark canoe

Our strength to dare, our course to turn ; 423
Yet boats a South Sea chief would burn*,
Sculk'd in the alder shade. Each bore,
Devoid of keel, or sail, or oar,
An upright fisherman, whose eye,
With Bramin-like solemnity,
Survey'd the surface either way,
And cleav'd it like a fly at play;
And crossways bore a balanc'd pole,
To drive the salmon from his hole;

---

* In Cæsar's Commentaries, mention is made of boats of this description, formed of a raw hide, (from whence, perhaps, their name Coricle,) which were in use among the natives. How little they dreamed of the vastness of modern perfection, and of the naval conflicts of latter days!

Then heedful leapt, without parade, 433
On shore, as luck or fancy bade;
And o'er his back, in gallant trim,
Swung the light shell that carried him;
Then down again his burden threw,
And launch'd his whirling bowl anew;
Displaying, in his bow'ry station,
The infancy of navigation.

   Soon round us spread the hills and dales,
Where GEOFFREY spun his magic tales,
And call'd them history. The land
Whence ARTHUR sprung, and all his band
Of gallant knights. Sire of romance,
Who led the fancy's mazy dance,
Thy tales shall please, thy name still be,
When Time forgets my verse and me.

Low sunk the sun, his ev'ning beam   449
Scarce reach'd us on the tranquil stream;
Shut from the world, and all its din,
Nature's own bonds had clos'd us in;
Wood, and deep dell, and rock, and ridge,
From smiling ROSS to MONMOUTH BRIDGE;
From morn, till twilight stole away,
A long, unclouded, glorious day.

END OF THE FIRST BOOK.

THE BANKS OF WYE.

BOOK II.

CONTENTS OF BOOK II.

Henry the Fifth.—Morning on the Water.—Landoga.—Ballad, " The Maid of Landoga."—Tintern Abbey.—Wind-Cliff.—Arrival at Chepstow.—Persfield.—Ballad, " Morris of Persfield."—View from Wind-Cliff.—Chepstow Castle by Moonlight.

THE BANKS OF WYE.

BOOK II.

HARRY of MONMOUTH, o'er thy page,
Great chieftain of a daring age,
The stripling soldier burns to see
The spot of thy nativity;
His ardent fancy can restore
Thy castle's turrets, now no more;
See the tall plumes of victory wave,
And call old valour from the grave;
Twang the strong bow, and point the lance,
That pierc'd the shatter'd hosts of France,

42 THE BANKS OF WYE.

When Europe, in the days of yore,   11
Shook at the rampant lion's roar.

  TEN hours were all we could command;
The Boat was moor'd upon the strand,
The midnight current, by her side,
Was stealing down to meet the tide;
The wakeful steersman ready lay,
To rouse us at the break of day;
It came—how soon! and what a sky,
To cheer the bounding traveller's eye!
To make him spurn his couch of rest,
To shout upon the river's breast;
Watching by turns the rosy hue
Of early cloud, or sparkling dew;
These living joys the verse shall tell,
HARRY, and MONMOUTH, fare-ye-well.

On upland farm, and airy height,   27
Swept by the breeze, and cloth'd in light,
The reapers, early from their beds,
Perhaps were singing o'er our heads.
For, stranger, deem not that the eye
Could hence survey the eastern sky;
Or mark the streak'd horizon's bound,
Where first the rosy sun wheels round;
Deep in the gulf beneath were we,
Whence climb'd blue mists o'er rock and tree;
A mingling, undulating crowd,
That form'd the dense or fleecy cloud;
Slow from the darken'd stream upborne,
They caught the quick'ning gales of morn;
There bade their parent WYE good day,
And ting'd with purple sail'd away.

The MUNNO join'd us all unseen,   43
TROY HOUSE, and BEAUFORT's bowers of green,
And nameless prospects, half defin'd,
Involv'd in mist, were left behind.
Yet as the boat still onward bore,
These ramparts of the eastern shore
Cower'd the high crest to many a sweep,
And bade us o'er each minor steep
Mark the bold KYMIN's sunny brow,
That, gleaming o'er our fogs below,
Lifted amain with giant power,
E'en to the clouds his NAVAL TOWER *;

---

* The Kymin Pavilion, erected in honour of the British Admirals, and their unparalleled victories.

Proclaiming to the morning sky, 55
Valour, and fame, and victory.

 THE air resign'd its hazy blue,
Just as LANDOGA came in view;
Delightful village! one by one,
Its climbing dwellings caught the sun.
So bright the scene, the air so clear,
Young Love and Joy seem'd station'd here;
And each with floating banners cried,
" Stop friends, you'll meet the slimy tide."
 Rude fragments, torn, disjointed, wild,
High on the Glo'ster shore are pil'd;
No ruin'd fane, the boast of years,
Unstain'd by time the group appears;
With foaming wrath, and hideous swell,
Brought headlong down a woodland dell,

When a dark thunder-storm had spread 71
Its terrors round the guilty head;
When rocks, earth-bound, themselves gave way,
When crash'd the prostrate timbers lay.
O, it had been a noble sight,
Crouching beyond the torrent's might,
To mark th' uprooted victims bow,
The grinding masses dash below,
And hear the long deep peal the while
Burst over TINTERN's roofless pile!
Then, as the sun regain'd his power,
When the last breeze from hawthorn bower,
Or Druid oak, had shook away
The rain-drops 'midst the gleaming day,
Perhaps the sigh of hope return'd
And love in some chaste bosom burn'd,

And softly trill'd the stream along,   87
Some rustic maiden's village song.

The Maid of Landoga.

RETURN, my Llewellyn, the glory
That heroes may gain o'er the sea,
    Though nations may feel
    Their invincible steel,
By falsehood is tarnish'd in story;
Why tarry, Llewellyn, from me?

Thy sails, on the fathomless ocean,
Are swell'd by the boisterous gale;
    How rests thy tir'd head
    On the rude rocking bed?

While here not a leaf is in motion, 99
And melody reigns in the dale.

The mountains of Monmouth invite thee;
The WYE, O how beautiful here!
   This woodbine, thine own,
    Hath the cottage o'ergrown,
O what foreign shore can delight thee,
And where is the current so clear?

Can lands where false pleasure assails thee,
And beauty invites thee to roam;
   Can the deep orange grove
    Charm with shadows of love?
Thy love at LANDOGA bewails thee;
Remember her truth and thy home.

Adieu, Landoga, scene most dear, 113
Farewell we bade to Ethel's Wier;
Round many a point then bore away,
Till morn was chang'd to beauteous day:
And forward on the lowland shore,
Silent majestic ruins wore
The stamp of holiness; this strand
The steersman hail'd, and touch'd the land.

Sudden the change; at once to tread
The grass-grown mansions of the dead!
Awful to feeling, where, immense,
Rose ruin'd, gray magnificence;
The fair-wrought shaft all ivy-bound,
The tow'ring arch with foliage crown'd,

That trembles on its brow sublime,
Triumphant o'er the spoils of time.
Here, grasping all the eye beheld,
Thought into mingling anguish swell'd,
And check'd the wild excursive wing,
O'er dust or bones of priest or king;
Or rais'd some STRONGBOW * warrior's ghost
To shout before his banner'd host.
But all was still.—The chequer'd floor
Shall echo to the step no more;
Nor airy roof the strain prolong,
Of vesper chant or choral song.

---

* They shew here a mutilated figure, which they call the famous Earl Strongbow; but it appears from Coxe that he was buried at Gloucester.

THE BANKS OF WYE.

TINTERN, thy name shall hence sustain 139
A thousand raptures in my brain;
Joys, full of soul, all strength, all eye,
That cannot fade, that cannot die.

No loitering here, lone walks to steal,
Welcome the early hunter's meal;
For time and tide, stern couple, ran
Their endless race, and laugh'd at man;
Deaf, had we shouted, " turn about?"
Or, " wait a while, till we come out;"
To humour them we check'd our pride,
And ten cheer'd hearts stow'd side by side;
Push'd from the shore with current strong,
And, " Hey for Chepstow," steer'd along.

Amidst the bright expanding day,
Solemnly deep, dark shadows lay,
Of that rich foliage, tow'ring o'er
Where princely abbots dwelt of yore.
The mind, with instantaneous glance,
Beholds his barge of state advance,
Borne proudly down the ebbing tide,
She turns the waving boughs aside;
She winds with flowing pendants drest,
And as the current turns south-west,
She strikes her oars, where full in view,
Stupendous WIND-CLIFF greets his crew.
But, Fancy, let thy day-dreams cease,
With fallen greatness be at peace;
Enough; for WIND-CLIFF still was found
To hail us as we doubled round.

Bold in primeval strength he stood; 169
His rocky brow, all shagg'd with wood,
O'er-look'd his base, where, doubling strong,
The inward torrent pours along;
Then ebbing turns, and turns again,
To meet the Severn and the Main,
Beneath the dark shade sweeping round,
Of beetling PERSFIELD's fairy ground,
By buttresses of rock upborne,
The rude APOSTLES all unshorn.

Long be the slaught'ring axe defy'd;
Long may they bear their waving pride;
Tree over tree, bower over bower,
In uncurb'd nature's wildest power;
Till WYE forgets to wind below,
And genial spring to bid them grow.

And shall we e'er forget the day,   185
When our last chorus died away?
When first we hail'd, then moor'd beside
Rock-founded CHEPSTOW's mouldering pride?
Where that strange bridge*, light, trembling, high,
Strides like a spider o'er the WYE;
When, for the joys the morn had giv'n,
Our thankful hearts were rais'd to heav'n?

---

* "On my arrival at Chepstow," says Mr. Coxe, "I walked to the bridge; it was low water, and I looked down on the river ebbing between forty and fifty feet beneath; six hours after it rose near forty feet, almost reached the floor of the bridge, and flowed upward with great rapidity. The channel in this place being narrow in proportion to the Severn, and confined between perpendicular cliffs, the great rise and fall of the river are peculiarly manifest."

Never;—that moment shall be dear, 193
While hills can charm, or sun-beams cheer.
   POLLETT, farewell! Thy dashing oar
Shall lull us into peace no more;
But where KYRL trimm'd his infant green,
Long mayst thou with thy bark be seen;
And happy be the hearts that glide
Through such a scene, with such a guide.

   THE verse of gravel walks that tells,
With pebble rocks and mole-hill swells,
May strain description's bursting cheeks,
And far out-run the goal it seeks.
Not so when ev'ning's purpling hours,
Hied us away to PERSFIELD bowers:
Here no such danger waits the lay,
Sing on, and truth shall lead the way;

Here sight may range, and hearts may glow, 209
Yet shrink from the abyss below;
Here echoing precipices roar,
As youthful ardour shouts before;
Here a sweet paradise shall rise
At once to greet poetic eyes.
Then why does he dispel, unkind,
The sweet illusion from the mind,
That giant, with the goggling eye,
Who strides in mock sublimity?
Giants, identified, may frown,
Nature and taste would knock them down;
Blocks that usurp some noble station,
As if to curb imagination,
That, smiling at the chissel's pow'r,
Makes better monsters every hour.

THE BANKS OF WYE.

Beneath impenetrable green,   225
Down 'midst the hazel stems was seen
The turbid stream, with all that past;
The lime-white deck, the gliding mast;
Or skiff with gazers darting by,
Who rais'd their hands in extasy.
Impending cliffs hung overhead;
The rock-path sounded to the tread,
Where twisted roots, in many a fold,
Through moss, disputed room for hold.
 The stranger thus who steals one hour
To trace thy walks from bower to bower,
Thy noble cliffs, thy wildwood joys,
Nature's own work that never cloys,
Who, while reflection bids him roam,
Exclaims not, " PERSFIELD is my *home*,"

Can ne'er, with dull unconscious eye,   241
Leave them behind without a sigh.
Thy tale of truth then, Sorrow, tell,
Of one who bade *this home* farewell;
MORRIS of PERSFIELD.—Hark, the strains!
Hark! 'tis some Monmouth bard complains!
The deeds, the worth, he knew so well,
The force of nature bids him tell.

Morris of Persfield.

WHO was lord of yon beautiful seat;
    Yon woods which are tow'ring so high?
Who spread the rich board for the great,
    Yet listen'd to pity's soft sigh?

Who gave alms with a spirit so free? 253
   Who succour'd distress at his door?
Our MORRIS of PERSFIELD was he,
   Who dwelt in the hearts of the poor.

But who e'en of wealth shall make sure,
   Since wealth to misfortune has bow'd?
Long cherish'd untainted and pure,
   The stream of his charity flow'd.
But all his resources gave way,
   O what could his feelings controul?
What shall curb, in the prosperous day,
   Th' excess of a generous soul?

He bade an adieu to the town,
   O, can I forget the sad day?
When I saw the poor widows kneel down,
   To bless him, to weep, and to pray.

Though sorrow was mark'd in his eye, 269
　　This trial he manfully bore;
Then pass'd o'er the bridge of the WYE,
　　To return to his PERSFIELD no more.

Yet surely another may feel,
　　And poverty still may be fed;
I was one who rung out the dumb peal,
　　For to us noble MORRIS was dead.

He had not lost sight of his home,
　　Yon domain that so lovely appears,
When he heard it, and sunk overcome;
　　He could feel, and he burst into tears.

The lessons of prudence have charms,
　　And slighted, may lead to distress;
But the man whom benevolence warms,
　　Is an angel who lives but to bless.

If ever man merited fame,   285
  If ever man's failings went free,
Forgot at the sound of his name,
  Our MORRIS of PERSFIELD was he*.

CLEFT from the summit, who shall say
When WIND-CLIFF's other half gave way?
Or when the sea-waves roaring strong,
First drove the rock-bound tide along?
To studious leisure be resign'd,
The task that leads the wilder'd mind

---

* The author is equally indebted to Mr. Coxe's County History for this anecdote, as for the greater part of the notes subjoined throughout the Journal.

From time's first birth throughout the range   295
Of Nature's everlasting change.
Soon from his all-commanding brow,
Lay PERSFIELD's rocks and woods below.
  Back over MONMOUTH who could trace
The WYE's fantastic mountain race?
Before us, sweeping far and wide,
Lay out-stretch'd SEVERN's ocean tide,
Through whose blue mists, all upward blown,
Broke the faint lines of heights unknown;
And still, though clouds would interpose,
The COTSWOLD promontories rose
In dark succession: STINCHCOMB's brow,
With BERKLEY CASTLE crouch'd below;
And stranger spires on either hand,
From THORNBURY, on the Glo'ster strand;

THE BANKS OF WYE.

With black-brow'd woods, and yellow fields, 311
The boundless wealth that summer yields,
Detain'd the eye, that glanc'd again
O'er KINGROAD anchorage to the main.
 Or was the bounded view preferr'd,
Far, far beneath the spreading herd
Low'd as the cow-boy stroll'd along,
And cheerly sung his last new song.
But cow-boy, herd, and tide, and spire,
Sunk into gloom, the tinge of fire,
As westward roll'd the setting day,
Fled like a golden dream away.
Then CHEPSTOW's ruin'd fortress caught
The mind's collected store of thought,
And seem'd, with mild but jealous frown,
To promise peace, and warn us down.

'Twas well; for he has much to boast,   327
Much still that tells of glories lost,
Though rolling years have form'd the sod,
Where once the bright-helm'd warrior trod
From tower to tower, and gaz'd around,
While all beneath him slept profound.
E'en on the walls where pac'd the brave,
High o'er his crumbling turrets wave
The rampant seedlings.—Not a breath
Past through their leaves; when, still as death,
We stopp'd to watch the clouds—for night
Grew splendid with encreasing light,
Till, as time loudly told the hour,
Gleam'd the broad front of MARTEN's TOWER *,

---

* Henry Marten, whose signature appears upon the death-

MARTINS TOWER, CHEPSTOW CASTLE.

Bright silver'd by the moon.—Then rose   341
The wild notes sacred to repose;
Then the lone owl awoke from rest,
Stretch'd his keen talons, plum'd his crest,
And from his high embattl'd station,
Hooted a trembling salutation.

---

warrant of Charles the First, finished his days here in prison. Marten lived to the advanced age of seventy-eight, and died by a stroke of apoplexy, which seized him while he was at dinner, in the twentieth year of his confinement. He was buried in the chancel of the parish church at Chepstow. Over his ashes was placed a stone with an inscription, which remained there until one of the succeeding vicars declaring his abhorrence that the monument of a rebel should stand so near the altar, removed the stone into the body of the church!

Rocks caught the "halloo" from his tongue, 347
And PERSFIELD back the echoes flung
Triumphant o'er th' illustrious dead,
Their history lost, their glories fled.

END OF THE SECOND BOOK.

THE BANKS OF WYE.

BOOK III.

CONTENTS OF BOOK III.

Departure for Ragland.—Ragland Castle.—Abergavenny.—Expedition up the "Pen-y-Vale," or Sugar-Loaf Hill.—Invocation to the Spirit of Burns.—View from the Mountain.—Castle of Abergavenny.—Departure for Brecon,—Pembrokes of Crickhowel.—Tre-Tower Castle.—Jane Edwards.

THE BANKS OF WYE.

BOOK III.

Peace to your white-wall'd cots, ye vales,
Untainted fly your summer gales;
Health, thou from cities lov'st to roam,
O make the Monmouth hills your home!
Great spirits of her bards of yore,
While harvests triumph, torrents roar,
Train her young shepherds, train them high
To sing of mountain liberty:
Give them the harp and modest maid;
Give them the sacred village shade.

Long be Llandenny, and Llansoy,
Names that import a rural joy;
Known to our fathers, when May-day
Brush'd a whole twelvemonth's cares away.
   Oft on the lisping infant's tongue
Reluctant information hung,
Till, from a belt of woods full grown,
Arose immense thy turrets brown,
Majestic RAGLAND! Harvests wave
Where thund'ring hosts their watch-word gave,
When cavaliers, with downcast eye,
Struck the last flag of loyalty *:

---

  * This castle, with a garrison commanded by the Marquis of Worcester, was the last place of strength which held out for the unfortunate Charles the First.

Then, left by gallant WORC'STER's band, 23
To devastation's cruel hand
The beauteous fabric bow'd, fled all
The splendid hours of festival.
No smoke ascends; the busy hum
Is heard no more; no rolling drum,
No high-ton'd clarion sounds alarms,
No banner wakes the pride of arms *;

---

* " These magnificent ruins, including the citadel, occupy a tract of ground not less than one-third of a mile in circumference."

" In addition to the injury the castle sustained from the parliamentary army, considerable dilapidations have been occasioned by the numerous tenants in the vicinity, who conveyed away the stone and other materials for the construction of farm-houses, barns, and other buildings. No less than twenty-three staircases were taken down by these de-

But ivy, creeping year by year, 31
Of growth enormous, triumphs here.
Each dark festoon with pride upheaves
Its glossy wilderness of leaves
On sturdy limbs, that, clasping, bow
Broad o'er the turrets utmost brow,
Encompassing, by strength alone,
In fret-work bars, the sliding stone,
That tells how years and storms prevail,
And spreads its dust upon the gale.

---

vastators; but the present Duke of Beaufort no sooner succeeded to his estate, than he instantly gave orders that not a stone should be moved from its situation, and thus preserved these noble ruins from destruction."

History of Monmouthshire, page 148.

The man who could unmov'd survey 41
What ruin, piecemeal, sweeps away;
Works of the pow'rful and the brave,
All sleeping in the silent grave;
Unmov'd reflect that here were sung
Carols of joy, by beauty's tongue,
Is fit, where'er he deigns to roam,
And hardly fit—to stay at home.
Spent here in peace one solemn hour,
'Midst legends of the YELLOW TOWER,
Truth and tradition's mingled stream,
Fear's start, and superstition's dream *

---

* A village woman, who very officiously pointed out all that she knew respecting the former state of the castle, desired us to remark the descent to a vault, apparently of large dimen-

Is pregnant with a thousand joys,   53
That distance, place, nor time destroys;
That with exhaustless stores supply
Food for reflection till we die.

 ONWARD the rested steeds pursu'd
The cheerful route, with strength renew'd,
For onward lay the gallant town,
Whose name old custom hath clipp'd down,
With more of music left than many,
So handily to ABERGANY.

---

sions, in which she had heard that no candle would continue burning; " and," added she, " they say it is because of the damps; but for my part, I think the devil is there."

And as the sidelong, sober light 63
Left valleys darken'd, hills less bright,
Great BLORENGE rose to tell his tale;
And the dun peak of PEN-Y-VALE
Stood like a centinel, whose brow
Scowl'd on the sleeping world below;
Yet even sleep itself outspread
The mountain paths we meant to tread,
'Midst fresh'ning gales all unconfin'd,
Where USK's broad valley shrinks behind.

Joyous the crimson morning rose,
As joyous from the night's repose
Sprung the light heart, the glancing eye
Beheld, amidst the dappl'd sky,

Exulting PEN-Y-VALE. But how
Could females climb his gleaming brow,
Rude toil encount'ring? how defy
The wintry torrent's course, when dry,
A rough-scoop'd bed of stones? or meet
The powerful force of August heat?
Wheels might assist, could wheels be found
Adapted to the rugged ground:
'Twas done; for prudence bade us start
With three Welch ponies, and a cart;
A red-cheek'd mountaineer *, a wit,
Full of rough shafts, that sometimes hit,

---

* The driver, Powell, I believe, occupied a cottage, or small farm, which we past during the ascent, and where goats milk was offered for refreshment.

Trudg'd by their side, and twirl'd his thong, 89
And cheer'd his scrambling team along.

 At ease to mark a scene so fair,
And treat their steeds with mountain air,
Some rode apart, or led before,
Rock after rock the wheels upbore;
The careful driver slowly sped,
To many a bough we duck'd the head,
And heard the wild inviting calls
Of summer's tinkling waterfalls,
In wooded glens below; and still,
At every step the sister hill,
BLORENGE, grew greater, half unseen
At times from out our bowers of green,
That telescopic landscapes made,
From the arch'd windows of its shade;

For woodland tracts begirt us round;   105
The vale beyond was fairy ground,
That verse can never paint.   Above
Gleam'd something like the mount of Jove,
(But how much let the learned say
Who take Olympus in their way)
Gleam'd the fair, sunny, cloudless peak
That simple strangers ever seek.
And are they simple?   Hang the dunce
Who would not doff his cap at once
In extasy, when, bold and new,
Bursts on his sight a mountain-view.

 Though vast the prospect here became,
Intensely as the love of fame
Glow'd the strong hope, that strange desire,
That deathless wish of climbing higher,

Where heather clothes his graceful sides, 121
Which many a scatter'd rock divides,
Bleach'd by more years than hist'ry knows,
Mov'd by no power but melting snows,
Or gushing springs, that wash away
Th' embedded earth that forms their stay.
The heart distends, the whole frame feels,
Where, inaccessible to wheels,
The utmost storm-worn summit spreads
Its rocks grotesque, its downy beds;
Here no false feeling sense belies,
Man lifts the weary foot, and sighs;
Laughter is dumb; hilarity
Forsakes at once th' astonish'd eye;
E'en the clos'd lip, half useless grown,
Drops but a word, " Look down; look down."

Good Heav'ns! must scenes like these expand,
Scenes so magnificently grand, 138
And millions breathe, and pass away,
Unbless'd, throughout their little day,
With one short glimpse? By place confin'd,
Shall many an anxious ardent mind,
Sworn to the Muses, cow'r its pride,
Doom'd but to sing with pinions tied?

Spirit of Burns! the daring child
Of glorious freedom, rough and wild,
How have I wept o'er all thy ills,
How blest thy Caledonian hills!
How almost worshipp'd in my dreams
Thy mountain haunts,—thy classic streams!
How burnt with hopeless, aimless fire,
To mark thy giant strength aspire

In patriot themes! and tun'd the while 153
Thy " *Bonny Doon,*" or " *Balloch Mile.*"
Spirit of BURNS! accept the tear
That rapture gives thy mem'ry here
On the bleak mountain top. Here thou
Thyself had rais'd the gallant brow
Of conscious intellect, to twine
Th' imperishable verse of thine,
That charm'st the world. Or can it be,
That scenes like these were nought to thee?
That Scottish hills so far excel,
That so deep sinks the Scottish dell,
That boasted PEN-Y-VALE had been *,
For thy loud northern lyre too mean;

---

* The respective heights of these mountains above the

G

Broad-shoulder'd BLORENGE a mere knoll,   167
And SKYRID, let him smile or scowl,
A dwarfish bully, vainly proud
Because he breaks the passing cloud?
If even so, thou bard of fame,
The consequences rest the same:
For, grant that to thy infant sight
Rose mountains of stupendous height;
Or grant that Cambrian minstrels taught
'Mid scenes that mock the lowland thought;

---

mouth of the Gavany, was taken barometrically by General Roy.

	Feet.
The summit of the Sugar-Loaf	1852
Of the Blorenge	1720
Of the Skyrid	1498

Grant that old TALLIESIN flung 177
His thousand raptures, as he sung
From huge PLYNLIMON's awful brow,
Or CADER IDRIS, capt with snow;
Such Alpine scenes with them or thee
Well suited.—*These* are Alps to me.

LONG did we, noble BLORENGE, gaze
On thee, and mark the eddying haze
That strove to reach thy level crown,
From the rich stream, and smoking town;
And oft, old SKYRID, hail'd thy name,
Nor dar'd deride thy holy fame [*].

---

[*] There still remains, on the summit of the Skyrid, or
St. Michael's Mount, the foundation of an ancient chapel,

Long follow'd with untiring eye 189
Th' illumin'd clouds, that o'er the sky
Drew their thin veil, and slowly sped,
Dipping to every mountain's head,
Dark-mingling, fading, wild, and thence,
Till admiration, in suspense,
Hung on the verge of sight. Then sprung,
By thousands known, by thousands sung,
Feelings that earth and time defy,
That cleave to immortality.

---

to which the inhabitants formerly ascended on Michaelmas Eve, in a kind of pilgrimage. A prodigious cleft, or separation in the hill, tradition says, was caused by the earthquake at the crucifixion, it was therefore termed the Holy Mountain.

A light gray haze enclos'd us round;   199
Some momentary drops were found,
Borne on the breeze; soon all dispell'd;
Once more the glorious prospect swell'd
Interminably fair *. Again
Stretch'd the BLACK MOUNTAIN's dreary chain!
When eastward turn'd the straining eye,
Great MALVERN met the cloudless sky:
Southward arose th' embattled shores,
Where Ocean in his fury roars,

---

* This hill commands a view of the counties of Radnor, Salop, Brecknock, Glamorgan, Hereford, Worcester, Gloucester, Somerset, and Wilts.

And rolls abrupt his fearful tides, 209
Far still from MENDIP's fern-clad sides;
From whose vast range of mingling blue,
The weary, wand'ring sight withdrew,
O'er fair GLAMORGAN's woods and downs,
O'er glitt'ring streams, and farms, and towns,
Back to the TABLE ROCK, that lours
O'er old CRICKHOWEL's ruin'd towers.

   Here perfect stillness reign'd. The breath
A moment hush'd, 'twas mimic death.
The ear, from all assaults releas'd,
As motion, sound, and life, had ceas'd.
The beetle rarely murmur'd by,
No sheep-dog sent his voice so high,
Save when, by chance, far down the steep,
Crept a live speck, a straggling sheep;

THE BANKS OF WYE.

Yet one lone object, plainly seen,   225
Curv'd slowly, in a line of green,
On the brown heath: no demon fell,
No wizard foe, with magic spell,
To chain the senses, chill the heart,
No wizard guided POWEL's cart;
He of our nectar had the care,
All our ambrosia rested there.
At leisure, but reluctant still,
We join'd him by a mountain rill;
And there, on springing turf, all seated,
Jove's guests were never half so treated;
Journies they had, and feastings many,
But never came to ABERGANY;
Lucky escape:—the wrangling crew,
Mischief to cherish, or to brew,

Was all their sport: and when, in rage, 241
They chose 'midst warriors to engage,
" Our chariots of fire," they cried,
And dash'd the gates of heav'n aside,
Whirl'd through the air, and foremost stood
'Midst mortal passions, mortal blood,
Celestial power with earthly mix'd;
Gods by the arrow's point transfix'd!
Beneath us frown'd no deadly war,
And POWEL's wheels were safer far;
As on them, without flame or shield,
Or bow to twang, or lance to wield,
We left the heights of inspiration,
And relish'd a mere mortal station;
Our object, not to fire a town,
Or aid a chief, or knock him down;

But safe to sleep from war and sorrow,   257
And drive to BRECKNOCK on the morrow.

HEAVY and low'ring, crouds on crouds,
Drove adverse hosts of dark'ning clouds
Low o'er the vale, and far away,
Deep gloom o'erspread the rising day;
No morning beauties caught the eye,
O'er mountain top, or stream, or sky,
As round the castle's ruin'd tower,
We mus'd for many a solemn hour;
And, half-dejected, half in spleen,
Computed idly, o'er the scene,
How many murders there had dy'd
Chiefs and their minions, slaves of pride;

THE BANKS OF WYE.

When perjury, in every breath,   271
Pluck'd the huge falchion from its sheath,
And prompted deeds of ghastly fame,
That hist'ry's self might blush to name *.

At length, through each retreating shower,
Burst, with a renovating power,
Light, life, and gladness; instant fled
All contemplations on the dead.

Who hath not mark'd, with inward joy,
The efforts of the diving boy;
And, waiting while he disappear'd,
Exulted, trembled, hop'd, and fear'd?

---

* In Jones's History of Brecknockshire, the castle of Abergavenny is noticed as having been the scene of the most shocking enormities.

Then felt his heart, 'midst cheering cries, 283
Bound with delight to see him rise?
Who hath not burnt with rage, to see
Falshood's vile cant, and supple knee;
Then hail'd, on some courageous brow,
The power that works her overthrow;
That, swift as lightning, seals her doom,
With, " Miscreant vanish!—truth is come?"
So PEN-Y-VALE upheav'd his brow,
And left the world of fog below;
So SKYRID, smiling, broke his way
To glories of the conqu'ring day;
With matchless grace, and giant pride,
So BLORENGE turn'd the clouds aside,
And warn'd us, not a whit too soon,
To chase the flying car of noon,

Where herds and flocks unnumber'd fed, 299
Where Usk her wand'ring mazes led.

 Here on the mind, with powerful sway,
Press'd the bright joys of yesterday;
For still, though doom'd no more t' inhale
The mountain air of PEN-Y-VALE,
His broad dark-skirting woods o'erhung
Cottage and farm, where careless sung
The labourer, where the gazing steer
Low'd to the mountains, deep and clear.

 SLOW less'ning BLORENGE, left behind,
Reluctantly his claims resign'd,
And stretch'd his glowing front entire,
As forward peep'd CRICKHOWEL spire;

But no proud castle turrets gleam'd; 313
No warrior Earl's gay banner stream'd;
E'en of thy palace, grief to tell!
A tower without a dinner bell;
An arch where jav'lin'd centries bow'd
Low to their chief, or fed the croud,
Are all that mark where once a train
Of *barons* grac'd thy rich domain,
Illustrious PEMBROKE *! drain'd thy bowl,
And caught the nobleness of soul
The harp-inspir'd, indignant blood
That prompts to arms and hardihood.

---

* Part of the original palace of the powerful Earls of Pembroke is still undemolished by time.

To muse upon the days gone by, 325
Where desolation meets the eye,
Is double life; truth, cheaply bought,
The nurse of sense, the food of thought,
Whence judgment, ripen'd, forms, at will,
Her estimates of good or ill;
And brings contrasted scenes to view,
And weighs the *old* rogues with the *new;*
Imperious tyrants, gone to dust,
With tyrants whom the world hath curs'd
Through modern ages. By what power
Rose the strong walls of old Tre Tower?
Deep in the valley, whose clear rill
Then stole through wilds, and wanders still
Through village shades, unstain'd with gore,
Where war-steeds bathe their hoofs no more.

THE BANKS OF WYE.

Empires have fallen, armies bled, 341
Since yon old wall, with upright head,
Met the loud tempest; who can trace
When first the rude mass, from its base,
Stoop'd in that dreadful form? E'en thou,
JANE, with the placid silver brow,
Know'st not the day, though thou hast seen
An hundred * springs of cheerful green,
An hundred winters' snows increase
That brook, the emblem of thy peace.

---

* Jane Edwards, or as she pronounced it, *Etwarts*, a tall, bony, upright woman, leaning both hands on the head of her stick, and in her manners venerably impressive, was then at the age of one hundred. She was living in 1807, then one hundred and two.

Most venerable dame! and shall 351
The plund'rer, in his gorgeous hall,
His fame, with Moloch-frown prefer,
And scorn *thy* harmless character?
Who scarcely hear'st of his renown,
And never sack'd nor burnt a town;
But should he crave, with coward cries,
To be Jane Edwards when he dies,
Thou'lt be the conqueror, old lass,
So take thy alms, and let us pass.

Forth from the calm sequester'd shade,
Once more approaching twilight bade;
When, as the sigh of joy arose,
And while e'en fancy sought repose,

One vast transcendent object sprung,   365
Arresting every eye and tongue;
Strangers, fair BRECON, wondering, scan
The peaks of thy stupendous VANN:
But how can strangers, chain'd by time,
Through floating clouds his summit climb?
Another day had almost fled;
A clear horizon, glowing red,
Its promise on all hearts impress'd,
Bright sunny hours, and Sabbath rest.

END OF THE THIRD BOOK.

THE BANKS OF WYE.

BOOK IV.

CONTENTS OF BOOK IV.

The Gaer, a Roman Station.—Brunless Castle.—The Hay.—Funeral Song, "Mary's Grave."—Clifford Castle.—Return by Hereford, Malvern Hills, Cheltenham, and Gloucester, to Uley.—Conclusion.

THE BANKS OF WYE.

BOOK IV.

'Tis sweet to hear the soothing chime,
And, by thanksgiving, measure time;
When hard-wrought poverty awhile
Upheaves the bending back to smile;
When servants hail, with boundless glee,
The sweets of love and liberty;
For guiltless love will ne'er disown
The cheerful Sunday's market town,

Clean, silent, when his power's confess'd,   9
And trade's contention lull'd to rest.
   Seldom has worship cheer'd my soul
With such invincible controul!
It was a bright benignant hour,
The song of praise was full of power;
And, darting from the noon-day sky,
Amidst the tide of harmony,
O'er aisle and pillar glancing strong,
Heav'ns radiant light inspir'd the song.
The word of peace, that can disarm
Care with its own peculiar charm,
Here flow'd a double stream, to cheer
The Saxon * and the Mountaineer,

---

   * Divine service is performed alternately in English and

Of various stock, of various name,   23
Now join'd in rites, and join'd in fame.

   Ye who religion's duty teach,
What constitutes a Sabbath breach?
Is it, when joy the bosom fills,
To wander o'er the breezy hills?
Is it, to trace around your home
The footsteps of imperial Rome?
Then guilty, guilty let us plead,
Who, on the cheerful rested steed,

Welsh. That they still call us Saxons, need hardly be mentioned. I observed the army to be equally as accommodating as the church, for the posting-bills, for recruits, are printed in both languages.

In thought absorb'd, explor'd, with care, 33
The wild lanes round the silent GAER*,
Where conqu'ring eagles took their stand;
Where heathen altars stain'd the land;

---

* A road must have led from Abergavenny, through the Vale of the Usk, north-west to the " Gaer," situated two miles north-west of Brecon, on a gentle eminence, at the conflux of the rivers E-ker and Usk. Mr. Wyndham traced parts of walls, which he describes as exactly resembling those at Caerleon; and Mr. Lemon found several bricks, bearing the inscription of LEG. II. AVG.—*Coxe.*

In addition to the above, it may be acceptable to state, that Mr. Price, a very intelligent farmer on the spot, has in his possession several of the above kind of bricks, bearing the same inscription, done, evidently, by stamping the clay, while moist, with an instrument. These have been turned up by the plough, together with several small Roman lamps.

Where soldiers of Augustus pin'd, 37
Perhaps, for pleasures left behind,
And measur'd, from this lone abode,
The new-form'd, stoney, forest road,
Back to Caerleon's southern train,
Their barks, their home, beyond the main;
Still by the Vann reminded strong
Of Alpine scenes, and mountain song,
The olive groves, and cloudless sky,
And golden vales of Italy.

With us 'twas peace, we met no foes;
With us far diff'rent feelings rose.
Still onward inclination bade;
The wilds of Mona's Druid shade,
Snowdon's sublime and stormy brow,
His land of Britons stretch'd below,

THE BANKS OF WYE.

And Penman Mawr's huge crags, that greet   53
The thund'ring ocean at his feet,
Were all before us. Hard it prov'd,
To quit a land so dearly lov'd;
Forego each bold terrific boast
Of northern Cambria's giant coast.
Friends of the harp and song, forgive
The deep regret that, whilst I live,
Shall dwell upon my heart and tongue;
Go, joys untasted, themes unsung,
Another scene, another land,
Hence shall the homeward verse demand.
Yet fancy wove her flow'ry chain,
Till " farewell Brecon" left a pain;
A pain that travellers may endure,
Change is their food, and change their cure.

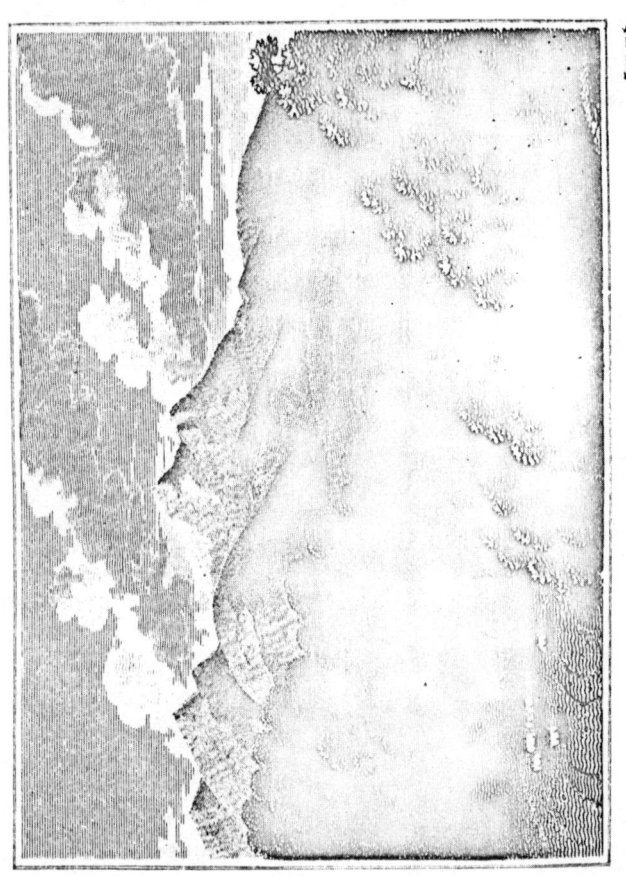

VAN MOUNTAIN, near BRECKNOCK from the PRIORY WOODS.

Yet, oh, how dream-like, far away, 69
To recollect so bright a day!
Dream-like those scenes the townsmen love,
Their tumbling Usk, their Priory Grove,
View'd while the moon cheer'd, calmly bright,
The freshness of a summer's night.

High o'er the town, in morning smiles,
The blue Vann heav'd his deep defiles;
And rang'd, like champions for the fight,
Basking in sun-beams on our right,
Rose the Black Mountains, that surround
That far-fam'd spot of holy ground,
Llanthony, dear to monkish tale,
And still the pride of Ewais Vale.
No road-side cottage smoke was seen,
Or rarely, on the village green

No youths appear'd, in spring-tide dress,   85
In ardent play, or idleness.
Brown wav'd the harvest, dale and slope
Exulting bore a nation's hope;
Sheaves rose as far as sight could range,
And every mile was but a change
Of peasants lab'ring, lab'ring still,
And climbing many a distant hill.
Some talk'd, perhaps, of spring's bright hour,
And how they pil'd, in BRUNLESS TOWER *,
The full-dried hay. Perhaps they told
Tradition's tales, and taught how old

---

* The only remaining tower of Brunless Castle now makes an excellent hay-loft; and almost every building on the spot is composed of fragments.

The ruin'd castle! False or true, 97
They guess it, just as others do.

  Lone tower! though suffer'd yet to stand,
Dilapidation's wasting hand
Shall tear thy pond'rous walls, to guard
The slumb'ring steed, or fence the yard;
Or wheels shall grind thy pride away
Along the turnpike road to HAY,
Where fierce GLENDOW'R's rude mountaineers
Left war's attendants, blood and tears,
And spread their terrors many a mile,
And shouted round the flaming pile.
May heav'n preserve our native land
From blind ambition's murdering hand;
From all the wrongs that can provoke
A people's wrath, and urge the stroke

That shakes the proudest throne! Guard, heav'n,
The sacred birth-right thou hast given;
Bid justice curb, with strong controul,
The desp'rate passions of the soul.

Here ivy'd fragments, lowering, throw
Broad shadows on the poor below,
Who, while they rest, and when they die,
Sleep on the rock-built shores of WYE.

To tread o'er nameless mounds of earth,
To muse upon departed worth,
To credit still the poor distress'd,
For feelings never half express'd,
Their hopes, their faith, their tender love,
Faith that sustain'd, and hope that strove,
Is sacred joy; to heave a sigh,
A debt to poor mortality.

Funereal rites are clos'd; 'tis done; 129
Ceas'd is the bell; the priest is gone;
What then if bust or stone denies
To catch the pensive loit'rer's eyes,
What course can poverty pursue?
What can the *poor* pretend to do?
O boast not, quarries, of your store;
Boast not, O man, of wealth or lore,
The flowers of nature here shall thrive,
Affection keep those flowers alive;
And they shall strike the melting heart,
Beyond the utmost power of art;
Planted on graves *, their stems entwine,
And every blossom is a line

---

* To the custom of scattering flowers over the graves of

Indelibly impress'd, that tends, 143
In more than language comprehends,
To teach us, in our solemn hours,
That we ourselves are dying flowers.

   What if a father buried here
His earthly hope, his friend most dear,

---

departed friends, David ap Gwillym beautifully alludes in one of his odes. " O whilst thy season of flowers, and thy tender sprays thick of leaves remain, I will pluck the roses from the brakes, the flowerets of the meads, and gems of the wood; the vivid trefoil, beauties of the ground, and the gaily-smiling bloom of the verdant herbs, to be offered to the memory of a chief of fairest fame. Humbly will I lay them on the grave of Ivor."

  On a grave in the church-yard at Hay, or the Hay, as it is commonly spoken, flowers had evidently been *planted*, but only one solitary sprig of sweet-briar had taken root.

His only child? Shall his dim eye, 149
At poverty's command, be dry?
No, he shall muse, and think, and pray,
And weep his tedious hours away;
Or weave the song of woe to tell,
How dear that child he lov'd so well.

Mary's Grave.

No child have I left, I must wander alone,
   No light-hearted Mary to sing as I go,
Nor loiter to gather bright flowers newly blown,
   She delighted, sweet maid, in these emblems of woe.

Then the stream glided by her, or playfully boil'd
   O'er its rock-bed unceasing, and still it goes free;
But her infant life was arrested, unsoil'd   161
   As the dew-drop when shook by the wing of the
      bee.

Sweet flowers were her treasures, and flowers shall
      be mine;
   I bring them from Radnor's green hills to her
      grave;
Thus planted in anguish, oh let them entwine
   O'er a heart once as gentle as heav'n e'er gave.
Oh, the glance of her eye, when at mansions of wealth
   I pointed, suspicious, and warn'd her of harm;
She smil'd in content, 'midst the bloom of her health,
   And closer and closer still hung on my arm.

What boots it to tell of the sense she possess'd, 171
   The fair buds of promise that mem'ry endears?
The mild dove, affection, was queen of her breast,
   And I had her love, and her truth, and her tears;
She was mine. But she goes to the land of the good,
   A change which I must, and yet dare not deplore;
I'll bear the rude shock like the oak of the wood,
   But the green hills of Radnor will charm me no more.

   Ruins of greatness, all farewell;
No Chepstows here, no Raglands tell,
By mound, or foss, or mighty tower,
Achievements high in hall or bower;

Or give to fancy's vivid eye, 183
The helms and plumes of chivalry.
CLIFFORD has fall'n, howe'er sublime,
Mere fragments wrestle still with time;
Yet as they perish, sure and slow,
And rolling dash the stream below,
They raise tradition's glowing scene,
The clue of silk, the wrathful queen,
And link, in mem'ry's firmest bond,
The love-lorn tale of Rosamond *.

How placid, how divinely sweet,
The flow'r-grown brook that, by our feet,

---

* Clifford Castle is supposed to have been the birth place of Fair Rosamond.

Winds on a summer's day; e'en where 195
Its name no classic honours share,
Its springs untrac'd, its course unknown,
Seaward for ever rambling down!
Here, then, how sweet, pelucid, chaste;
'Twas this bright current bade us taste
The fulness of its joy. Glide still,
Enchantress of PLYNLIMON HILL,
Meandering WYE! Still let me dream,
In raptures, o'er thy infant stream;
For could th' immortal soul forego
Its cumbrous load of earthly woe,
And clothe itself in fairy guise,
Too small, too pure, for human eyes,
Blithe would we seek thy utmost spring,
Where mountain-larks first try the wing;

There, at the crimson dawn of day,
Launch a scoop'd leaf, and sail away,
Stretch'd at our ease, or crouch below,
Or climb the green transparent prow,
Stooping where oft the blue bell sips
The passing stream, and shakes and dips;
And when the heifer came to drink,
Quick from the gale our bark would shrink,
And huddle down amidst the brawl
Of many a five-inch waterfall,
Till the expanse should fairly give
The bow'ring hazel room to live;
And as each swelling junction came,
To form a riv'let worth a name,
We'd dart beneath, or brush away
Long-beaded webs, that else might stay

THE BANKS OF WYE.

Our silent course; in haste retreat,   227
Where whirlpools near the bull-rush meet;
Wheel round the ox of monstrous size;
And count below his shadowy flies;
And sport amidst the throng; and when
We met the barks of giant men,
Avoid their oars, still undescried,
And mock their overbearing pride;
Then vanish by some magic spell,
And shout, " Delicious WYE, farewell!"

'TWAS noon, when o'er thy mountain stream,
The carriage roll'd, each pow'rful gleam
Struck on thy surface, where, below,
Spread the deep heaven's azure glow;

And water-flowers, a mingling croud,   241
Wav'd in the dazzling silver cloud.
Again farewell! The treat is o'er;
For me shall Cambria smile no more;
Yet truth shall still the song sustain,
And touch the springs of joy again.

   Hail! land of cyder, vales of health!
Redundant fruitage, rural wealth;
Here, did *Pomona* still retain,
Her influence o'er a British plain,
Might temples rise, spring blossoms fly,
Round the capricious deity;
Or autumn sacrifices bound,
By myriads, o'er the hallow'd ground,
And deep libations still renew
The fervours of her dancing crew.

Land of delight! let mem'ry strive
To keep thy flying scenes alive;
Thy grey-limb'd orchards, scattering wide
Their treasures by the highway side;
Thy half-hid cottages, that show
The dark green moss, the resting bough,
At broken panes, that taps and flies,
Illumes and shades the maiden's eyes
At day-break, and, with whisper'd joy,
Wakes the light-hearted shepherd boy:
These, with thy noble woods and dells,
The hazel copse, the village bells,
Charm'd more the passing sultry hours
Than HEREFORD, with all her towers.

 Sweet was the rest, with welcome cheer,
But a far nobler scene was near;

And when the morrow's noon had spread, 273
O'er orchard stores, the deep'ning red,
Behind us rose the billowy cloud,
That dims the air to city croud.

And deem not that, where cyder reigns
The beverage of a thousand plains,
Malt, and the liberal harvest horn,
Are all unknown, or laugh'd to scorn;
A spot that all delights might bring,
A palace for an eastern king,
CANFROME *, shall from her vaults display
John Barleycorn's resistless sway.

---

* The noble seat of —— Hopton, Esq. which exhibits, in a striking manner, the real old English magnificence and hospitality of the last age.

To make the odds of fortune even, 285
Up bounc'd the cork of "*seventy-seven,*"
And sent me back to school; for then,
Ere yet I learn'd to wield the pen;
The pen that should all crimes assail,
The pen that leads to fame—or jail;
Then steem'd the malt, whose spirit bears
The frosts and suns of thirty years!

 Through LEDBURY, at decline of day,
The wheels that bore us, roll'd away,
To cross the MALVERN HILLS. 'Twas night;
Alternate met the weary sight
Each steep, dark, undulating brow,
And WORC'STER's gloomy vale below:
Gloomy no more, when eastward sprung
The light that gladdens heart and tongue;

THE BANKS OF WYE.

When morn glanc'd o'er the shepherd's bed, 301
And cast her tints of lovely red
Wide o'er the vast expanding scene,
And mix'd her hues with mountain green;
Then, gazing from a height so fair,
Through miles of unpolluted air,
Where cultivation triumphs wide,
O'er boundless views on every side,
Thick planted towns, where toils ne'er cease,
And far-spread silent village peace,
As each succeeding pleasure came,
The heart acknowledg'd MALVERN's fame.

Oft glancing thence to Cambria still,
Thou yet wert seen, my fav'rite hill,
Delightful PEN-Y-VALE! Nor shall
Great MALVERN's high imperious call

Wean me from thee, or turn aside 317
My earliest charm, my heart's strong pride.
 Boast MALVERN, that thy springs revive
The drooping patient, scarce alive;
Where, as he gathers strength to toil,
Not e'en thy heights his spirit foil,
But nerve him on to bless, t' inhale,
And triumph in the morning gale;
Or noon's transcendent glories give
The vigorous touch that bids him live.
Perhaps e'en now he stops to breathe,
Surveying the expanse beneath?
Now climbs again, where keen winds blow,
And holds his beaver to his brow;
Waves to the *Wrecken* his white hand,
And, borrowing Fancy's magic wand,

Skims over WORC'STER's spires away, 333
Where sprung the blush of rising day;
And eyes, with joy, sweet *Hagley Groves*,
That taste reveres and virtue loves;
And stretch'd upon thy utmost ridge,
Marks Severn's course, and UPTON-bridge,
That leads to home, to friends, or wife,
And all thy sweets, domestic life;
He drops the tear, his bosom glows,
That consecrated *Avon* flows
Down the blue distant vale, to yield
Its stores by TEWKESBURY's deadly field,
And feels whatever can inspire,
From history's page or poet's fire.

 BRIGHT vale of Severn! shall the song
That wildly devious roves along,

The charms of nature to explore, 349
On history rest, or themes of yore?
More joy the thoughts of home supply,
Short be the glance at days gone by,
Though gallant TEWKESBURY, clean and gay,
Hath much to tempt the traveller's stay,
Her noble abbey, with its dead,
A powerful claim; a silent dread,
Sacred as holy virtue springs
Where rests the dust of chiefs and kings;
With his who by foul murder died,
The fierce Lancastrian's hope and pride,
When brothers brothers could destroy
Heroic Margaret's *red-rose* boy.*

* Prince Edward, son of Henry the Sixth, taken prisoner

THE BANKS OF WYE.

Muse, turn thee from the field of blood,   363
Rest to the brave, peace to the good;
Avon, with all thy charms, adieu!
For CHELTENHAM mocks thy pilgrim crew;
And like a girl in beauty's power,
Flirts in the fairings of an hour.

Queen of the valley! soon behind
Gleam'd thy bright fanes, in sun and wind,
Fair Glo'ster. Though thy fabric stands,
The boast of Severn's winding sands
If grandeur, beauty, grace, can stay
The traveller on his homeward way.

---

with his mother, Margaret of Anjou, at the battle of Tewkesbury, and murdered by the Duke of Gloucester, afterwards Richard the Third.

There rests the Norman prince who rose 375
In zeal against the christian's foes,
Yet doom'd at home to pine and die,
Of birthright rob'd, and liberty;
Foil'd was the lance he well could fling,
Robert *, who should have been a king;
His tide of wrongs he could not stem,
His brothers filch'd his diadem.
There sleeps the king who aim'd to spurn
The daring Scots, at Bannockburn,
But turn'd him back, with humbled fame,
And *Berkley's* " *shrieks* " † declare his name.

---

* The eldest son of William the Conqueror was imprisoned eight-and-twenty years by his own brother!
† " Shrieks of an agonizing king."

THE BANKS OF WYE.

Cease, cease the lay, the goal is won, 387
But silent memory revels on;
Fast clos'd the day, the last bright hour,
The setting sun, on DURSLEY tower,
Welcom'd us home, and forward bade,
To ULEY valley's peaceful shade.

WHO so unfeeling, who so bold,
To judge that fictions, idly told,
Deform the verse that only tries
To consecrate realities?
If e'er th' unworthy thought should come,
Let strong conviction strike them dumb.
Go to the proof; your steed prepare,
Drink nature's cup, the rapture share;

If dull you find your devious course, 401
Your tour is useless—sell your horse.
  Ye who, ingulph'd in trade, endure
What gold alone can never cure;
The constant sigh for scenes of peace,
From the world's trammels free release,
Wait not, for reason's sake attend,
Wait not in chains till times shall mend;
Till the clear voice, grown hoarse and gruff,
Cries, " Now I'll go, I'm rich enough;"
Youth, and the prime of manhood, seize,
Steal ten days absence, ten days ease;
Bid ledgers from your minds depart;
Let mem'ry's treasures cheer the heart;
And when your children round you grow,
With opening charms and manly brow,

THE BANKS OF WYE.

Talk of the Wye as some old dream,   417
Call it the wild, the wizard stream;
Sink in your broad arm-chair to rest,
And youth shall smile to see you bless'd.
  Artists, betimes your powers employ,
And take the pilgrimage of joy;
The eye of genius may behold
A thousand beauties here untold;
Rock, that defies the winter's storm;
Wood, in its most imposing form,
That climbs the mountain, bows below,
Where deep th' unsullied waters flow.
Here *Gilpin's* eye transported scan'd
Views by no tricks of fancy plan'd;
Gray here, upon the stream reclin'd,
Stor'd with delight his ardent mind.

THE BANKS OF WYE.

But let the vacant trifler stray 433
From thy enchantments far away;
For should, from fashion's rainbow train,
The idle and the vicious vain,
In sacrilege presume to move
Through these dear scenes of peace and love,
The *spirit of the stream* would rise
In wrathful mood, and tenfold size,
And nobly guard his COLDWELL SPRING,
And bid his inmost caverns ring;
Loud thund'ring on the giddy crew,
" My stream was never meant for you."
But ye, to nobler feelings born,
Who sense and nature dare not scorn,
Glide gaily on, and ye shall find
The blest serenity of mind

134 THE BANKS OF WYE.

That springs from silence; or shall raise 449
The hand, the eye, the voice of praise.
Live then, sweet stream! and henceforth be
The darling of posterity;
Lov'd for thyself, for ever dear,
Like beauty's smile and virtue's tear,
Till time his striding race give o'er,
And verse itself shall charm no more.

THE END.

BOOKS

PRINTED FOR VERNOR, HOOD, AND SHARPE,
31, POULTRY.

BLOOMFIELD'S FARMER'S BOY, RURAL TALES, and WILD FLOWERS.
Elegantly printed in Two Vols. post 18mo. with a Head of the Author, price 8s. boards.
BLOOMFIELD'S FARMER'S BOY, f. c. 4s. boards.
———————— RURAL TALES, f. c. 4s. boards.
———————— WILD FLOWERS, f. c. 4s. 6d. boards.

COTTON'S VISIONS IN VERSE, for the Amusement and Instruction of Younger Minds.
A new Edition, f. c. 12mo. with Six elegant Plates, price 3s.

THE FISHER BOY, a Poem: comprising his several Avocations during the Four Seasons of the Year.

Inest sua gratia parvis.

By H. C. Esq.

*Si je n'ai point d'autres charmes
J'ai au moins la Verité,——*

Foolscap 8vo. with Five Plates, from Bird's Designs, new Edition, price 6s. boards.

" This story is in the highest degree affecting, and is told with all the native simplicity of truth. The Author discovers traits of native genius, genuine benevolence, and sound principles of morality, with such a diffidence of his own powers, as usually accompanies real merit.

" The FISHER BOY, indeed, is one of the most pleasing, instructive, and at the same time, cheap Poems we have seen since the FARMER's BOY appeared."

Antijacobin Review, October.

BOOKS PRINTED FOR VERNOR, HOOD, AND SHARPE.

THE SAILOR BOY; a Poem, in Four Cantos; illustrative of the Navy of Great Britain. By H. C. Esq. Author of the Fisher Boy.

Foolscap 8vo. with an elegant Frontispiece, from a Design by Bird, price 5s. boards.

THE REMAINS OF HENRY KIRKE WHITE, late of St. John's College, Cambridge. With an Account of his Life, by ROBERT SOUTHEY.

A new Edition, in Two Vols. 8vo. with entire new Plates, price 16s. boards.

THE FABLES of JOHN GAY. In Two Parts; with Notes. By W. COXE, A. M. F. R. S. F. A. S. Rector of Bemerton. Fourth Edition.

In royal 18mo. a new Edition, with a new Set (52) of Wood Cuts, price 3s. 6d. bound.

N. B. Great Allowance to Schools.

THE SORROWS OF SEDUCTION, in Eight Delineations; with other Poems.

> Forbid, great God! that Vice, in Virtue's guise,
> Should e'er unguarded Innocence surprise;
> Despoil of every charm that decks her brow,
> And give her up to unavailing woe.

A new Edition, being the Third, with Plates, price 5s. boards.

THE SEASONS, ODES, HYMN, AND SONGS, of JAMES THOMSON. With his Life, and a Glossary.

Elegantly printed from Stereotype Plates, and embellished with elegant Wood Cuts, price 5s. boards.

Fine Paper, ornamented with Four highly finished Engravings, price 10s. 6d. boards.

Printed by T. Hood and Co. St. John's Square, London.

MAY DAY

WITH

THE MUSES.

BY

ROBERT BLOOMFIELD,

AUTHOR OF THE FARMER'S BOY,
RURAL TALES, &c.

LONDON:

PRINTED FOR THE AUTHOR; AND FOR BALDWIN,
CRADOCK, AND JOY.

1822.

PREFACE.

I AM of opinion that Prefaces are very useless things in cases like the present, where the Author must talk of himself, with little amusement to his readers. I have hesitated whether I should say any thing or nothing; but as it is the fashion to say something, I suppose I must comply. I am well aware that many readers will exclaim—" It is not the common practice of English baronets to remit half a year's rent to their tenants for poetry, or for any thing else." This may be very true; but I have found a character in the Rambler, No. 82, who made a very different bargain, and who says, " And as Alfred received the tri-
" bute of the Welsh in wolves' heads, I allowed
" my tenants to pay their rents in butterflies, till

"I had exhausted the papilionaceous tribe. I then directed them to the pursuit of other animals, and obtained, by this easy method, most of the grubs and insects which land, air, or water can supply. . . . . I have, from my own ground, the longest blade of grass upon record, and once accepted, as a half year's rent for a field of wheat, an ear, containing more grains than had been seen before upon a single stem."

I hope my old Sir Ambrose stands in no need of defence from me or from any one; a man has a right to do what he likes with his own estate. The characters I have introduced as candidates may not come off so easily; a cluster of poets is not likely to be found in one village, and the following lines, written by my good friend T. Park, Esq. of Hampstead, are not only true, but beautifully true, and I cannot omit them.

PREFACE.

WRITTEN IN THE ISLE OF THANET,
August, 1790.

The bard, who paints from rural plains,
    Must oft himself the void supply
Of damsels pure and artless swains,
    Of innocence and industry:

For sad experience shows the heart
    Of human beings much the same;
Or polish'd by insidious art,
    Or rude as from the clod it came.

And he who roams the village round,
    Or strays amid the harvest sere,
Will hear, as now, too many a sound
    Quiet would never wish to hear.

The wrangling rustics' loud abuse,
    The coarse, unfeeling, witless jest,
The threat obscene, the oath profuse,
    And all that cultured minds detest.

Hence let those Sylvan poets glean,
    Who picture life without a flaw;
Nature may form a perfect scene,
    But Fancy must the figures draw.

The word " fancy" connects itself with my very childhood, fifty years back. The fancy of those who wrote the songs which I was obliged to hear in infancy was a very inanimate and sleepy fancy. I could enumerate a dozen songs at least which all described sleeping shepherds and shepherdesses, and, in one instance, where they both went to sleep: this is not fair certainly; it is not even " watch and watch."

" As Damon and Phillis were keeping of sheep,
" Being free from all care they retired to sleep," &c.

I must say, that if I understand any thing at all about keeping sheep, this is not the way to go to work with them. But such characters and such writings were fashionable, and fashion will beat common sense at any time.

With all the beauty and spirit of Cunningham's " Kate of Aberdeen," and some others, I never found any thing to strike my mind so

PREFACE.

forcibly as the last stanza of Dibdin's " Sailor's Journal"—

" At length, 'twas in the month of May,
   " Our crew, it being lovely weather,
" At three A. M. discovered day
   " And England's chalky cliffs together!
" At seven, up channel how we bore,
   " Whilst hopes and fears rush'd o'er each fancy!
" At twelve, I gaily jump'd on shore,
   " And to my throbbing heart press'd Nancy."

This, to my feelings, is a balm at all times; it is spirit, animation, and imagery, all at once.

I will plead no excuses for any thing which the reader may find in this little volume, but merely state, that I once met with a lady in London, who, though otherwise of strong mind and good information, would maintain that " it is impossible for a blind man to fall in love." I always thought her wrong, and the present tale of " Alfred and Jennet" is written to elucidate my side of the question.

PREFACE.

I have been reported to be dead; but I can assure the reader that this, like many other reports, is not true. I have written these tales in anxiety, and in a wretched state of health; and if these formidable foes have not incapacitated me, but left me free to meet the public eye with any degree of credit, that degree of credit I am sure I shall gain.

I am, with remembrance of what is past,

Most respectfully,

ROBERT BLOOMFIELD.

Shefford, Bedfordshire,
April 10*th,* 1822.

MAY-DAY WITH THE MUSES.

THE INVITATION.

O for the strength to paint my joy once more!
That joy I feel when Winter's reign is o'er;
When the dark despot lifts his hoary brow,
And seeks his polar-realm's eternal snow.
Though black November's fogs oppress my brain,
Shake every nerve, and struggling fancy chain;
Though time creeps o'er me with his palsied hand,
And frost-like bids the stream of passion stand,

THE INVITATION.

And through his dry teeth sends a shivering blast,
And points to more than fifty winters past,
Why should I droop with heartless, aimless eye?
Friends start around, and all my phantoms fly,
And Hope, upsoaring with expanded wing,
Unfolds a scroll, inscribed " Remember Spring."
Stay, sweet enchantress, charmer of my days,
And glance thy rainbow colours o'er my lays;
Be to poor Giles what thou hast ever been,
His heart's warm solace and his sovereign queen;
Dance with his rustics when the laugh runs high,
Live in the lover's heart, the maiden's eye;
Still be propitious when his feet shall stray
Beneath the bursting hawthorn-buds of May;
Warm every thought, and brighten every hour,
And let him feel thy presence and thy power.

Sir Ambrose Higham, in his eightieth year,
With memory unimpair'd, and conscience clear,
His English heart untrammell'd, and full blown
His senatorial honours and renown,

THE INVITATION.

Now, basking in his plenitude of fame,
Resolved, in concert with his noble dame,
To drive to town no more—no more by night
To meet in crowded courts a blaze of light,
In streets a roaring mob with flags unfurl'd,
And all the senseless discord of the world,—
But calmly wait the hour of his decay,
The broad bright sunset of his glorious day;
And where he first drew breath at last to fall,
Beneath the towering shades of Oakly Hall*.

Quick spread the news through hamlet, field, and farm,
The labourer wiped his brow and staid his arm;
'Twas news to him of more importance far
Than change of empires or the yells of war;
It breathed a hope which nothing could destroy,
Poor widows rose, and clapp'd their hands for joy,
Glad voices rang at every cottage door,
" Good old Sir Ambrose goes to town no more."

* The seat of Sir Ambrose is situated in the author's imagination only; the reader must build Oakly Hall where he pleases.

THE INVITATION.

Well might the village bells the triumph sound,
Well might the voice of gladness ring around;
Where sickness raged, or want allied to shame,
Sure as the sun his well-timed succour came;
Food for the starving child, and warmth and wine
For age that totter'd in its last decline.
From him they shared the embers' social glow;
He fed the flame that glanced along the snow,
When winter drove his storms across the sky,
And pierced the bones of shrinking poverty.

Sir Ambrose loved the Muses, and would pay
Due honours even to the ploughman's lay;
Would cheer the feebler bard, and with the strong
Soar to the noblest energies of song;
Catch the rib-shaking laugh, or from his eye
Dash silently the tear of sympathy.
Happy old man!—with feelings such as these
The seasons all can charm, and trifles please;
And hence a sudden thought, a new-born whim,
Would shake his cup of pleasure to the brim,

THE INVITATION.

Turn scoffs and doubts and obstacles aside,
And instant action follow like a tide.

Time past, he had on his paternal ground
With pride the latent sparks of genius found
In many a local ballad, many a tale,
As wild and brief as cowslips in the dale,
Though unrecorded as the gleams of light
That vanish in the quietness of night.
" Why not," he cried, as from his couch he rose,
" To cheer my age, and sweeten my repose,
" Why not be just and generous in time,
" And bid my tenants pay their rents in rhyme?
" For one half year they shall.—A feast shall bring
" A crowd of merry faces in the spring;—
" Here, pens, boy, pens; I'll weigh the case no more,
" But write the summons:—go, go, shut the door.

" ' All ye on Oakly manor dwelling,
  ' Farming, labouring, buying, selling,

THE INVITATION.

' Neighbours! banish gloomy looks,
' My grey old steward shuts his books.
' Let not a thought of winter's rent
' Destroy one evening's merriment;
' I ask not gold, but tribute found
' Abundant on Parnassian ground.
' Choose, ye who boast the gift, your themes
' Of joy or pathos, tales or dreams,
' Choose each a theme;—but, harkye, bring
' No stupid ghost, no vulgar thing;
' Fairies, indeed, may wind their way,
' And sparkle through the brightest lay:
' I love their pranks, their favourite green,
' And, could the little sprites be seen,
' Were I a king, I'd sport with them,
' And dance beneath my diadem.
' But surely fancy need not brood
' O'er midnight darkness, crimes, and blood,
' In magic cave or monk's retreat,
' Whilst the bright world is at her feet;

THE INVITATION.

' Whilst to her boundless range is given,
' By night, by day, the lights of heaven,
' And all they shine upon; whilst Love
' Still reigns the monarch of the grove,
' And real life before her lies
' In all its thousand, thousand dies.
' Then bring me nature, bring me sense,
' And joy shall be your recompense:
' On Old May-day I hope to see
' All happy:—leave the rest to me.
' A general feast shall cheer us all
' Upon the lawn that fronts the hall,
' With tents for shelter, laurel boughs
' And wreaths of every flower that blows.
' The months are wending fast away;
' Farewell,—remember Old May-day.' "

Surprise, and mirth, and gratitude, and jeers,
The clown's broad wonder, th' enthusiast's tears,
Fresh gleams of comfort on the brow of care,
The sectary's cold shrug, the miser's stare,

Were all excited, for the tidings flew
As quick as scandal the whole country through.
" Rent paid by rhymes at Oakly may be great,
" But rhymes for taxes would appal the state,"
Exclaim'd th' exciseman, — " and then tithes, alas!
" Why there, again, 'twill never come to pass."—
Thus all still ventured, as the whim inclined,
Remarks as various as the varying mind:
For here Sir Ambrose sent a challenge forth,
That claim'd a tribute due to sterling worth;
And all, whatever might their host regale,
Agreed to share the feast and drink his ale.

Now shot through many a heart a secret fire,
A new born spirit, an intense desire
For once to catch a spark of local fame,
And bear a poet s honourable name!
Already some aloft began to soar,
And some to think who never thought before;

THE INVITATION.

But O, what numbers all their strength applied,
Then threw despairingly the task aside
With feign'd contempt, and vow'd they 'd never tried.
Did dairy-wife neglect to turn her cheese,
Or idling miller lose the favouring breeze;
Did the young ploughman o'er the furrows stand,
Or stalking sower swing an empty hand,
One common sentence on their heads would fall,
'Twas Oakly banquet had bewitch'd them all.
Loud roar'd the winds of March, with whirling snow,
One brightening hour an April breeze would blow;
Now hail, now hoar-frost bent the flow'ret's head,
Now struggling beams their languid influence shed,
That scarce a cowering bird yet dared to sing
'Midst the wild changes of our island spring.
Yet, shall the Italian goatherd boasting cry,
" Poor Albion! when hadst thou so clear a sky!"
And deem that nature smiles for him alone;
Her renovated beauties all his own?
No:—let our April showers by night descend,
Noon's genial warmth with twilight stillness blend;

THE INVITATION.

The broad Atlantic pour her pregnant breath,
And rouse the vegetable world from death;
Our island spring is rapture's self to me,
All I have seen, and all I wish to see.

Thus came the jovial day, no streaks of red
O'er the broad portal of the morn were spread,
But one high-sailing mist of dazzling white,
A screen of gossamer, a magic light,
Doom'd instantly, by simplest shepherd's ken,
To reign awhile, and be exhaled at ten.
O'er leaves, o'er blossoms, by his power restored,
Forth came the conquering sun and look'd abroad;
Millions of dew-drops fell, yet millions hung,
Like words of transport trembling on the tongue
Too strong for utt'rance:—Thus the infant boy,
With rosebud cheeks, and features tuned to joy,
Weeps while he struggles with restraint or pain,
But change the scene, and make him laugh again,
His heart rekindles, and his cheek appears
A thousand times more lovely through his tears.

THE INVITATION.

From the first glimpse of day a busy scene
Was that high swelling lawn, that destined green,
Which shadowless expanded far and wide,
The mansion's ornament, the hamlet's pride;
To cheer, to order, to direct, contrive,
Even old Sir Ambrose had been up at five;
There his whole household labour'd in his view,—
But light is labour where the task is new.
Some wheel'd the turf to build a grassy throne
Round a huge thorn that spread his boughs alone,
Rough-rined and bold, as master of the place;
Five generations of the Higham race
Had pluck'd his flowers, and still he held his sway,
Waved his white head, and felt the breath of May.
Some from the green-house ranged exotics round,
To bask in open day on English ground:
And 'midst them in a line of splendour drew
Long wreaths and garlands, gather'd in the dew.
Some spread the snowy canvas, propp'd on high
O'er shelter'd tables with their whole supply;

14 THE INVITATION.

Some swung the biting scythe with merry face,
And cropp'd the daisies for a dancing space.
Some roll'd the mouldy barrel in his might,
From prison'd darkness into cheerful light,
And fenced him round with cans; and others bore
The creaking hamper with its costly store,
Well cork'd, well flavour'd, and well tax'd, that came
From Lusitanian mountains, dear to fame,
Whence GAMA steer'd, and led the conquering way
To eastern triumphs and the realms of day.
A thousand minor tasks fill'd every hour,
'Till the sun gain'd the zenith of his power,
When every path was throng'd with old and young,
And many a sky-lark in his strength upsprung
To bid them welcome.—Not a face was there
But for May-day at least had banish'd care;
No cringing looks, no pauper tales to tell,
No timid glance, they knew their host too well,—
Freedom was there, and joy in every eye:
Such scenes were England's boast in days gone by.

THE INVITATION.

Beneath the thorn was good Sir Ambrose found,
His guests an ample crescent form'd around;
Nature's own carpet spread the space between,
Where blithe domestics plied in gold and green.
The venerable chaplain waved his wand,
And silence follow'd as he stretch'd his hand,
And with a trembling voice, and heart sincere,
Implored a blessing on th' abundant cheer.
Down sat the mingling throng, and shared a feast
With hearty welcomes given, by love increased;
A patriarch family, a close-link'd band,
True to their rural chieftain, heart and hand:
The deep carouse can never boast the bliss,
The animation of a scene like this.

At length the damask cloths were whisk'd away,
Like fluttering sails upon a summer's day;
The hey-day of enjoyment found repose;
The worthy baronet majestic rose;
They view'd him, while his ale was filling round,
The monarch of his own paternal ground.

THE INVITATION.

His cup was full, and where the blossoms bow'd
Over his head, Sir Ambrose spoke aloud,
Nor stopp'd a dainty form or phrase to cull—
His heart elated, like his cup, was full:—
" Full be your hopes, and rich the crops that fall;
" Health to my neighbours, happiness to all."
Dull must that clown be, dull as winter's sleet,
Who would not instantly be on his feet:
An echoing health to mingling shouts gave place,
" Sir Ambrose Higham, and his noble race."

Avaunt, Formality! thou bloodless dame,
With dripping besom quenching nature's flame;
Thou cankerworm, who liv'st but to destroy,
And eat the very heart of social joy;—
Thou freezing mist round intellectual mirth,
Thou spell-bound vagabond of spurious birth,
Away! away! and let the sun shine clear,
And all the kindnesses of life appear.

With mild complacency, and smiling brow,
The host look'd round, and bade the goblets flow;

THE INVITATION.

Yet curiously anxious to behold
Who first would pay in rhymes instead of gold;
Each eye inquiring through the ring was glanced
To see who dared the task, who first advanced;
That instant started Philip from the throng,
Philip, a farmer's son, well known for song,—
And, as the mingling whispers round him ran,
He humbly bow'd, and timidly began:—

THE DRUNKEN FATHER.

THE DRUNKEN FATHER.

Poor Ellen married Andrew Hall,
    Who dwells beside the moor,
Where yonder rose-tree shades the wall,
    And woodbines grace the door.

Who does not know how blest, how loved
    Were her mild laughing eyes
By every youth!—but Andrew proved
    Unworthy of his prize.

THE DRUNKEN FATHER.

In tippling was his whole delight,
    Each sign-post barr'd his way;
He spent in muddy ale at night
    The wages of the day.

Though Ellen still had charms, was young,
    And he in manhood's prime,
She sad beside her cradle sung,
    And sigh'd away her time.

One cold bleak night, the stars were hid,
    In vain she wish'd him home;
Her children cried, half cheer'd, half chid,
    " O when will father come!"

'Till Caleb, nine years old, upsprung,
    And kick'd his stool aside,
And younger Mary round him clung,
    " I'll go, and you shall guide."

THE DRUNKEN FATHER.

The children knew each inch of ground,
    Yet Ellen had her fears;
Light from the lantern glimmer'd round,
    And show'd her falling tears.

" Go by the mill and down the lane;
    " Return the same way home:
" Perhaps you'll meet him, give him light;
    " O how I *wish* he'd come."

Away they went, as close and true
    As lovers in the shade,
And Caleb swung his father's staff
    At every step he made.

The noisy mill-clack rattled on,
    They saw the water flow,
And leap in silvery foam along,
    Deep murmuring below.

24 THE DRUNKEN FATHER.

" We 'll soon be there," the hero said,
  " Come on, 'tis but a mile,—
" Here 's where the cricket-match was play'd,
  " And here 's the shady stile.

" How the light shines up every bough!
  " How strange the leaves appear!
" Hark!—What was that?—'tis silent now,
  " Come, Mary, never fear."

The staring oxen breathed aloud,
  But never dream'd of harm;
A meteor glanced along the cloud
  That hung o'er Wood-Hill Farm.

Old Cæsar bark'd and howl'd hard by,
  All else was still as death,
But Caleb was ashamed to cry,
  And Mary held her breath.

THE DRUNKEN FATHER.

At length they spied a distant light,
    And heard a chorus brawl;
Wherever drunkards stopp'd at night,
    Why there was Andrew Hall.

The house was full, the landlord gay,
    The bar-maid shook her head,
And wish'd the boobies far away
    That kept her out of bed.

There Caleb enter'd, firm, but mild,
    And spoke in plaintive tone:—
" My mother could not leave the child,
    " So we are come alone."

E'en drunken Andrew felt the blow
    That innocence can give,
When its resistless accents flow
    To bid affection live.

26 THE DRUNKEN FATHER.

"I'm coming, loves, I'm coming now,"—
   Then, shuffling o'er the floor,
Contrived to make his balance true,
   And led them from the door.

The plain broad path that brought him there
   By day, though faultless then,
Was up and down and narrow grown,
   Though wide enough for ten.

The stiles were wretchedly contrived,
   The stars were all at play,
And many a ditch had moved itself
   Exactly in his way.

But still conceit was uppermost,
   That stupid kind of pride:—
" Dost think I cannot see a post?
" Dost think I want a guide?

THE DRUNKEN FATHER.

" Why, Mary, how you twist and twirl!
　" Why dost not keep the track?
" I 'll carry thee home safe, my girl,"—
　Then swung her on his back.

Poor Caleb muster'd all his wits
　To bear the light ahead,
As Andrew reel'd and stopp'd by fits,
　Or ran with thund'ring tread.

Exult, ye brutes, traduced and scorn'd,
　Though true to nature's plan;
Exult, ye bristled, and ye horn'd,
　When infants govern man.

Down to the mill-pool's dangerous brink
　The headlong party drove;
The boy alone had power to think,
　While Mary scream'd above.

THE DRUNKEN FATHER.

"Stop!" Caleb cried, "you've lost the path;
 "The water's close before;
"I see it shine, 'tis very deep,—
 "Why, don't you hear it roar?"

And then in agony exclaim'd,
 "O where's my mother *now*?"
The Solomon of hops and malt
 Stopp'd short and made a bow:

His head was loose, his neck disjointed,
 It cost him little trouble;
But, to be stopp'd and disappointed,
 Poh! danger was a bubble.

Onward he stepp'd, the boy alert,
 Calling his courage forth,
Hung like a log on Andrew's skirt,
 And down he brought them both.

THE DRUNKEN FATHER.

The tumb'ling lantern reach'd the stream,
    Its hissing light soon gone;
'Twas night, without a single gleam,
    And terror reign'd alone.

A general scream the miller heard,
    Then rubb'd his eyes and ran,
And soon his welcome light appear'd,
    As grumbling he began:—

" What have we here, and whereabouts?
    " Why what a hideous squall!
" Some drunken fool! I thought as much—
    " 'Tis only Andrew Hall!

" Poor children!" tenderly he said,
    " But now the danger's past."
They thank'd him for his light and aid,
    And drew near home at last.

THE DRUNKEN FATHER.

But who upon the misty path
    To meet them forward press'd?
'Twas Ellen, shivering, with a babe
    Close folded to her breast.

Said Andrew, " Now you're glad, I know,
    " To se-se-see us come;—
" But I have taken care of both,
    " And brought them bo-bo-both safe home."

With Andrew vex'd, of Mary proud,
    But prouder of her boy,
She kiss'd them both, and sobb'd aloud,—
    The children cried for joy.

But what a home at last they found!
    Of comforts all bereft;
The fire out, the last candle gone,
    And not one penny left!

THE DRUNKEN FATHER.

But Caleb quick as light'ning flew,
    And raised a light instead;
And as the kindling brands he blew,
    His father snored in bed.

No brawling, boxing termagant
    Was Ellen, though offended;
Who ever knew a fault like this
    By violence amended?

No:—she was mild as April morn,
    And Andrew loved her too;
She rose at daybreak, though forlorn,
    To try what love could do.

And as her waking husband groan'd,
    And roll'd his burning head,
She spoke with all the power of truth,
    Down kneeling by his bed.

THE DRUNKEN FATHER.

" Dear Andrew, hear me,—though distress'd
 " Almost too much to speak,—
" This infant starves upon my breast—
 " To scold I am too weak.

" I work, I spin, I toil all day,
 " Then leave my work to cry,
" And start with horror when I think
 " You wish to see me die.

" But *do* you wish it? can that bring
 " More comfort, or more joy?
" Look round the house, how destitute!
 " Look at your ragged boy!

" That boy should make a father proud,
 " If any feeling can;
" Then save your children, save your wife,
 " Your honour as a man.

THE DRUNKEN FATHER.

" Hear me, for God's sake hear me now,
    " And act a father's part!"
The culprit bless'd her angel tongue,
    And clasp'd her to his heart;

And would have vow'd, and would have sworn,
    But Ellen kiss'd him dumb,—
" Exert your mind, vow to *yourself,*
    " And better days will come.

" I shall be well when you are kind,
    " And you'll be better too."—
" I'll drink no more,"—he quick rejoin'd,—
    " Be't poison if I do."

From that bright day his plants, his flowers,
    His crops began to thrive,
And for three years has Andrew been
    The soberest man alive.

34

Soon as he ended, acclamations 'rose,
Endang'ring modesty and self-repose,
Till the good host his prudent counsel gave,
Then listen'd all, the flippant and the grave.
" Let not applauses vanity inspire,
" Deter humility, or damp desire;
" Neighbours we are, then let the stream run fair,
" And every couplet be as free as air;
" Be silent when each speaker claims his right,
" Enjoy the day as I enjoy the sight:
" They shall not class us with the knavish elves,
" Who banish shame, and criticise themselves."

Thenceforward converse flow'd with perfect ease,
Midst country wit, and rustic repartees.
One drank to Ellen, if such might be found,
And archly glanced at female faces round.
If one with tilted can began to bawl,
Another cried, " Remember Andrew Hall."

35

Then, multifarious topics, corn and hay,
Vestry intrigues, the rates they had to pay,
The thriving stock, the lands too wet, too dry,
And all that bears on fruitful husbandry,
Ran mingling through the crowd — a crowd that might,
Transferr'd to canvas, give the world delight;
A scene that WILKIE might have touch'd with pride—
The May-day banquet then had never died.

But who is he, uprisen, with eye so keen,
In garb of shining plush of grassy green—
Dogs climbing round him, eager for the start,
With ceaseless tail, and doubly beating heart?
A stranger, who from distant forests came,
The sturdy keeper of the Oakly game.
Short prelude made, he pointed o'er the hill,
And raised a voice that every ear might fill;
His heart was in his theme, and in the forest still.

THE FORESTER.

THE FORESTER.

Born in a dark wood's lonely dell,
    Where echoes roar'd, and tendrils curl'd
Round a low cot, like hermit's cell,
    Old Salcey Forest was my world.
I felt no bonds, no shackles then,
    For life in freedom was begun;
I gloried in th' exploits of men,
    And learn'd to lift my father's gun.

THE FORESTER.

O what a joy it gave my heart!
   Wild as a woodbine up I grew;
Soon in his feats I bore a part,
   And counted all the game he slew.
I learn'd the wiles, the shifts, the calls,
   The language of each living thing;
I mark'd the hawk that darting falls,
   Or station'd spreads the trembling wing.

I mark'd the owl that silent flits,
   The hare that feeds at eventide,
The upright rabbit, when he sits
   And mocks you, ere he deigns to hide.
I heard the fox bark through the night,
   I saw the rooks depart at morn,
I saw the wild deer dancing light,
   And heard the hunter's cheering horn.

Mad with delight, I roam'd around
   From morn to eve throughout the year,

THE FORESTER.

But still, midst all I sought or found,
   My favourites were the spotted deer.
The elegant, the branching brow,
   The doe's clean limbs and eyes of love;
The fawn as white as mountain snow,
   That glanced through fern and brier and grove.

One dark, autumnal, stormy day,
   The gale was up in all its might,
The roaring forest felt its sway,
   And clouds were scudding quick as light:
A ruthless crash, a hollow groan,
   Aroused each self-preserving start,
The kine in herds, the hare alone,
   And shagged colts that grazed apart.

Midst fears instinctive, wonder drew
   The boldest forward, gathering strength
As darkness lour'd, and whirlwinds blew,
   To where the ruin stretch'd his length.

THE FORESTER.

The shadowing oak, the noblest stem
    That graced the forest's ample bound,
Had cast to earth his diadem;
    His fractured limbs had delved the ground.

He lay, and still to fancy groan'd;
    He lay like Alfred when he died—
Alfred, a king by Heaven enthroned,
    His age's wonder, England's pride!
Monarch of forests, great as good,
    Wise as the sage,—thou heart of steel!
Thy name shall rouse the patriot's blood
    As long as England's sons can feel.

From every lawn, and copse, and glade,
    The timid deer in squadrons came,
And circled round their fallen shade
    With all of language but its name.
Astonishment and dread withheld
    The fawn and doe of tender years,

THE FORESTER.

But soon a triple circle swell'd,
    With rattling horns and twinkling ears.

Some in his root's deep cavern housed,
    And seem'd to learn, and muse, and teach,
Or on his topmost foliage browsed,
    That had for centuries mock'd their reach.
Winds in their wrath these limbs could crash,
    This strength, this symmetry could mar;
A people's wrath can monarchs dash
    From bigot throne or purple car.

When Fate's dread bolt in Clermont's bowers
    Provoked its million tears and sighs,
A nation wept its fallen flowers,
    Its blighted hopes, its darling prize.—
So mourn'd my antler'd friends awhile,
    So dark, so dread, the fateful day;
So mourn'd the herd that knew no guile,
    Then turn'd disconsolate away!

44 THE FORESTER.

Who then of language will be proud?
 Who arrogate that gift of heaven?
To wild herds when they bellow loud,
 To all the forest-tribes 'tis given.
I've heard a note from dale or hill
 That lifted every head and eye;
I've heard a scream aloft, so shrill
 That terror seized on all that fly.

Empires may fall, and nations groan,
 Pride be thrown down, and power decay;
Dark bigotry may rear her throne,
 But science is the light of day.
Yet, while so low my lot is cast,
 Through wilds and forests let me range;
My joys shall pomp and power outlast—
 The voice of nature cannot change.

45

A soberer feeling through the crowd he flung,
Clermont was uppermost on every tongue;
But who can live on unavailing sighs?
The inconsolable are not the wise.
Spirit, and youth, and worth, demand a tear—
That day was past, and sorrow was not here;
Sorrow the contest dared not but refuse
'Gainst Oakly's open cellar and the muse.

Sir Ambrose cast his eye along the line,
Where many a cheerful face began to shine,
And, fixing on his man, cried, loud and clear,
" What have you brought, John Armstrong? let us hear."
Forth stepp'd his shepherd;—scanty locks of grey
Edged round a hat that seem'd to mock decay;
Its loops, its bands, were from the purest fleece,
Spun on the hills in silence and in peace.
A staff he bore carved round with birds and flowers,
The hieroglyphics of his leisure hours;

46

And rough form'd animals of various name,
Not just like BEWICK'S, but they meant the same.
Nor these alone his whole attention drew,
He was a poet,—this Sir Ambrose knew,—
A strange one too;—and now had penn'd a lay,
Harmless and wild, and fitting for the day.
No tragic tale on stilts;—his mind had more
Of boundless frolic than of serious lore;—
Down went his hat, his shaggy friend close by
Dozed on the grass, yet watch'd his master's eye.

THE SHEPHERD'S DREAM:
OR, FAIRIES' MASQUERADE.

THE SHEPHERD'S DREAM:
OR, FAIRIES' MASQUERADE.

I HAD folded my flock, and my heart was o'erflowing,
I loiter'd beside the small lake on the heath;
The red sun, though down, left his drapery glowing,
And no sound was stirring, I heard not a breath:
I sat on the turf, but I meant not to sleep,
And gazed o'er that lake which for ever is new,
Where clouds over clouds appear'd anxious to peep
From this bright double sky with its pearl and its blue.

D

50 THE SHEPHERD'S DREAM:

Forgetfulness, rather than slumber, it seem'd,
When in infinite thousands the fairies arose
All over the heath, and their tiny crests gleam'd
In mock'ry of soldiers, our friends and our foes.
There a stripling went forth, half a finger's length
    high,
And led a huge host to the north with a dash;
Silver birds upon poles went before their wild cry,
While the monarch look'd forward, adjusting his
    sash.

Soon after a terrible bonfire was seen,
The dwellings of fairies went down in their ire,
But from all I remember, I never could glean
Why the woodstack was burnt, or who set it on fire.
The flames seem'd to rise o'er a deluge of snow,
That buried its thousands,—the rest ran away;
For the hero had here overstrain'd his long bow,
Yet he honestly own'd the mishap of the day.

Then the fays of the north like a hailstorm came on,
And follow'd him down to the lake in a riot,
Where they found a large stone which they fix'd him upon,
And threaten'd, and coax'd him, and bade him be quiet.
He that conquer'd them all, was to conquer no more,
But the million beheld he could conquer alone;
After resting awhile, he leap'd boldly on shore,
When away ran a fay that had mounted his throne.

'Twas pleasant to see how they stared, how they scamper'd,
By furze-bush, by fern, by no obstacle stay'd,
And the few that held council, were terribly hamper'd,
For some were vindictive, and some were afraid.
I saw they were dress'd for a masquerade train,
Colour'd rags upon sticks they all brandish'd in view,
And of such idle things they seem'd mightily vain,
Though they nothing display'd but a bird split in two.

52 THE SHEPHERD'S DREAM:

Then out rush'd the stripling in battle array,
And both sides determined to fight and to maul:
Death rattled his jawbones to see such a fray,
And glory personified laugh'd at them all.
Here he fail'd,—hence he fled, with a few for his sake,
And leap'd into a cockle-shell floating hard by;
It sail'd to an isle in the midst of the lake,
Where they mock'd fallen greatness, and left him to
    die.

Meanwhile the north fairies stood round in a ring,
Supporting his rival on guns and on spears,
Who, though not a soldier, was robed like a king;
Yet some were exulting, and some were in tears.
A lily triumphantly floated above,
The crowd press'd, and wrangling was heard through
    the whole;
Some soldiers look'd surly, some citizens strove
To hoist the old nightcap on liberty's pole.

But methought in my dream some bewail'd him that fell,
And liked not his victors so gallant, so clever,
Till a fairy stepp'd forward, and blew through a shell,
" Bear misfortune with firmness, you'll triumph for
    ever."
I woke at the sound, all in silence, alone,
The moor-hens were floating like specks on a glass,
The dun clouds were spreading, the vision was gone,
And my dog scamper'd round 'midst the dew on the
    grass.

I took up my staff, as a knight would his lance,
And said, " Here's my sceptre, my baton, my spear,
" And there's my prime minister far in advance,
" Who serves me with truth for his food by the year."
So I slept without care till the dawning of day,
Then trimm'd up my woodbines and whistled amain;
My minister heard as he bounded away,
And we led forth our sheep to their pastures again.

54

Scorch'd by the shadeless sun on Indian plains,
Mellow'd by age, by wants, and toils, and pains,
Those toils still lengthen'd when he reach'd that shore
Where Spain's bright mountains heard the cannons roar,
A pension'd veteran, doom'd no more to roam,
With glowing heart thus sung the joys of home.

THE SOLDIER'S HOME.

THE SOLDIER'S HOME.

My untried muse shall no high tone assume,
Nor strut in arms;—farewell my cap and plume:
Brief be my verse, a task within my power,
I tell my feelings in one happy hour;
But what an hour was that! when from the main
I reach'd this lovely valley once again!
A glorious harvest fill'd my eager sight,
Half shock'd, half waving in a flood of light;

58   THE SOLDIER'S HOME.

On that poor cottage roof where I was born
The sun look'd down as in life's early morn.
I gazed around, but not a soul appear'd,
I listen'd on the threshold, nothing heard;
I call'd my father thrice, but no one came;
It was not fear or grief that shook my frame,
But an o'erpowering sense of peace and home,
Of toils gone by, perhaps of joys to come.
The door invitingly stood open wide,
I shook my dust, and set my staff aside.
How sweet it was to breathe that cooler air,
And take possession of my father's chair!
Beneath my elbow, on the solid frame,
Appear'd the rough initials of my name,
Cut forty years before!—the same old clock
Struck the same bell, and gave my heart a shock
I never can forget. A short breeze sprung,
And while a sigh was trembling on my tongue,
Caught the old dangling almanacks behind,
And up they flew, like banners in the wind;

THE SOLDIER'S HOME.

Then gently, singly, down, down, down, they went,
And told of twenty years that I had spent
Far from my native land:—that instant came
A robin on the threshold; though so tame,
At first he look'd distrustful, almost shy,
And cast on me his coal-black stedfast eye,
And seem'd to say (past friendship to renew)
" Ah ha! old worn-out soldier, is it you?"
Through the room ranged the imprison'd humble bee,
And bomb'd, and bounced, and struggled to be free,
Dashing against the panes with sullen roar,
That threw their diamond sunlight on the floor;
That floor, clean sanded, where my fancy stray'd
O'er undulating waves the broom had made,
Reminding me of those of hideous forms
That met us as we pass'd the *Cape of Storms,*
Where high and loud they break, and peace comes
  never;
They roll and foam, and roll and foam for ever.
But *here* was peace, that peace which home can yield;
The grasshopper, the partridge in the field,

THE SOLDIER'S HOME.

And ticking clock, were all at once become
The substitutes for clarion, fife, and drum.
While thus I mused, still gazing, gazing still
On beds of moss that spread the window sill,
I deem'd no moss my eyes had ever seen
Had been so lovely, brilliant, fresh, and green,
And guess'd some infant hand had placed it there,
And prized its hue, so exquisite, so rare.
Feelings on feelings mingling, doubling rose,
My heart felt every thing but calm repose;
I could not reckon minutes, hours, nor years,
But rose at once, and bursted into tears;
Then, like a fool, confused, sat down again,
And thought upon the past with shame and pain;
I raved at war and all its horrid cost,
And glory's quagmire, where the brave are lost.
On carnage, fire, and plunder, long I mused,
And cursed the murdering weapons I had used.

Two shadows then I saw, two voices heard,
One bespoke age, and one a child's appear'd.—

THE SOLDIER'S HOME.

In stepp'd my father with convulsive start,
And in an instant clasp'd me to his heart.
Close by him stood a little blue-eyed maid,
And, stooping to the child, the old man said,
" Come hither, Nancy, kiss me once again,
" This is your uncle Charles, come home from Spain."
The child approach'd, and with her fingers light,
Stroked my old eyes, almost deprived of sight.—
But why thus spin my tale, thus tedious be?
Happy old Soldier! what's the world to me?

Change is essential to the youthful heart,
It cannot bound, it cannot act its part
To one monotonous delight a slave;
E'en the proud poet's lines become its grave:
By innate buoyancy, by passion led,
It acts instinctively, it will be fed.

62

A troop of country lasses paced the green,
Tired of their seats, and anxious to be seen;
They pass'd Sir Ambrose, turn'd, and pass'd again,
Some lightly tripp'd, to make their meaning plain:
The old man knew it well, the thoughts of youth
Came o'er his mind like consciousness of truth,
Or like a sunbeam through a lowering sky,
It gave him youth again, and ecstacy;
He joy'd to see them in this favourite spot,
Who of fourscore, or fifty score, would not?
He wink'd, he nodded, and then raised his hand,—
'Twas seen and answer'd by the Oakly band.
Forth leap'd the light of heart and light of heel,
E'en stiff limb'd age the kindling joy could feel.
They form'd, while yet the music started light;
The grass beneath their feet was short and bright,
Where thirty couple danced with all their might.
The Forester caught lasses one by one,
And twirl'd his glossy green against the sun;
The Shepherd threw his doublet on the ground,
And clapp'd his hands, and many a partner found:

63

His hat-loops bursted in the jocund fray,
And floated o'er his head like blooming May.
Behind his heels his dog was barking loud,
And threading all the mazes of the crowd;
And had he boasted one had wagg'd his tail,
And plainly said, " What can my master ail?"
To which the Shepherd, had he been more cool,
Had only said, " 'Tis Oakly feast, you fool."

But where was Philip, he who danced so well?
Had he retired, had pleasure broke her spell?
No, he had yielded to a tend'rer bond,
He sat beside his own sick Rosamond,
Whose illness long deferr'd their wedding hour;
She wept, and seem'd a lily in a shower;
She wept to see him 'midst a crowd so gay,
For her sake lose the honours of the day.
But could a gentle youth be so unkind?
Would Philip dance, and leave his girl behind?
She in her bosom hid a written prize,
Inestimably rich in Philip's eyes;

64

The warm effusion of a heart that glow'd
With joy, with love, and hope by Heaven bestow'd.
He woo'd, he soothed, and every art assay'd,
To hush the scruples of the bashful maid,
Drawing, at length, against her weak command,
Reluctantly the treasure from her hand:
And would have read, but passion chain'd his tongue,
He turn'd aside, and down the ballad flung;
And paused so long from feeling and from shame,
That old Sir Ambrose halloo'd him by name:
" Bring it to me, my lad, and never fear,
" I never blamed true love, or scorn'd a tear;
" They well become us, e'en where branded most."
He came, and made a proxy of his host,
Who, as the dancers cooling join'd the throng,
Eyed the fair writer as he read her song.

ROSAMOND'S SONG OF HOPE.

ROSAMOND'S SONG OF HOPE.

Sweet Hope, so oft my childhood's friend,
    I will believe thee still,
For thou canst joy with sorrow blend,
    Where grief alone would kill.

When disappointments wrung my heart,
    Ill brook'd in tender years,
Thou, like a sun, perform'dst thy part,
    And dried my infant tears.

When late I wore the bloom of health,
    And love had bound me fast,
My buoyant heart would sigh by stealth
    For fear it might not last.

68   ROSOMOND'S SONG OF HOPE.

My sickness came, my bloom decay'd,
  But Philip still was by;
And thou, sweet Hope, so kindly said,
  " He'll weep if thou should'st die."

Thou told'st me too, that genial Spring
  Would bring me health again;
I feel its power, but cannot sing
  Its glories yet for pain.

But thou canst still my heart inspire,
  And Heaven can strength renew;
I feel thy presence, holy fire!
  My Philip will be true.

69

All eyes were turn'd, all hearts with pity glow'd,
The maid stood trembling, and the lover bow'd
As rose around them, while she dried her tears,
" Long life to Rosamond, and happy years!"

Scarce had the voices ceased, when forth there came
Another candidate for village fame:
By gratitude to Heaven, by honest pride,
Impell'd to rise and cast his doubts aside,
A sturdy yeoman, button'd to the throat,
Faced the whole ring, and shook his leathern coat.
" I have a tale of private life to tell,
" 'Tis all of self and home, I know it well;
" In love and honour's cause I would be strong,
" Mine is a father's tale, perhaps too long,
" For fathers, when a duteous child's the theme,
" Can talk a summer's sun down, and then dream
" Of retrospective joys with hearts that glow
" With feelings such as parents only know."

ALFRED AND JENNET.

ALFRED AND JENNET.

Yes, let me tell of Jennet, my last child;
In her the charms of all the rest ran wild,
And sprouted as they pleased. Still by my side,
I own she was my favourite, was my pride,
Since first she labour'd round my neck to twine,
Or clasp'd both little hands in one of mine:
And when the season broke, I've seen her bring
Lapfuls of flowers, and then the girl would sing

74 ALFRED AND JENNET.

Whole songs, and halves, and bits, O, with such glee!
If playmates found a favourite, it was she.
Her lively spirit lifted her to joy;
To distance in the race a clumsy boy
Would raise the flush of conquest in her eye,
And all was dance, and laugh, and liberty.
Yet not hard-hearted, take me right, I beg,
The veriest romp that ever wagg'd a leg
Was Jennet; but when pity soothed her mind,
Prompt with her tears, and delicately kind.
The half-fledged nestling, rabbit, mouse, or dove,
By turns engaged her cares and infant love;
And many a one, at the last doubtful strife,
Warm'd in her bosom, started into life.

At thirteen she was all that Heaven could send,
My nurse, my faithful clerk, my lively friend;
Last at my pillow when I sunk to sleep,
First on my threshold soon as day could peep:
I heard her happy to her heart's desire,
With clanking pattens, and a roaring fire.

ALFRED AND JENNET.

Then, having store of new-laid eggs to spare,
She fill'd her basket with the simple fare,
And weekly trudged (I think I see her still)
To sell them at yon house upon the hill.
Oft have I watch'd her as she stroll'd along,
Heard the gate bang, and heard her morning song;
And, as my warm ungovern'd feelings rose,
Said to myself, " Heaven bless her! there she goes."
Long would she tarry, and then dancing home,
Tell how the lady bade her oft'ner come,
And bade her talk and laugh without control;
For Jennet's voice was music to the soul,
My tale shall prove it:—For there dwelt a son,
An only child, and where there is but one,
Indulgence like a mildew reigns, from whence
Mischief may follow if that child wants sense.
But Alfred was a youth of noble mind,
With ardent passions, and with taste refined;
All that could please still courted heart and hand,
Music, joy, peace, and wealth, at his command;

76   ALFRED AND JENNET.

Wealth, which his widow'd mother deem'd his own;
Except the poor, she lived for him alone.
Yet would she weep by stealth when he was near,
But check'd all sighs to spare his wounded ear;
For from his cradle he had never seen
Soul-cheering sunbeams, or wild nature's green.
But all life's blessings centre not in sight;
For Providence, that dealt him one long night,
Had given, in pity to the blooming boy,
Feelings more exquisitely tuned to joy.
Fond to excess was he of all that grew;
The morning blossom sprinkled o'er with dew,
Across his path, as if in playful freak,
Would dash his brow, and weep upon his cheek;
Each varying leaf that brush'd where'er he came,
Press'd to his rosy lip he call'd by name;
He grasp'd the saplings, measured every bough,
Inhaled the fragrance that the spring months throw
Profusely round, till his young heart confess'd
That all was beauty, and himself was bless'd.

ALFRED AND JENNET.

Yet when he traced the wide extended plain,
Or clear brook side, he felt a transient pain;
The keen regret of goodness, void of pride,
To think he could not roam without a guide.

Who, guess ye, knew these scenes of home delight
Better than Jennet, bless'd with health and sight?
Whene'er she came, he from his sports would slide,
And catch her wild laugh, listening by her side;
Mount to the tell-tale clock with ardent spring,
And *feel* the passing hour, then fondly cling
To Jennet's arm, and tell how sweet the breath
Of bright May-mornings on the open heath;
Then off they started, rambling far and wide,
Like Cupid with a wood-nymph by his side.

Thus months and months roll'd on, the summer pass'd,
And the long darkness, and the winter blast,
Sever'd the pair; no flowery fields to roam,
Poor Alfred sought his music and his home.

ALFRED AND JENNET.

What wonder then if inwardly he pined?
The anxious mother mark'd her stripling's mind
Gloomy and sad, yet striving to be gay
As the long tedious evenings pass'd away:
'Twas her delight fresh spirits to supply.—
My girl was sent for—just for company.

A tender governess my daughter found,
Her temper placid, her instruction sound;
Plain were her precepts, full of strength, their power
Was founded on the practice of the hour:
Theirs were the happy nights to peace resign'd,
With ample means to cheer th' unbended mind.
The Sacred History, or the volumes fraught
With tenderest sympathy, or towering thought,
The laughter-stirring tale, the moral lay,
All that brings dawning reason into day.
There Jennet learn'd by maps, through every land
To travel, and to name them at command;

ALFRED AND JENNET.

Would tell how great their strength, their bounds
    how far,
And show where uncle Charles was in the war.
The globe she managed with a timid hand,
Told which was ocean, which was solid land,
And said, whate'er their diff'rent climates bore,
All still roll'd round, though that I knew before.

Thus grown familiar, and at perfect ease,
What could be Jennet's duty but to please?
Yet hitherto she kept, scarce knowing why,
One powerful charm reserved, and still was shy.
When Alfred from his grand-piano drew
Those heavenly sounds that seem'd for ever new,
She sat as if to sing would be a crime,
And only gazed with joy, and nodded time.
Till one snug evening, I myself was there,
The whispering lad inquired, behind my chair,
" Bowman, can Jennet sing?" " At home," said I,
" She sings from morn till night, and seems to fly

ALFRED AND JENNET.

" From tune to tune, the sad, the wild, the merry,
" And moulds her lip to suit them like a cherry;
" She learn'd them here."—" O ho!" said he, " O ho!"
And rubb'd his hands, and stroked his forehead, so.
Then down he sat, sought out a tender strain,
Sung the first words, then struck the chords again;
" Come, Jennet, help me, you *must* know this song
" Which I have sung, and you have heard so long."
I mark'd the palpitation of her heart,
Yet she complied, and strove to take a part,
But faint and fluttering, swelling by degrees,
Ere self-composure gave that perfect ease,
The soul of song:—then, with triumphant glee,
Resting her idle work upon her knee,
Her little tongue soon fill'd the room around
With such a voluble and magic sound,
That, 'spite of all her pains to persevere,
She stopp'd to sigh, and wipe a starting tear;
Then roused herself for faults to make amends,
While Alfred trembled to his fingers' ends.

ALFRED AND JENNET.

But when this storm of feeling sunk to rest,
Jennet, resuming, sung her very best,
And on the ear, with many a dying fall,
She pour'd th' enchanting " Harp of Tara's Hall."
Still Alfred hid his raptures from her view,
Still touch'd the keys, those raptures to renew,
And led her on to that sweet past'ral air,
The Highland Laddie with the yellow hair.
She caught the sound, and with the utmost ease
Bade nature's music triumph, sure to please:
Such truth, such warmth, such tenderness express'd,
That my old heart was dancing in my breast.
Upsprung the youth, " O Jennet, where's your hand?
" There's not another girl in all the land,
" If she could bring me empires, bring me sight,
" Could give me such unspeakable delight:
" You little baggage! not to tell before
" That you could sing; mind—you go home no more.

Thus I have seen her from my own fire-side
Attain the utmost summit of her pride;

82 ALFRED AND JENNET.

For, from that singing hour, as time roll'd round,
At the great house my Jennet might be found,
And, while I watch'd her progress with delight,
She had a father's blessing every night,
And grew in knowledge at that moral school
Till I began to guess myself a fool.
Music! why she could play as well as he!
At least I thought so,—but we'll let that be:
She read the poets, grave and light, by turns,
And talk'd of Cowper's "Task," and Robin Burns;
Nay, read without a book, as I may say,
As much as some could with in half a day.
'Twas thus I found they pass'd their happy time,
In all their walks, when nature in her prime
Spread forth her scents and hues, and whisper'd love
And joy to every bird in every grove;
And though their colours could not meet his eye,
She pluck'd him flowers, then talk'd of poetry.

Once on a sunbright morning, 'twas in June,
I felt my spirits and my hopes in tune,

ALFRED AND JENNET.

And idly rambled forth, as if t' explore
The little valley just before my door;
Down by yon dark green oak I found a seat
Beneath the clustering thorns, a snug retreat
For poets, as I deem'd, who often prize
Such holes and corners far from human eyes;
I mark'd young Alfred, led by Jennet, stray
Just to the spot, both chatting on their way:
They came behind me, I was still unseen;
He was the elder, Jennet was sixteen.
My heart misgave me, lest I should be deem'd
A prying listener, never much esteem'd,
But this fear soon subsided, and I said,
" I'll hear this blind lad and my little maid."
That instant down she pluck'd a woodbine wreath,
The loose leaves rattled on my head beneath;
This was for Alfred, which he seized with joy,
" O, thank you, Jennet," said the generous boy.
Much was their talk, which many a theme supplied,
As down they sat, for every blade was dried.

ALFRED AND JENNET.

I would have skulk'd away, but dare not move,
" Besides," thought I, " they will not talk of love;"
But I was wrong, for Alfred, with a sigh,
A little tremulous, a little shy,
But, with the tenderest accents, ask'd his guide
A question which might touch both love and pride.
" This morning, Jennet, why did you delay,
" And talk to that strange clown upon your way,
" Our homespun gardener? how can you bear
" His screech-owl tones upon your perfect ear?
" I cannot like that man, yet know not why,
" He's surely quite as old again as I;
" He's ignorant, and cannot be your choice,
" And ugly too, I'm certain, by his voice,
" Besides, he call'd you pretty."—" Well, what then?
" I cannot hide my face from all the men;
" Alfred, indeed, indeed, you are deceived,
" He never spoke a word that I believed;
" Nay, can he think that I would leave a home
" Full of enjoyment, present, and to come,

ALFRED AND JENNET.

" While your dear mother's favours daily prove
" How sweet the bonds of gratitude and love?
" No, while beneath her roof I shall remain,
" I'll never vex you, never give you pain."
" Enough, my life," he cried, and up they sprung;
By Heaven, I almost wish'd that I was young;
It was a dainty sight to see them pass,
Light as the July fawns upon the grass,
Pure as the breath of spring when forth it spreads,
Love in their hearts, and sunshine on their heads.

Next day I felt what I was bound to do,
To weigh the adventure well, and tell it too;
For Alfred's mother must not be beguiled,
He was her earthly hope, her only child;
I had no wish, no right to pass it by,
It might bring grief, perhaps calamity.
She was the judge, and she alone should know
Whether to check the flame or let it grow.
I went with fluttering heart, and moisten'd eye,
But strong in truth, and arm'd for her reply.

ALFRED AND JENNET.

" Well, master Bowman, why that serious face?"
Exclaim'd the lovely dame, with such a grace,
That had I knelt before her, I had been
Not quite the simplest votary ever seen.
I told my tale, and urged that well-known truth,
That the soft passion in the bloom of youth
Starts into power, and leads th' unconscious heart
A chase where reason takes but little part;
Nothing was more in nature, or more pure,
And from their habits nothing was more sure.
Whether the lady blush'd from pride or joy,
I could but guess;—at length she said—" My boy
" Dropp'd not a syllable of this to me!
" What was I doing, that I could not see?
" Through all the anxious hours that I have known,
" His welfare still was dearer than my own;
" How have I mourn'd o'er his unhappy fate!
" Blind as he is! the heir to my estate!
" I now might break his heart, and Jennet's too;
" What must I, Bowman, or what can I do?"—

ALFRED AND JENNET.

"Do, madam?" said I, boldly, "if you trace
"Impending degradation or disgrace
"In this attachment, let us not delay;
"Send my girl home, and check it while you may."
"I will," she said, but the next moment sigh'd;
Parental love was struggling hard with pride.

I left her thus, deep musing, and soon found
My daughter, for I traced her by the sound
Of Alfred's flageolet; no cares had they,
But in the garden bower spent half the day.
By starts he sung, then wildest trillings made,
To mock a piping blackbird in the glade.
I turn'd a corner and approach'd the pair;
My little rogue had roses in her hair!
She whipp'd them out, and with a downcast look,
Conquer'd a laugh by poring on her book.
My object was to talk with her aside,
But at the sight my resolution died;
They look'd so happy in their blameless glee,
That, as I found them, I e'en let them be;

ALFRED AND JENNET.

Though Jennet promised a few social hours
'Midst her old friends, my poultry, and my flowers.
She came,—but not till fatal news had wrung
Her heart through sleepless hours, and chain'd her tongue.
She came, but with a look that gave me pain,
For, though bright sunbeams sparkled after rain,
Though every brood came round, half run, half fly,
I knew her anguish by her alter'd eye;
And strove, with all my power, where'er she came,
To soothe her grief, yet gave it not a name.
At length a few sad bitter tears she shed,
And on both hands reclined her aching head.
'Twas then my time the conqueror to prove,
I summon'd all my rhetoric, all my love.
" Jennet, you must not think to pass through life
" Without its sorrows, and without its strife;
" Good, dutiful, and worthy, as you are,
" You must have griefs, and you must learn to bear."
Thus I went on, trite moral truths to string,—
All chaff, mere chaff, where love has spread his wing:

ALFRED AND JENNET.

She cared not, listen'd not, nor seem'd to know
What was my aim, but wiped her burning brow,
Where sat more eloquence and living power
Than language could embody in an hour.
With soften'd tone I mention'd Alfred's name,
His wealth, our poverty, and that sad blame
Which would have weigh'd me down, had I not told
The secret which I dare not keep for gold,
Of Alfred's love, o'erheard the other morn,
The gardener, and the woodbine, and the thorn;
And added, " Though the lady sends you home,
" You are but young, child, and a day may come"—
" She has *not* sent me home," the girl replied,
And rose with sobs of passion from my side;
" She has *not* sent me home, dear father, no;
" She gives me leave to tarry or to go;
" She has not *blamed* me,—yet she weeps no less,
" And every tear but adds to my distress;
" I am the cause,—thus all that she has done
" Will bring the death or misery of her son.

ALFRED AND JENNET.

" Jealous he might be, could he but have seen
" How other lads approach'd where I have been;
" But this man's voice offends his very soul,
" That strange antipathy brooks no control;
" And should I leave him now, or seem unkind,
" The thought would surely wreck his noble mind;
" To leave him thus, and in his utmost need!
" Poor Alfred! then you will be blind indeed!
" I will not leave him."—" Nay, child, do not rave,
" What, would you be his menial, be his slave?"
" Yes," she exclaim'd, and wiped each streaming eye,
" Yes, be his slave, and serve him till I die;
" He is too just to act the tyrant's part,
" He's truth itself." O how my burthen'd heart
Sigh'd for relief!—soon that relief was found;
Without one word we traced the meadow round,
Her feverish hand in mine, and weigh'd the case,
Nor dared to look each other in the face;
Till, with a sudden stop, as if from fear,
I roused her sinking spirit, " Who comes here?"

ALFRED AND JENNET.

Down the green slope before us, glowing warm,
Came Alfred, tugging at his mother's arm;
Willing she seem'd, but he still led the way,
She had not walk'd so fast for many a day;
His hand was lifted, and his brow was bare,
For now no clust'ring ringlets wanton'd there,
He threw them back in anger and in spleen,
And shouted " Jennet" o'er the daisied green.
Boyish impatience strove with manly grace
In ev'ry line and feature of his face;
His claim appear'd resistless as his choice,
And when he caught the sound of Jennet's voice,
And when with spotless soul he clasp'd the maid,
My heart exulted while my breath was staid.
" Jennet, we must not part! return again;
" What have I done to merit all this pain?
" Dear mother, share my fortune with the poor,
" Jennet is mine, and *shall* be—say no more;
" Bowman, you know not what a friend I'll be;
" Give me your daughter, Bowman, give her me;

ALFRED AND JENNET.

" Jennet, what will my days be if you go?
" A dreary darkness, and a life of woe:
" My dearest love, come *home,* and do not cry;
" You are my daylight, Jennet, I shall die."
To such appeals all prompt replies are cold,
And stately prudence snaps her cobweb hold.
Had the good widow tried, or wish'd to speak,
This was a bond she could not, dared not break;
Their hearts (you never saw their likeness, never)
Were join'd, indissolubly join'd for ever.
Why need I tell how soon our tears were dried,
How Jennet blush'd, how Alfred with a stride
Bore off his prize, and fancied every charm,
And clipp'd against his ribs her trembling arm;
How mute we seniors stood, our power all gone?
Completely conquer'd, Love the day had won,
And the young vagrant triumph'd in our plight,
And shook his roguish plumes, and laugh'd outright.
Yet, by my life and hopes, I would not part
With this sweet recollection from my heart;

ALFRED AND JENNET.

I would not now forget that tender scene
To wear a crown, or make my girl a queen.
Why need be told how pass'd the months along,
How sped the summer's walk, the winter's song,
How the foil'd suitor all his hopes gave up,
How Providence with rapture fill'd their cup?
No dark regrets, no tragic scenes to prove,
The gardener was too old to die for love.
A thousand incidents I cast aside
To tell but one—I gave away the bride—
Gave the dear youth what kings could not have given;
Then bless'd them both, and put my trust in Heaven.
There the old neighbours laugh'd the night away,
Who talk of Jennet's wedding to this day.
And could you but have seen the modest grace,
The half-hid smiles that play'd in Jennet's face,
Or mark'd the bridegroom's bounding heart o'erflow,
You might have wept for joy, as I could now:
I speak from memory of days long past;
Though 'tis a father's tale, I've done at last.

Here rest thee, rest thee, Muse, review the scene
Where thou with me from peep of dawn hast been:
We did not promise that this motley throng
Should every *one* supply a votive song,
Nor every tenant:—yet thou hast been kind,
For untold tales must still remain behind,
Which might o'er listening patience still prevail,
Did fancy waver not, nor daylight fail.
" The Soldier's Wife," her toils, his battles o'er,
" Love in a Shower," the riv'let's sudden roar;
Then, " Lines to Aggravation" form the close,
Parent of murders, and the worst of woes.
But while the changeful hours of daylight flew,
Some homeward look'd, and talk'd of evening dew;
Some watch'd the sun's decline, and stroll'd around,
Some wish'd another dance, and partners found;

95

When in an instant every eye was drawn
To one bright object on the upper lawn;
A fair procession from the mansion came,
Unknown its purport, and unknown its aim.
No gazer could refrain, no tongue could cease,
It seem'd an embassy of love and peace.
Nearer and nearer still approach'd the train,
Age in the van transform'd to youth again.
Sir Ambrose gazed, and scarce believed his eyes;
'Twas magic, memory, love, and blank surprise,
For there his venerable lady wore
The very dress which, sixty years before,
Had sparkled on her sunshine bridal morn,
Had sparkled, ay, beneath this very thorn!
Her hair was snowy white, o'er which was seen,
Emblem of what her bridal cheeks had been,
A twin red rose—no other ornament
Had pride suggested, or false feeling lent;
She came to grace the triumph of her lord,
And pay him honours at his festive board.

96

Nine ruddy lasses follow'd where she stepp'd;
White were their virgin robes, that lightly swept
The downy grass; in every laughing eye
Cupid had skulk'd, and written " victory."
What heart on earth its homage could refuse?
Each tripp'd, unconsciously, a blushing Muse.
A slender chaplet of fresh blossoms bound
Their clustering ringlets in a magic round.
And, as they slowly moved across the green,
Each in her beauty seem'd a May-day queen.
The first a wreath bore in her outstretch'd hand,
The rest a single rose upon a wand;
Their steps were measured to that grassy throne
Where, watching them, Sir Ambrose sat alone.
They stopp'd,—when she, the foremost of the row,
Curtsied, and placed the wreath upon his brow;
The rest, in order pacing by his bower,
In the loop'd wreath left each her single flower,—
Then stood aside.—What broke the scene's repose?
The whole assembly clapp'd their hands and rose.

97

The Muses charm'd them as they form'd a ring,
And look'd the very life and soul of Spring!
But still the white hair'd dame they view'd with pride,
Her love so perfect, and her truth so tried.
Oh, sweet it is to hear, to see, to name,
Unquench'd affection in the palsied frame—
To think upon the boundless raptures past,
And love, triumphant, conquering to the last!

Silenced by feeling, vanquish'd by his tears,
The host sprung up, nor felt the weight of years;
Yet utterance found not, though in virtue's cause,
But acclamations fill'd up nature's pause,
Till, by one last and vigorous essay,
His tide of feeling roll'd itself away;
The language of delight its bondage broke,
And many a warm heart bless'd him as he spoke.

" Neighbours and friends, by long experience proved,
" Pardon this weakness; I was too much moved:

98

" My dame, you see, can youth and age insnare,
" In vain I strove, 'twas more than I could bear,—
" Yet hear me,—though the tyrant passions strive,
" The words of truth, like leading stars, survive;
" I thank you all, but will accomplish more—
" Your verses shall not die as heretofore;
" Your local tales shall not be thrown away,
" Nor war remain the theme of every lay.
" Ours is an humbler task, that may release
" The high-wrought soul, and mould it into peace.
" These pastoral notes some victor's ear may fill,
" Breathed amidst blossoms, where the drum is still:
" I purpose then to send them forth to try
" The public patience, or its apathy.
" The world shall see them; why should I refrain?
" 'Tis all the produce of my own domain.
" Farewell!" he said, then took his lady's arm,
On his shrunk hand her starting tears fell warm;

99

Again he turn'd to view the happy crowd,
And cried, " Good night, good night, good night,"
    aloud,
" Health to you all! for see, the evening closes,"
Then march'd to rest, beneath his crown of roses.
" Happy old man! with feelings such as these,
" The seasons all can charm, and trifles please."
An instantaneous shout re-echoed round,
'Twas wine and gratitude inspired the sound:
Some joyous souls resumed the dance again,
The aged loiter'd o'er the homeward plain,
And scatter'd lovers rambled through the park,
And breathed their vows of honour in the dark;
Others a festal harmony preferr'd,
Still round the thorn the jovial song was heard;
Dance, rhymes, and fame, they scorn'd such things as
    these,
But drain'd the mouldy barrel to its lees,
As if 'twere worse than shame to want repose:
Nor was the lawn clear till the moon arose,

And on each turret pour'd a brilliant gleam
Of modest light, that trembled on the stream;
The owl awoke, but dared not yet complain,
And banish'd silence re-assumed her reign.

THE END.

LONDON:
PRINTED BY THOMAS DAVISON, WHITEFRIARS.